295 Delicious Baking Recipes

(295 Delicious Baking Recipes - Volume 1)

Sandra Neal

Content

CHAPTER 8: AWESOME BAKING RECIPES..181

Chapter 1: Easter Baking Recipes

***

| 1. | Brooklyn Blackout Cake |

Serving: Cuts into 12 slices | Prep: 30mins | Cook: 40mins | Ready in:

Ingredients

- For the cake
- 140g unsalted butter, plus extra for greasing
- 100ml vegetable oil
- 140g buttermilk
- 100ml coffee, made with 1 tsp espresso powder
- 2 large eggs, at room temperature
- 1 tsp vanilla extract
- 250g light muscovado sugar
- 250g plain flour
- 1 tsp bicarbonate of soda
- 2 tsp baking powder
- 50g cocoa powder
- For the custard filling and covering
- 250g golden caster sugar
- 500ml full-fat milk
- 140g chocolate, 85% cocoa solids, broken into cubes
- 50g cornflour
- 2 tsp espresso powder
- 2 tsp vanilla extract

Direction

- Make the custard first as it needs to chill. Put all the ingredients, except the vanilla, in a large pan and bring gently to the boil, whisking all the time, until the chocolate has melted and you have a silky, thick custard. It will take 5-7 mins from cold. Stir in the vanilla and a generous pinch of salt, then scrape the custard into a wide, shallow bowl. Cover the surface with cling film, cool, then chill for at least 3 hrs or until cold and set.
- Heat oven to 180C/160C fan/gas 4. Grease then line the bases of 2 x 20cm sandwich tins. Melt the butter in a pan, then remove from the heat and beat in the oil, buttermilk, coffee and eggs. In a large bowl, whisk the dry ingredients togetherplus 1/4 tsp salt (saves sifting) and squish any resistant lumps of sugar with your fingers. Tip in the wet ingredients and whisk until smooth.
- Divide the batter between the prepared tins and bake for 25-30 mins until risen and a skewer inserted into the middle of the cakes comes out clean. Cool for 10 mins, then transfer to a rack to cool completely, parchment-side down.
- Remove the parchment linings from the cakes. If the cakes are domed, trim them flat. Now cut each cake across the middle using a large serrated knife. Put your least successful layer and any trimmings into a processor and pulse it to crumbs. Tip into a large bowl.
- Sit one layer on a cake plate and spread it with a quarter of the custard. Sandwich the next layer on top, add another quarter of the custard, then top with the final layer of cake. Spoon the remaining custard on top of the cake, then spread it around the top and down the sides until smooth. Chill for 15 mins to firm up the custard again.
- Hold the cake over the bowl containing the crumbs, then sprinkle and gently press a layer of crumbs all over the cake. Brush any excess from the plate. You'll have some crumbs left. Chill for 2 hrs, or longer, before serving, and eat it cold. Can be made up to 2 days ahead. The cake gets fudgier and more enticing the longer you leave it.

Nutrition Information

- Calories: 548 calories
- Total Carbohydrate: 68 grams carbohydrates
- Sodium: 0.6 milligram of sodium
- Sugar: 47 grams sugar
- Saturated Fat: 12 grams saturated fat
- Protein: 7 grams protein
- Total Fat: 27 grams fat
- Fiber: 3 grams fiber

2. Bunny Carrot Cake

Serving: Cuts into 10-12 slices | Prep: 30mins | Cook: 1hours10mins | Ready in:

Ingredients

- 200g light soft brown sugar, plus 3 tbsp
- 150ml light rapeseed oil (we used Cooks & Co with natural butter flavour), plus extra for greasing
- 100g natural yogurt, plus extra to serve (optional)
- 3 large eggs
- 2 tsp vanilla extract
- zest 3 oranges, juice of 2 (save juice of last orange for the carrots, below)
- 300g self-raising flour
- 1 tbsp mixed spice
- 1 tsp ground cinnamon
- 250g coarsely grated carrot
- crème fraîche, to serve (optional)
- For the caramelised carrots
- 225-250g small or baby carrots, peeled and halved lengthways
- juice 1 orange (from cake ingredients)
- 25g butter
- 4 tbsp light soft brown sugar

Direction

- First, make the caramelised carrots. Put the carrots in a saucepan so they can sit in just about a single layer. Add the orange juice, butter, sugar and enough water to cover the tops of the carrots by just 1cm. Bring to the boil, then cook until the water has almost evaporated and the carrots are left in a sticky syrup – you may want to reduce the heat if the liquid looks more syrupy, and go a little slower at the end so the carrots don't catch. Can be made up to 1 day ahead.
- Heat oven to 160C/140C fan/gas 3. Grease a 23cm cake tin. Lift the candied carrots from the pan and syrup, and arrange in the base of the tin, cut-side down. Keep the pan and syrup for later.
- Whisk together the 200g brown sugar, the oil, yogurt, eggs, vanilla and zest from 2 oranges. Mix the flour, mixed spice, cinnamon and grated carrot in a big mixing bowl. Stir in the whisked mixture until smooth, then spoon over the carrots in the tin – be careful not to dislodge their arrangement too much. Bake for 45-50 mins until a skewer poked in comes out clean. Cool in the tin for 20 mins.
- Meanwhile, add the orange juice to the syrup pan with the 3 tbsp brown sugar. Simmer together until slightly reduced, then stir in the remaining zest.
- Turn the cake out onto a plate and spoon over the syrup. Eat just warm or at room temperature with more yogurt or crème fraîche.

Nutrition Information

- Calories: 359 calories
- Sodium: 0.4 milligram of sodium
- Total Fat: 16 grams fat
- Fiber: 2 grams fiber
- Total Carbohydrate: 50 grams carbohydrates
- Sugar: 32 grams sugar
- Saturated Fat: 3 grams saturated fat
- Protein: 5 grams protein

3. Carrot Cake Monkey Bread

Serving: Serves 12 | Prep: 1hours20mins | Cook: 45mins | Ready in:

Ingredients

- 150ml whole milk
- 135g unsalted butter, softened, plus extra for the tin
- 550g strong white bread flour, plus extra for dusting
- 1 orange, zested
- 2 tsp mixed spice
- 200g carrots (about 2 large), grated
- 7g sachet fast-action dried yeast
- 50g golden caster sugar
- 2 large eggs, at room temperature
- oil, for the bowl
- 1 tbsp cinnamon
- 100g walnuts, toasted and finely chopped
- 150g light brown soft sugar
- 100g golden marzipan
- For the icing
- ½ orange, zested and juiced
- 100g icing sugar

Direction

- Gently heat the milk and 85g of the butter in a medium pan until the butter has melted and the milk has started to simmer. Leave to cool to room temperature. Tip the flour, orange zest, mixed spice, carrots, yeast, caster sugar and 1 tsp salt into a large bowl with the eggs, then add the cooled milk mixture and bring together into a sticky dough using your hands. Knead until combined, then tip onto a floured work surface and knead again for 5-10 mins until smooth and springy. Transfer the dough to a lightly oiled, large bowl, cover and leave to prove for 1 hr, or until doubled in size.
- Generously butter a 25cm bundt tin. Melt the remaining butter and leave to cool slightly. Mix the cinnamon, walnuts and brown sugar together in a medium bowl. Separate the proved dough into 40-50 x 25g pieces and roll into balls on a lightly floured surface. Roll the marzipan into small, pea-sized balls and set aside. Dunk the dough balls in the melted butter, then roll in the walnut and sugar mixture to coat. Drop the dough balls into the prepared tin, dotting around some of the marzipan balls as you go. Repeat until you've used up all the dough balls and marzipan. Cover and prove again for 45 mins until the dough has risen slightly.
- Heat the oven to 180C/160C fan/gas 4. Uncover the tin and bake for 40-45 mins, or until well risen and golden. Carefully loosen the bread from the edges using a skewer or butter knife, and leave to cool in the tin for 20 mins. Invert onto a serving plate, keeping the tin in place, and leave for 5-10 mins (the bread will naturally shrink away from the sides), then remove the tin.
- Gradually whisk the orange juice into the icing sugar to make a thick icing, then drizzle over the bread, letting it drip down the sides. Scatter over the orange zest and serve warm.

Nutrition Information

- Calories: 477 calories
- Total Carbohydrate: 67 grams carbohydrates
- Sodium: 0.5 milligram of sodium
- Protein: 10 grams protein
- Sugar: 32 grams sugar
- Total Fat: 18 grams fat
- Saturated Fat: 7 grams saturated fat
- Fiber: 3 grams fiber

4. Carrot Patch Cake

Serving: 12 | Prep: 25mins | Cook: 1hours10mins | Ready in:

Ingredients

- 175ml vegetable oil, plus extra for the tin
- 75g natural yogurt
- 3 large eggs
- 1 tsp vanilla extract
- 200g self-raising flour
- 250g light muscovado sugar
- 2 tsp ground cinnamon

- ¼ fresh nutmeg, finely grated
- 200g carrots (about three), grated
- 100g sultanas or raisins
- 100g pistachios, finely chopped (or slivered if you can get them)
- For the icing
- 100g slightly salted butter, softened
- 200g icing sugar
- 100g full-fat cream cheese
- 100g fondant icing or marzipan
- orange food colouring

Direction

- Heat oven to 180C/160C fan/gas 4. Oil and line a 900g loaf tin with baking parchment. Whisk the oil, yogurt, eggs and vanilla in a jug. Mix the flour, sugar, cinnamon and nutmeg with a good pinch of salt in a bowl. Squeeze any lumps of sugar through your fingers, shaking the bowl a few times to bring the lumps to the surface.
- Add the wet ingredients to the dry, along with the carrots, raisins and half the pistachios. Mix well to combine, then scrape into the tin. Bake for 1 hr 10 mins or until a skewer inserted into the centre of the cake comes out clean. If any wet mixture clings to the skewer, return to the oven for 5 mins, then check again. Leave to cool in the tin.
- To make the icing, beat the butter and sugar together until smooth. Add half the cream cheese and beat again, then add the rest (adding it bit by bit prevents the icing from splitting). Remove the cake from the tin and spread the icing thickly on top. Scatter with some of the remaining pistachios. Dye the fondant or marzipan orange by kneading in a drop of food colouring. Roll into little carrot shapes, then use a skewer to make indentations and poke a few pistachios in to look like fronds. Top the cake with the carrots, then serve. Will keep in the fridge for up to five days (eat at room temperature).

Nutrition Information

- Calories: 546 calories
- Protein: 6 grams protein
- Total Fat: 30 grams fat
- Saturated Fat: 8 grams saturated fat
- Fiber: 3 grams fiber
- Sodium: 0.5 milligram of sodium
- Total Carbohydrate: 63 grams carbohydrates
- Sugar: 49 grams sugar

---

5. Chocolate & Spice Hot Cross Buns

Serving: Makes 12 | Prep: 40mins | Cook: 25mins | Ready in:

Ingredients

- zest and juice 1 large orange
- sunflower oil, for greasing
- For the dough and crosses
- 225ml semi-skimmed milk
- 50g unsalted butter, plus extra for greasing
- 1 large egg
- 450g strong white bread flour, plus extra for dusting
- 2 tsp fast-action yeast
- 50g golden caster sugar
- For the flavouring and glaze
- 140g raisins
- 100g chocolate, 70% cocoa solids
- 1 tsp ground cinnamon
- 4 tbsp golden caster sugar
- 100g plain flour

Direction

- Make the dough first. Heat the milk in a pan until steaming. Remove from the heat, and drop in the butter. After a couple of mins, beat in the egg and half the orange zest. The liquid should be just warm for step 2.
- Mix the strong flour, yeast, 1 tsp salt and the sugar in a large bowl, then tip in the liquid and stir to make a soft dough without dry patches. Flour the work surface and your

hands, then knead the dough for 5-10 mins until smooth and elastic. Use a stand mixer or processor if you like. Oil a large bowl, sit the dough inside it, then cover with oiled cling film. Rise in a warm place for about 1 hr or until doubled in size.

- Put the raisins and half the orange juice in a small pan or covered bowl, and either simmer for a few mins or microwave on High for 1 min until hot. Cool completely. Break the chocolate into a food processor with the cinnamon and 2 tbsp sugar, then pulse until very finely chopped. Mix in the rest of the zest. If you don't have a processor, chop it by hand or grate it, then mix with the other ingredients.

- Turn the risen dough onto a floured surface and press it out to a large rectangle, a little bigger than A4 paper. Scatter it evenly with the chocolate mix and the raisins, which should have absorbed all of the juice (drain them if not). Roll the dough up around the filling, then knead it well for a few mins until the chocolate and fruit are evenly spread. Some raisins and chocolate will try to escape, but keep kneading them back in.

- Grease then line a large baking sheet with baking parchment. Divide the dough into 12 equal pieces. Shape into buns by pinching each ball of dough into a purse shape, concentrating on making the underneath of the ball (which will be the top) as smooth as you can. Put the buns, smooth-side up, onto the baking sheet, leaving room for rising. Cover loosely with oiled cling film and prove in a warm place for 30-45 mins or until the dough has risen and doesn't spring back quickly when prodded gently.

- Heat oven to 190C/170C fan/gas 5. To make the paste for the crosses, gradually stir 6-7 tbsp water into the plain flour to make a smooth, thick paste, then put in a food bag and snip off the end to about 5mm. Pipe the crosses, then bake for 20-25 mins until the buns are risen and dark golden brown.

- Mix the rest of the orange juice with the remaining sugar and let it dissolve. Brush the syrup over the buns while they are hot, then

leave to cool. Eat on the day of baking, or toast the next day.

Nutrition Information

- Calories: 332 calories
- Total Carbohydrate: 55 grams carbohydrates
- Fiber: 2 grams fiber
- Saturated Fat: 5 grams saturated fat
- Sugar: 22 grams sugar
- Protein: 8 grams protein
- Total Fat: 8 grams fat
- Sodium: 0.5 milligram of sodium

6. Chocolate Checkerboard Hot Cross Buns

Serving: makes 12 | Prep: 45mins | Cook: 30mins | Ready in:

Ingredients

- 250ml whole milk
- 50g butter, chopped into chunks
- 2 tbsp cocoa powder
- 500g strong white flour, plus 100g for the crosses
- 1 tsp ground cinnamon
- 85g golden caster sugar
- 7g sachet fast-action dried yeast
- 1 large egg
- 150g mixed dried fruit
- 50g dark chocolate, chopped into small chunks
- 1 orange, zested
- 50g dried sour cherries
- 50g white chocolate, chopped into small chunks
- oil, for the bowls and baking tray
- 2 tbsp apricot jam (optional)

Direction

- Warm the milk in a saucepan until steaming. Remove from the heat, then add the butter.

Swirl to melt the butter and cool the milk a little. Mix the cocoa with 2 tbsp boiling water, then set aside to cool.

- Mix 500g flour, the cinnamon, sugar, yeast and ½ tsp salt in a bowl. When the milk mixture is still warm, add it to the flour bowl along with the egg, and mix to form a sticky dough (use a tabletop mixer if you have one). Continue mixing, then kneading, until the dough is less sticky and feels springy – about 8-10 mins. Add the dried fruit and mix again until the fruit is evenly spread through the dough.
- Put a clean bowl on your scales. Scrape the dough into this bowl to weigh the full quantity, then return half of it to the original bowl. Add the cocoa mixture, dark chocolate and orange zest to one bowl, and the white chocolate and cherries to the other. Knead each dough for a further minute or until well mixed. Return each dough to a cleaned, oiled bowl, cover with a tea towel or cling film and leave somewhere warm for 1-2 hrs (depending on your kitchen temperature) until the dough has roughly doubled in size.
- Knead and fold each dough a little bit to knock out some air. Divide each dough into six balls (use the scales if you want your buns to be perfectly sized.) To shape the buns, take a piece of dough in your palm, pull a corner into the middle and press to seal. Continue doing this around the edge of the dough to create a tight bun shape when you flip the dough over. Shape all the buns, then arrange them on a lightly oiled tray in a chequerboard pattern, leaving about 1.5cm around each one to allow space for rising. Cover the tray loosely with oiled cling film and set aside for 30 mins-1 hr until almost doubled in size again. Heat oven to 200C/180C fan/gas 6.
- Mix the remaining our with enough water to make a thick paste, about 80ml. Transfer the paste to a piping bag and snip a small opening. Uncover the buns and pipe a line along each row, then repeat in the other direction to make crosses. Bake for 25-30 mins until the buns are golden brown. Leave to cool.

- Warm the jam in a saucepan and brush over the buns for a glossy finish, if you like. To serve, split the buns, toast them under the grill and enjoy with salted butter.

Nutrition Information

- Calories: 362 calories
- Protein: 10 grams protein
- Sugar: 21 grams sugar
- Total Fat: 9 grams fat
- Saturated Fat: 5 grams saturated fat
- Sodium: 0.4 milligram of sodium
- Total Carbohydrate: 59 grams carbohydrates
- Fiber: 3 grams fiber

7. Chocolate Chip Traybake

Serving: Cuts into 32 small pieces | Prep: 20mins | Cook: 30mins | Ready in:

Ingredients

- 190ml rapeseed oil, plus extra for the tin
- 250g plain flour
- 80g cocoa powder
- 3 tsp baking powder
- 300g light brown soft sugar
- 350ml whole milk
- 2 tsp vanilla extract
- 2 large eggs
- 100g white chocolate chips
- For the icing
- 150g butter, cubed
- 200g icing sugar, sieved
- 4 tsp cocoa powder
- 2 tbsp milk

Direction

- Heat the oven to 180C/160C fan/gas 4. Oil the base and sides of a 33 x 23cm roasting tin that's at least 2.5cm deep. Line with baking parchment. Combine the flour, cocoa powder, baking powder, sugar and a good pinch of salt in a large bowl. Break up any sugar lumps with a whisk.

- Whisk the oil together with the milk, vanilla and eggs in a jug, and pour into the dry ingredients, then stir in the chocolate chips. Stir well using a spatula until there are no pockets of flour. Pour the mix into the prepared tin and bake for 25-30 mins until a skewer inserted into the centre comes out clean. If any wet mix clings to the skewer, return to the oven for 5 mins, then check again. Leave to cool in the tin for at least 20 mins.
- Meanwhile, make the icing. Melt the butter, then remove from the heat and stir in the icing sugar, cocoa powder and milk. The icing will be very runny, but will thicken a little as it cools. (If the icing has thickened too much before the cake has cooled, reheat it slightly to make it easier to pour.)
- Pour the chocolate icing over the cake and leave until it has set before slicing into sqaures.

Nutrition Information

- Calories: 220 calories
- Saturated Fat: 4 grams saturated fat
- Total Fat: 12 grams fat
- Protein: 3 grams protein
- Fiber: 1 grams fiber
- Sodium: 0.2 milligram of sodium
- Total Carbohydrate: 24 grams carbohydrates
- Sugar: 18 grams sugar

8. Chocolate Egg Baked Tart

Serving: 12 | Prep: 20mins | Cook: 30mins | Ready in:

Ingredients

- For the base
- 80g butter, softened

- 40g golden caster sugar
- 120g self raising flour
- For the filling
- 75g butter
- 100g dark chocolate (70% cocoa)
- 75g golden caster sugar
- 50g plain flour
- 4 large eggs, beaten
- 2 x 80g bags of chocolate eggs (we used Galaxy Golden Eggs)
- crème fraîche, to serve

Direction

- For the shortbread base, beat the butter and sugar together until light and creamy, then mix in the flour. Press the dough into the base of a 20-21cm tart tin and put in the fridge for 20 mins to harden.
- Heat oven to 180C/160C fan/ gas 4. Prick the base all over with a fork and bake in the centre of the oven for 15 mins until lightly golden.
- Meanwhile, melt the butter and chocolate together in a saucepan over a low heat. Once melted, stir in the sugar and flour, then gradually beat in the eggs. Pour the filling over the base and cover the top in chocolate eggs. Return to the oven and bake for 12-15 mins or until the fiilling is just set at the edges but the centre is still shiny and a bit wobbly. Remove from the oven and put in the fridge to chill. Can be made a day ahead and kept in the tin overnight. To release from the tin, warm the sides with a hot dishcloth for a couple of mins. Serve with crème fraîche.

Nutrition Information

- Calories: 332 calories
- Saturated Fat: 11 grams saturated fat
- Total Carbohydrate: 31 grams carbohydrates
- Sugar: 20 grams sugar
- Protein: 6 grams protein
- Fiber: 1 grams fiber
- Sodium: 0.4 milligram of sodium
- Total Fat: 20 grams fat

9. Dark & White Chocolate Cardamom Swirl Tart

Serving: Cuts into 12-15 slices | Prep: 30mins | Cook: 20mins | Ready in:

Ingredients

- For the ganaches
- 7 cardamom pods
- 400ml double cream
- 100g white caster sugar
- 200g bar white Belgian chocolate
- 180g pack Willie's Cacao Venezuelan Black 100% Carenero cacao, or try Lindt 99% cacao (both available from Waitrose)
- 25g unsalted butter, cut into small pieces and softened
- 1 tsp vanilla extract
- 150ml whole milk
- For the base
- 200g dark chocolate digestives
- 75g unsalted butter, melted, plus extra for greasing
- 3 tbsp caster sugar (white or golden)

Direction

- Crush the cardamom pods with a pestle and mortar, then put the seeds and the husks in a medium pan. Pour in the cream and sugar, stir, then heat gently until the cream begins to simmer. Remove the pan from the heat and leave to infuse for 30 mins.
- Meanwhile, finely chop the white chocolate in a food processor, then tip into a medium bowl. Repeat with the cacao, tip this into another bowl and add the butter. Season each chocolate with a pinch of salt.
- Heat oven to 180C/160C fan/gas 4 and lightly grease a 23cm fluted tart tin or springform tin. Without cleaning the processor, tip in the digestives and pulse to fine crumbs. Pulse in the melted butter and sugar until the mixture

looks like wet sand, then press firmly into the base of the tin. Slide it onto a baking sheet, bake for 10 mins, then cool completely.

- When the base is cold, reheat the infused cream to a simmer. Strain half the cream on top of the white chocolate and stir. Add the milk to what is left in the pan, reheat, then strain this over the chopped cacao and butter, and stir. It will take a few mins before each chocolate melts completely.
- Pour all but about 3 tbsp of the cacao ganache on top of the biscuit base and chill for 15 mins or until just set. Now flood the top with the white chocolate ganache. Finish with the reserved cacao mix, dropping 6 dollops on top like a clock face, and one in the middle. Use a skewer to swirl the colours together. Chill for at least 4 hrs or ideally overnight to let the ganache set firm, then bring it out of the fridge for 30 mins before serving.

Nutrition Information

- Calories: 445 calories
- Sodium: 0.3 milligram of sodium
- Protein: 4 grams protein
- Saturated Fat: 20 grams saturated fat
- Fiber: 1 grams fiber
- Total Fat: 34 grams fat
- Sugar: 26 grams sugar
- Total Carbohydrate: 33 grams carbohydrates

10. Duck Egg Sponge Cake

Serving: Cuts into 12 slices | Prep: 1hours | Cook: 35mins | Ready in:

Ingredients

- For the sponge
- 250g butter, melted, plus extra for greasing
- 5 duck eggs, or 250g weight of beaten hen's eggs
- 250g white caster sugar

- 1 tsp vanilla extract
- 250g self-raising flour
- 1 tsp baking powder
- For the buttercream
- 250g unsalted butter, chopped, at room temperature
- 600g icing sugar
- 2 tbsp milk
- 1 vanilla pod
- food colouring (optional)
- For the decoration
- cocoa powder, for dusting
- selection of mini chocolate eggs

Direction

- Heat oven to 180C/160C fan/gas 4. Grease then line 2 x 20cm cake tins with baking parchment and grease the parchment too.
- Crack the duck eggs into a large mixing bowl. Add the sugar and whisk for about 5 mins until pale and fluffy. Keep whisking as you add the melted butter, a little at a time, followed by the vanilla extract.
- Fold in the flour and baking powder with a large metal spoon until you can't see any pockets of flour. Divide the mixture between the two prepared tins and bake for 35 mins or until bouncy to the touch and a skewer poked into the middle of the cake comes out clean. Leave the cakes to cool in the tin, then turn out onto wire racks when cool enough to handle.
- To make the buttercream, tip the butter into a big bowl and whisk with an electric hand whisk. Add the icing sugar, 2-3 tbsp at a time, until it's all incorporated, adding the milk halfway through the process. Scrape the seeds out of a vanilla pod, add them in and whisk again. Transfer half the buttercream to another bowl and, if using, stir your food colouring into one of the mixtures. I used blue and a dash of green to create a classic duck egg shade.
- When the buttercream mixtures are ready and the cake is cold, level the cakes with a bread knife, cut each one in half through the middle and stick all the layers together with the

uncoloured buttercream. Cover the whole cake with a thin layer of the coloured buttercream – this will seal in any crumbs. Chill the cake for 30 mins, then cover with the rest of the buttercream and use a palette knife or pastry scraper to make the buttercream flat.

- To finish, sprinkle about 1/4 tsp of cocoa powder onto the cake to create a speckled design. Repeat this in different sections of the cake, then top with a cluster of mini chocolate eggs and serve. Will keep for 2-3 days.

Nutrition Information

- Calories: 717 calories
- Sugar: 71 grams sugar
- Fiber: 1 grams fiber
- Protein: 7 grams protein
- Total Carbohydrate: 86 grams carbohydrates
- Total Fat: 38 grams fat
- Sodium: 0.7 milligram of sodium
- Saturated Fat: 22 grams saturated fat

11. Easter Biscuits

Serving: makes 18 | Prep: 1hours15mins | Cook: 30mins | Ready in:

Ingredients

- 300g plain flour, plus extra for dusting
- 150g white caster sugar
- 150g slightly salted butter, chopped
- 1 large egg
- 2 tsp vanilla extract or vanilla bean paste
- For the iced option
- 500g royal icing sugar
- your favourite food colouring gels
- For the jammy middle option
- icing sugar, for dusting
- 400g apricot jam, or lemon curd

Direction

- Weigh the flour and sugar in a bowl. Add the butter and rub together with your fingertips until the mixture resembles wet sand, with no buttery lumps. Beat the egg with the vanilla, then add to the bowl. Mix briefly with a cutlery knife to combine, then use your hands to knead the dough together – try not to overwork the dough, or the biscuits will be tough. Shape into a disc, then wrap in cling film and chill for at least 15 mins. Heat oven to 180C/160C fan/gas 4. Line two baking sheets with baking parchment.
- Dust a work surface with flour. Halve the dough, then roll one half out to the thickness of a £1 coin. Use an egg-shaped cookie cutter (ours was 10cm long; you could also make a cardboard template to cut around) to stamp out as many cookies as you can, then transfer them to one of the baking sheets, leaving a little space between the biscuits. Repeat with the other half of the dough. If you want to make jammy biscuits, use a small circular cutter to stamp holes in half of the biscuits (where the yolk would be). If you intend to make both iced and jammy biscuits, only stamp holes in a quarter of the biscuits.
- Bake for 12-15 mins, until the biscuits are pale gold. Cool on the sheets for 10 mins, then transfer to a wire rack to cool fully. Once cool, decorate to your liking (see next steps). Will keep in an airtight container for up to five days.
- To decorate the biscuits with icing, add enough water to the icing sugar to make a thick icing – it should hold its shape without spreading when piped. Transfer about a third of the icing to a piping bag fitted with a very small round nozzle (or just snip a tiny opening at the tip). Pipe an outline around the biscuits, then draw patterns in the middle – lines, spots and zigzags work well. Leave to dry for 10 mins. Divide the remaining icing between as many colours as you'd like to use, then use the gels to dye them. Loosen each icing with a few drops of water, then transfer them to piping bags. Use the coloured icing to fill the empty spaces on the biscuits. You may need to use a cocktail stick to tease it into the corners. Once covered, leave to dry for a few hours.
- To make the jammy middle biscuits, dust the biscuits with holes in the middle with a heavy coating of icing sugar. Spread the jam or curd generously over the whole biscuits, then sandwich the dusted biscuits on top of them.

Nutrition Information

- Calories: 163 calories
- Sodium: 0.2 milligram of sodium
- Saturated Fat: 4 grams saturated fat
- Sugar: 8 grams sugar
- Total Carbohydrate: 21 grams carbohydrates
- Protein: 2 grams protein
- Total Fat: 7 grams fat
- Fiber: 1 grams fiber

12. Easter Chocolate Truffle Cake

Serving: 12 | Prep: 45mins | Cook: 40mins | Ready in:

Ingredients

- For the cake
- 150ml sunflower oil or groundnut oil, plus extra for greasing
- 175g self-raising flour, plus extra for dusting
- 4 tbsp cocoa powder
- 1 tsp baking powder
- 1 tsp bicarbonate of soda
- 140g golden caster sugar
- 2 tbsp golden syrup
- 2 eggs
- 150ml full-fat milk
- For the icing and filling
- 125ml double cream
- 1 tbsp soft butter
- 140g dark chocolate (about 70% cocoa solids)
- 4 tbsp raspberry jam or apricot jam
- For the truffles
- 100g milk chocolate, broken into chunks
- 1 tsp soft butter

- 50g digestive biscuits
- 2-3 tbsp coloured or chocolate sprinkles

Direction

- Heat oven to 160C/140C fan/gas 3. Grease two 20cm cake tins and dust with flour. Tip all the cake ingredients into a large bowl and beat well with an electric hand whisk or wooden spoon to give a smooth, thick batter consistency.
- Divide the mixture between the tins and bake in the oven for 30-35 mins until it springs back to the touch and a skewer inserted into the centre comes out clean. Leave to cool in the tins for about 10 mins, then turn out onto a wire rack.
- Meanwhile, make the truffles. In a bowl, gently melt the milk chocolate in the microwave or over a pan of simmering water. Stir in the butter. Put the biscuits in a sandwich bag and crush them to fine crumbs by bashing with a rolling pin. Mix into the chocolate and chill in the fridge for about 20 mins. When chilled, roll into 11 even-sized balls with your hands. Coat in sprinkles and set aside.
- For the icing, pour the cream into a saucepan and place over a medium heat. Once hot, stir in the butter until melted. Break the chocolate into small pieces, tip into a medium bowl and pour over the hot cream mixture. Stir well until the chocolate melts into the cream. Cool for about 30 mins.
- Once the cake is completely cool, sandwich the two sponges together with the jam in the middle. Spread the top and sides with the icing. Finish by placing the truffles around the outside of the cake.

Nutrition Information

- Calories: 478 calories
- Total Carbohydrate: 43 grams carbohydrates
- Protein: 6 grams protein
- Sugar: 28 grams sugar
- Saturated Fat: 12 grams saturated fat
- Sodium: 0.6 milligram of sodium
- Fiber: 3 grams fiber
- Total Fat: 30 grams fat

13. Easter Egg Cookies

Serving: Makes 20 | Prep: 20mins | Cook: 55mins | Ready in:

Ingredients

- 175g butter, softened
- 200g light brown soft sugar
- 100g golden caster sugar
- 1 tbsp vanilla extract
- 1 large egg
- 250g plain flour
- ½ tsp bicarbonate of soda
- 50g white chocolate, chopped into chunks
- 100g bar dark chocolate, chopped into chunks
- 100g mini chocolate eggs, lightly crushed with a rolling pin, leaving some larger pieces to decorate

Direction

- Heat oven to 190C/170C fan/gas 5. Line two baking sheets with baking parchment. Tip the butter, sugars and vanilla into a bowl. Beat with a hand-held electric whisk until pale and fluffy. Add the egg and beat again. Tip in the flour, bicarb and a pinch of salt, then use a spatula to mix together before adding the chocolate chunks and about half the crushed mini eggs (set aside the larger pieces) and mix again until everything is combined.
- Scoop golf-ball-sized mounds of cookie dough onto the baking sheets, making sure you leave plenty of space between each one. (You should fit 4-6 cookies on each, so you'll have to bake in batches to make the total 20 cookies.) Push the remaining mini egg pieces into the tops. Can be frozen at this point for up to three months. Defrost thoroughly in the fridge before baking. Bake for 15-18 mins, swapping

the sheets around halfway through. For soft and chewy cookies, the cookies should be golden around the edges but still pale and soft in the middle. If you prefer a biscuit texture, you will need to bake them a little longer.

- Remove from the oven and leave to cool for 10 mins before transferring to a wire rack, then bake the second batch. Continue until all the cookies are baked. Will keep in an airtight container for up to a week.

Nutrition Information

- Calories: 241 calories
- Fiber: 1 grams fiber
- Total Carbohydrate: 31 grams carbohydrates
- Sodium: 0.3 milligram of sodium
- Total Fat: 11 grams fat
- Saturated Fat: 7 grams saturated fat
- Sugar: 21 grams sugar
- Protein: 2 grams protein

14. Easter Simnel Cake

Serving: 12 | Prep: 30mins | Cook: 2hours | Ready in:

Ingredients

- 250g mixed dried fruit (a mixture of sultanas, currants, raisins and candied mixed peel)
- 1 orange, zested and juiced
- 500g pack marzipan
- 250g pack butter, softened
- 200g light brown soft sugar
- 4 eggs, plus 1 beaten to glaze
- 175g plain flour
- 100g ground almonds
- 1 tsp baking powder
- 1 lemon, zested
- 2 tsp mixed spice
- 1 tsp vanilla extract
- 100g glacé cherries, halved
- 3 tbsp apricot jam

Direction

- Put the mixed dried fruit in a bowl with the orange juice and zest and 2 tbsp water. Cover and microwave for 2 mins, then leave to cool completely. Alternatively, heat gently in a pan, stirring now and then until the liquid has been absorbed and leave to cool.
- Heat oven to 150C/130C fan/gas 2. Roll out a third of the marzipan and use the base of a deep 20cm cake tin as a template to cut out a circle. Wrap any offcuts and the remaining two-thirds of marzipan and set aside for later. Butter and line the cake tin with a double layer of parchment. Beat the butter and sugar together until creamy. Add the eggs, flour, almonds, baking powder, lemon zest, mixed spice and vanilla (all in one go) and mix until well combined. Mix in the cooled soaked dried fruit and fold in the cherries.
- Scrape half the cake mixture into the tin. Top with the disc of marzipan, then the remaining cake mixture, and level the top with a spatula. Bake for 2 hrs. Check it's cooked by inserting a skewer to the centre of the cake, if any wet mixture clings to the skewer, return to the oven for another 10 mins, then check again. Cool in the tin for 15 mins, then turn out onto a wire rack and leave to cool completely.
- Brush the top of the cake with apricot jam. Roll out half of the remaining marzipan and use the base of the cake as a template to cut out another disc. Place it on top of the cake and crimp the edges, if you like. Roll the remaining marzipan into 11 equal-sized balls for the apostles. Brush the marzipan with beaten egg and arrange the apostles in a circle on top around the outside, and brush them with a little egg too. Put under a hot grill for a minute or two until just starting to caramelise – be very careful as the marzipan will burn easily. Leave to cool and wrap a ribbon around the cake, if you like. Will keep for up to a week in a sealed tin.

Nutrition Information

- Calories: 619 calories
- Saturated Fat: 12 grams saturated fat
- Total Carbohydrate: 77 grams carbohydrates
- Sodium: 0.65 milligram of sodium
- Sugar: 60 grams sugar
- Fiber: 2 grams fiber
- Total Fat: 29 grams fat
- Protein: 10 grams protein

15. Easy Easter Biscuits

Serving: Makes 40 | Prep: 30mins | Cook: 15mins | Ready in:

Ingredients

- 250g unsalted butter, softened
- 140g golden caster sugar, plus extra for sprinkling
- 1 medium egg, separated and beaten
- 1 lemon, zested
- generous grating of nutmeg
- 300g plain flour, plus extra for dusting
- ½ tsp fine salt
- 60g currants

Direction

- Heat the oven to 180C/160 fan/gas 4. Place the butter and sugar in a bowl and beat together with a wooden spoon until well combined. Add the egg yolk, lemon zest and nutmeg and beat again.
- Add the flour, salt and currants and mix everything together to make a firm dough, using your hands if necessary. Form into a puck-shape, wrap and chill in the fridge for 30 mins.
- Line two large baking sheets with baking parchment and lightly dust your work surface with flour. Cut the dough in half and roll out to a ½ cm thickness. Cut out biscuits using a 6cm fluted cutter, lift onto one of the baking sheets with a palette knife, leaving a little space in between. Repeat with the remaining

pastry to make a second tray of biscuits, re-rolling the off-cuts. Chill for 30 mins.
- Bake for 7 mins, then remove from the oven, brush with egg white, sprinkle with extra sugar and return to the oven for 7-8 mins or until lightly golden brown. Leave to cool on the trays for 5 mins then carefully transfer to a wire rack to cool completely.

Nutrition Information

- Calories: 100 calories
- Saturated Fat: 3 grams saturated fat
- Fiber: 0.4 grams fiber
- Protein: 1 grams protein
- Total Fat: 5 grams fat
- Sugar: 6 grams sugar
- Total Carbohydrate: 12 grams carbohydrates
- Sodium: 0.07 milligram of sodium

16. Easy Easter Nests

Serving: Makes 12 | Prep: 25mins | Cook: 8mins | Ready in:

Ingredients

- 200g milk chocolate, broken into pieces
- 85g shredded wheat, crushed
- 2 x 100g bags mini chocolate eggs
- You'll also need
- cupcake cases

Direction

- Melt the chocolate in a small bowl placed over a pan of barely simmering water. Pour the chocolate over the shredded wheat and stir well to combine.
- Spoon the chocolate wheat into 12 cupcake cases and press the back of a teaspoon in the centre to create a nest shape. Place 3 mini chocolate eggs on top of each nest. Chill the nests in the fridge for 2 hrs until set.

Nutrition Information

- Calories: 139 calories
- Protein: 2 grams protein
- Total Fat: 7 grams fat
- Saturated Fat: 4 grams saturated fat
- Total Carbohydrate: 18 grams carbohydrates
- Sugar: 13 grams sugar
- Fiber: 1 grams fiber

17. Edd Kimber's Bakewell Ombre Cake

Serving: Cuts into 12 slices | Prep: 2hours15mins | Cook: 30mins | Ready in:

Ingredients

- For the almond cake layers
- 325g plain flour
- 25g cornflour
- 4 ½ tsp baking powder
- 225g butter, at room temperature
- 400g golden caster sugar
- 1 tsp vanilla extract
- 2 tsp almond extract
- 5 medium egg whites, lightly beaten
- 300ml whole milk
- For the raspberry cream cheese frosting
- 300g butter, at room temperature
- 625g icing sugar
- 450g full-fat cream cheese
- 300g seedless raspberry jam
- red paste food colouring

Direction

- Heat oven to 180C/160C fan/gas 4. Grease 3 x 20cm round cake tins and line the bases with baking parchment, greasing the parchment, too.
- In a medium bowl, stir together the flour, cornflour, baking powder and ½ tsp salt, then set aside. Put the butter in a large bowl and beat for about 3 mins until smooth and creamy. Add the caster sugar and beat for about 5 mins until light and fluffy. Add the extracts and mix to combine.
- Add the egg white a little at a time, beating until fully combined. Sift in the flour mixture in 3 additions, alternating with the milk, but starting and finishing with the flour.
- Divide the mixture equally between the prepared tins, gently levelling out. Bake for 25-30 mins, or until the cake springs back when lightly touched. Allow the cakes to cool in the tins for 10 mins before inverting onto a wire rack to cool completely. The sponge is quite delicate, so take care when working with the cooled cake.
- For the frosting, beat the butter for about 3 mins until light and creamy. Add the icing sugar, a little bit at a time, until fully combined. Beat the frosting until light and smooth, then add the cream cheese and half the jam. Mix until just smooth – don't overmix as it will get thinner the more you stir.
- Put the first cake on a serving plate and spread a layer of the frosting over the top. Then spread half the remaining jam evenly over the frosting. Repeat with the second cake and finally place the third cake on top. Cover the outside of the whole cake with a thin layer of frosting using a palette knife, and put it in the fridge while you prepare the frosting for the decoration.
- Divide the remaining frosting between 3 small bowls. Add about ½ tsp of red paste colouring to one of the bowls and about 1 tsp colouring to another bowl, leaving the third bowl as it is. You want to have three bowls of frosting with clearly different colours.
- To decorate the cakes, put each frosting into a piping bag fitted with a small round piping tip. Pipe 6 dots of frosting up the cake, 2 of each colour, with the darkest at the base of the cake. Use a teaspoon or small palette knife to smear the frosting to the right. Repeat the piping process, moving the dots up one so that as you pipe around the cake the colour will graduate in a swirl. For the top, pipe 2 rings of the darker pink dots around the outside,

spreading the frosting in the same fashion, followed by 2 rings of the medium pink dots, and finish with the lighter frosting in the middle. Will keep for up to 3 days, chilled.

Nutrition Information

- Calories: 1006 calories
- Sodium: 1.1 milligram of sodium
- Saturated Fat: 34 grams saturated fat
- Protein: 6 grams protein
- Total Fat: 55 grams fat
- Sugar: 103 grams sugar
- Fiber: 1 grams fiber
- Total Carbohydrate: 123 grams carbohydrates

18. Flowerpot Chocolate Chip Muffins

Serving: Makes 10 mini muffins | Prep: 10mins | Cook: 15mins | Ready in:

Ingredients

- 3 tbsp vegetable oil
- 125g plain flour
- 1 tsp baking powder
- 25g cocoa powder
- 100g golden caster sugar
- 1 large egg
- 100ml milk
- 150g milk chocolate chips
- 25g chocolate cake decorations such as vermicelli sprinkles or chocolate-coated popping candy
- 20 rice paper wafer daisies (these come in packs of 12, so get 2 packs)
- You will need
- 10 mini teracotta pots (see tip)

Direction

- Heat oven to 180C/160C fan/gas 4. Lightly oil the inside of the terracotta pots with a little vegetable oil and place on a baking tray. Place a paper mini muffin case in the bottom of each pot.
- Put the flour, baking powder and cocoa in a bowl and stir in the sugar.
- Crack the egg into a jug and whisk with the milk and remaining oil. Pour this over the flour and cocoa mixture, and stir in with 50g of the chocolate chips. Be careful not to overmix – you want a loose but still quite lumpy mixture. Spoon into the pots up to three-quarters full. Place in the middle of the oven and bake for 12-15 mins until risen and firm. Transfer to a wire rack (still in the pots) and leave to cool.
- Put the rest of the chocolate chips in a small bowl and melt over a small pan of gently simmering water (don't let the water touch the bowl), or put in a microwave-proof bowl and heat on High for 1 min until melted.
- Spread the tops of the muffins with the melted chocolate. Sprinkle over the chocolate decorations and add 2 rice paper wafer daisies to each pot to serve. Will keep for 2 days in an airtight container.

Nutrition Information

- Calories: 215 calories
- Sugar: 19 grams sugar
- Saturated Fat: 4 grams saturated fat
- Protein: 4 grams protein
- Sodium: 0.2 milligram of sodium
- Total Fat: 9 grams fat
- Total Carbohydrate: 28 grams carbohydrates
- Fiber: 1 grams fiber

19. Fruity Simnel Squares

Serving: Cuts into 15 squares | Prep: 40mins | Cook: 1hours | Ready in:

Ingredients

- 250g mixed dried fruit
- 100g dried apricot, chopped
- 85g glacé cherry, chopped
- zest 2 oranges, juice 1 orange (use the second in the topping)
- 200g butter, softened, plus extra for the tin
- 200g light muscovado sugar
- 4 large eggs
- 200g self-raising flour
- 50g ground almond
- 2 tsp mixed spice
- 1 tsp ground cinnamon
- ½ tsp freshly grated nutmeg
- 500g marzipan, 200g/7oz cut into 2cm chunks, the rest for the topping
- For the topping
- 50g butter
- 50g light muscovado sugar
- 100g plain flour
- 100g flaked almond
- 3 tbsp golden syrup
- 85g icing sugar, sieved
- 2-3 tsp orange juice

Direction

- Soak all the dried fruit in the orange juice for 2 hrs, or overnight.
- Butter and line a 20 x 30cm tin with baking parchment. Heat oven to 160C/ 140C fan/gas 3. In a large bowl, beat the butter and sugar with an electric whisk until pale and fluffy. Add the eggs one at a time; mix well between each addition.
- Sift the flour into the bowl and mix in the ground almonds and spices. Add the marzipan chunks, zest and dried fruit with any remaining juice, and give everything a good stir to combine.
- Tip the cake mix into the prepared tin, level the surface, and bake for 45 mins – the cake may still be a little gooey in the centre at this point. Remove from the oven and increase the heat to 200C/ 180C fan/gas 6.
- Make the topping. Rub the butter, sugar and flour together with your fingers to a crumbly breadcrumb texture. Grate in 200g reserved marzipan, add the flaked almonds and golden syrup. Mix everything with a fork, making sure it stays crumbly and doesn't clump. Sprinkle over the cake and return to the oven for 12-15 mins. Meanwhile, divide the rest of the marzipan into 11 and roll into balls.
- Remove the cake from the oven once cooked through, arrange the marzipan balls on top and allow to cool in the tin. Mix the icing sugar with enough orange juice to give a runny icing, drizzle it all over the cake, then let it set a little before slicing it.

Nutrition Information

- Calories: 576 calories
- Total Fat: 25 grams fat
- Saturated Fat: 10 grams saturated fat
- Total Carbohydrate: 79 grams carbohydrates
- Sugar: 65 grams sugar
- Fiber: 3 grams fiber
- Protein: 9 grams protein
- Sodium: 0.5 milligram of sodium

20. Hot Cross Bread & Lemon Pudding

Serving: 4 | Prep: 20mins | Cook: 40mins | Ready in:

Ingredients

- knob of butter, for the dish
- 4 stale hot cross buns
- 200g lemon curd
- 2 large eggs
- 200ml double cream
- 200ml milk
- ½ tsp vanilla extract
- 4 tbsp caster sugar
- little lemon zest
- cream or vanilla ice cream, to serve (optional)

Direction

- Butter a 1-litre baking dish that will quite snugly fit the buns. Cut each bun into 3 slices, and sandwich back together with a generous spreading of curd. Arrange buns in the dish.
- Whisk egg, cream, milk and remaining curd, then sieve into a jug with the vanilla and 3 tbsp of the sugar. Pour over the buns and stand at room temperature for 30 mins for the custard to soak in.
- Heat oven to 160C/140C fan/ gas 3. Scatter the remaining sugar and lemon zest over the pudding. Bake for 30-40 mins until the top is golden and the custard gently set. Stand for 5 mins, then serve with cream or vanilla ice cream, if you like.

Nutrition Information

- Calories: 676 calories
- Fiber: 1 grams fiber
- Protein: 10 grams protein
- Sodium: 0.4 milligram of sodium
- Total Fat: 38 grams fat
- Sugar: 49 grams sugar
- Saturated Fat: 20 grams saturated fat
- Total Carbohydrate: 74 grams carbohydrates

21. Hot Cross Buns

Serving: Makes 15 | Prep: 30mins | Cook: 20mins | Ready in:

Ingredients

- For the buns
- 300ml full-fat milk, plus 2 tbsp more
- 50g butter
- 500g strong bread flour
- 1 tsp salt
- 75g caster sugar
- 1 tbsp sunflower oil
- 7g sachet fast-action or easy-blend yeast
- 1 egg, beaten
- 75g sultanas
- 50g mixed peel
- zest 1 orange
- 1 apple, peeled, cored and finely chopped
- 1 tsp ground cinnamon
- For the cross
- 75g plain flour, plus extra for dusting
- For the glaze
- 3 tbsp apricot jam

Direction

- Bring 300ml full-fat milk to the boil, then remove from the heat and add 50g butter. Leave to cool until it reaches hand temperature. Put 500g strong bread flour, 1 tsp salt, 75g caster sugar and 7g sachet fast-action or easy-blend yeast into a bowl. Make a well in the centre. Pour in the warm milk and butter mixture, then add 1 beaten egg. Using a wooden spoon, mix well, then bring everything together with your hands until you have a sticky dough.
- Tip on to a lightly floured surface and knead by holding the dough with one hand and stretching it with the heal of the other hand, then folding it back on itself. Repeat for 5 mins until smooth and elastic. Put the dough in a lightly oiled bowl. Cover with oiled cling film and leave to rise in a warm place for 1 hr or until doubled in size and a finger pressed into it leaves a dent.
- With the dough still in the bowl, tip in 75g sultanas, 50g mixed peel, zest of 1 orange, 1 finely chopped apple and 1 tsp ground cinnamon. Knead into the dough, making sure everything is well distributed. Leave to rise for 1 hr more, or until doubled in size, again covered by some well-oiled cling film to stop the dough getting a crust.
- Divide the dough into 15 even pieces (about 75g per piece). Roll each piece into a smooth ball on a lightly floured work surface. Arrange the buns on one or two baking trays lined with parchment, leaving enough space for the dough to expand. Cover (but don't wrap) with more oiled cling film, or a clean tea towel, then set aside to prove for 1 hr more.

- Heat oven to 220C/200C fan/gas 7. Mix 75g plain flour with about 5 tbsp water to make the paste for the cross - add the water 1 tbsp at a time, so you add just enough for a thick paste. Spoon into a piping bag with a small nozzle. Pipe a line along each row of buns, then repeat in the other direction to create crosses. Bake for 20 mins on the middle shelf of the oven, until golden brown.
- Gently heat 3 tbsp apricot jam to melt, then sieve to get rid of any chunks. While the jam is still warm, brush over the top of the warm buns and leave to cool.

Nutrition Information

- Calories: 226 calories
- Total Carbohydrate: 41 grams carbohydrates
- Total Fat: 4 grams fat
- Saturated Fat: 2 grams saturated fat
- Sugar: 14 grams sugar
- Protein: 5 grams protein
- Sodium: 0.5 milligram of sodium
- Fiber: 2 grams fiber

22. Hot Cross Cinnamon Buns

Serving: Makes 12 | Prep: 25mins | Cook: 25mins | Ready in:

Ingredients

- 250ml whole milk
- 1 lemon, zested
- 150g butter, cubed
- 640g strong white flour, plus extra for dusting
- 2 tsp cinnamon
- 85g golden caster sugar
- 7g sachet fast-action dried yeast
- 2 medium eggs, beaten separately
- a little vegetable or sunflower oil, for proving
- 50g light brown soft sugar
- 100g mixed dried fruit
- 100g cream cheese

- 75g icing sugar

Direction

- Warm the milk and lemon zest in a small saucepan until steaming. Remove from the heat and add 25g butter, swirling until it has melted and the milk has cooled slightly.
- Mix 500g flour, 1 tsp cinnamon, the caster sugar, yeast and 1 tsp salt in a large bowl. Pour in the milk mixture and one of the beaten eggs, then combine with a wooden spoon until the mixture clumps together. Tip out onto your work surface and knead until smooth and elastic, about 10 mins – the dough should bounce back when pressed with your finger. Transfer to an oiled bowl, cover with a tea towel and leave to rise for 2 hrs or until doubled in size.
- While the dough rises, make your cinnamon butter. Mash the remaining butter and cinnamon with the light brown sugar.
- Dust your largest baking tray with flour. Tip the dough onto the work surface and knead again to knock out any air bubbles. Roll the dough to a rectangle roughly 30 x 40cm. Spread the cinnamon butter over the dough, covering the whole surface. Scatter over the dried fruit. From one of the longer edges, roll up the dough into a tight sausage shape. Use a sharp knife to cut the dough into 12 equal-sized pieces. Arrange them on the tray, leaving a small gap between each one and making sure the open end of the scroll is facing inwards to prevent them springing open as they cook. Cover loosely and leave somewhere warm to prove for 1 hr or until almost doubled in size – the buns should be just touching.
- Heat oven to 180C/160C fan/gas 4. Brush the buns with a little beaten egg. Mix the remaining 140g flour with enough water to make a thick, smooth paste, then transfer to a piping bag fitted with a small round nozzle (or use a sandwich bag with a corner snipped off). Use the paste to pipe crosses over the buns, then bake for 25 mins until deep golden brown and cooked through.

- Leave to cool for 10 mins on the tray. Meanwhile, mix the cream cheese and icing sugar, then brush the mixture over the warm buns. If you have any excess, you can serve this on the side for spreading over. Eat the buns warm from the oven or leave to cool. Will keep for up to two days in an airtight container.

Nutrition Information

- Calories: 431 calories
- Total Carbohydrate: 64 grams carbohydrates
- Sugar: 24 grams sugar
- Fiber: 2 grams fiber
- Protein: 9 grams protein
- Sodium: 0.8 milligram of sodium
- Total Fat: 15 grams fat
- Saturated Fat: 9 grams saturated fat

23. Lemon & Marzipan Hot Cross Buns

Serving: Makes 12 | Prep: 45mins | Cook: 30mins | Ready in:

Ingredients

- 250ml full-fat milk
- zest 2 lemons
- 50g butter,cubed
- 500g strong white flour, plus 140g/5oz for the crosses and extra for dusting
- ½ tsp ground cinnamon
- 85g golden caster sugar
- 7g sachet fast-action dried yeast
- 1 large egg, beaten, plus 1 egg to glaze
- vegetable oil or sunflower oil, for greasing
- 200g marzipan, chilled
- 100g mixed dried fruit
- 50g candied lemon peel (or use mixed peel)
- 1 tbsp lemon curd, to glaze, plus extra to serve
- salted butter, to serve

Direction

- Warm the milk and lemon zest in a small saucepan until steaming. Remove from the heat and add the butter, swirling the pan until it has melted and the milk has cooled slightly.
- Mix the flour, cinnamon, sugar, yeast and 1 tsp salt in a large bowl. Pour in the milk mixture and the beaten egg, and combine with a wooden spoon until the mixture clumps together. Tip out onto your work surface and knead until smooth and elastic, about 10 mins – the dough should bounce back when pressed with your finger. Transfer to a clean oiled bowl, cover with cling film or a tea towel and leave to rise for 2 hrs or until doubled in size.
- Dust your largest baking tray with flour. Tip the dough onto the work surface and knead again to knock out any air bubbles. Roll the dough to a rectangle roughly 30 x 40cm. Grate the marzipan on the coarse side of a cheese grater, straight onto the dough, covering the whole surface. Scatter over the dried fruit and candied peel too. From one of the longer edges, roll up the dough into a tight sausage shape. Use a sharp knife to cut the dough into 12 equal pieces, then lightly roll each piece into a smooth ball, closing the cut edges. Try not to overwork the dough or you'll lose the layers of marzipan. Instead, pinch the sides together in a purse shape, concentrating on creating a smooth surface on the bottom (which will become the top). Arrange the balls on the tray, smooth-side up, leaving a small gap between each one. Cover loosely with a piece of oiled cling film and leave somewhere warm to prove for 1 hr or until almost doubled in size – the buns should be just touching.
- Heat oven to 180C/160C fan/gas 4. Brush the buns with a little beaten egg. Mix the 140g flour with enough water to make a thick, smooth paste, then transfer to a piping bag fitted with a small round nozzle (or use a sandwich bag and snip off one corner). Use the paste to pipe crosses over the buns. Bake for 25 mins until deep golden brown and cooked through.

- Mix the lemon curd with 1-2 tsp water to loosen it a little, then brush over the top of the buns. Leave to cool for 10 mins on the baking tray. Serve warm from the oven or toasted, with butter and lemon curd. Will keep for up to 3 days in a tin, or freeze for up to 2 months.

Nutrition Information

- Calories: 389 calories
- Protein: 9 grams protein
- Total Carbohydrate: 68 grams carbohydrates
- Sugar: 27 grams sugar
- Total Fat: 8 grams fat
- Saturated Fat: 3 grams saturated fat
- Fiber: 3 grams fiber
- Sodium: 0.6 milligram of sodium

24. Lemon Curd & Orange Cake

Serving: 10 | Prep: 15mins | Cook: 20mins |Ready in:

Ingredients

- 170g soft salted butter
- 150g golden caster sugar
- 2 eggs
- 70g natural yogurt
- 150g self-raising flour
- 50g ground almonds
- 1 large orange, zested
- 2-3 tbsp milk
- 10 tbsp lemon curd
- 20g flaked almonds
- lemon zest, to decorate

Direction

- Heat the oven to 180C/160C fan/gas 4. Butter a 1-litre loaf tin and line with baking parchment.
- Put the butter, sugar, eggs, yogurt, self-raising flour, ground almonds, orange zest, milk and 5 tbsp lemon curd in a large bowl

and whisk until smooth. Put another 5 tbsp lemon curd in a second bowl and whisk to loosen.

- Spoon half the batter into the prepared tin, dollop over the lemon curd and top with the remaining batter. Scatter over the flaked almonds and bake for 50 mins, or until risen and golden. Leave to cool on a wire rack, scatter over some lemon zest and slice.

Nutrition Information

- Calories: 365 calories
- Total Carbohydrate: 40 grams carbohydrates
- Sugar: 26 grams sugar
- Fiber: 1 grams fiber
- Saturated Fat: 10 grams saturated fat
- Sodium: 0.6 milligram of sodium
- Total Fat: 20 grams fat
- Protein: 6 grams protein

25. Lemon Drizzle Simnel Slices

Serving: cuts into 16 pieces | Prep: 35mins | Cook: 40mins |Ready in:

Ingredients

- oil, for the tin
- 250g butter, softened
- 250g golden caster sugar, plus 50g for the topping
- 2 large lemons, zested and juiced
- 3 large eggs
- 200g plain flour
- 100g ground almonds
- 2 ½ tsp baking powder
- 50ml milk
- 100g mixed dried fruit
- 300g marzipan, chilled
- 50g icing sugar

Direction

- Heat oven to 180C/160C fan/gas 4. Oil and line a 20cm x 30cm baking tin with baking parchment. Beat the butter and sugar with most of the lemon zest until pale and fluffy. Add the eggs one at a time, mixing constantly, then add the flour, almonds and baking powder, and keep mixing until you have a smooth cake batter. Stir in the milk and dried fruit.
- Scrape half the cake batter into the tin and level the surface. Coarsely grate half the marzipan onto the batter to create an even layer, then cover with the rest of the batter, trying not to disturb the marzipan too much. Level the top and bake for 35-40 mins or until a skewer inserted into the centre comes out clean. If any wet cake mixture clings to the skewer, return the cake to the oven for 5 mins, then check again. Mix the remaining caster sugar with a quarter of the lemon juice, then drizzle over the cake while still warm. Leave the cake to cool in the tin.
- Mix the icing sugar with enough lemon juice to make a drizzly icing – 2-3 tsp should be enough. Divide the rest of the marzipan into 11 even lumps and roll into balls. Drizzle the icing over the cake, top with the marzipan balls and sprinkle with the remaining lemon zest. Will keep in an airtight container for up to five days.

Nutrition Information

- Calories: 401 calories
- Saturated Fat: 9 grams saturated fat
- Total Fat: 20 grams fat
- Total Carbohydrate: 48 grams carbohydrates
- Sodium: 0.5 milligram of sodium
- Protein: 6 grams protein
- Sugar: 39 grams sugar
- Fiber: 1 grams fiber

26. Little Carrot Cakes With Orange & Honey Syrup

Serving: Makes 12 | Prep: 15mins | Cook: 20mins | Ready in:

Ingredients

- 150ml sunflower oil, plus a little for the tin
- 175g light muscovado sugar
- 200g self-raising flour
- 1 tsp bicarbonate of soda
- 2 tsp mixed spice
- 1 orange, zested and juiced (save the juice for the syrup)
- 2 large eggs
- 50g natural yogurt
- 200g carrots, about 2 large ones, peeled and grated
- For the syrup and icing
- 50ml runny honey, plus extra to drizzle (optional)
- 150g mascarpone
- 100g thick natural yogurt
- 75g icing sugar, sieved
- edible flowers or extra orange zest, to decorate

Direction

- Heat oven to 180C/160C fan/gas 4 and oil a 12-hole muffin tin, or line it with muffin cases. In a large mixing bowl, mix the sugar, flour, bicarb, mixed spice and orange zest. Whisk together the eggs, oil and yogurt, then stir into the dry ingredients along with the grated carrots. Pour the mixture into the prepared tin, or divide between the cases, if using, then bake for 20-22 mins until a skewer inserted in to the middle comes out clean. Turn the cakes out onto a wire rack and leave them to cool a little.
- Meanwhile, to make the syrup, heat the honey and orange juice in a pan. Bring to the boil, then simmer for a minute until syrupy. Spoon a few tsp over each cake while still warm, then leave to cool completely. For the icing, mix the mascarpone, yogurt and icing sugar until just

combined (if you over-mix, it will become runny). Use a palette or cutlery knife to swirl the icing on top of the cakes, drizzle with a little more honey, if you like, and decorate with edible flowers or orange zest.

Nutrition Information

- Calories: 356 calories
- Protein: 4 grams protein
- Total Fat: 20 grams fat
- Sodium: 0.5 milligram of sodium
- Sugar: 27 grams sugar
- Saturated Fat: 6 grams saturated fat
- Total Carbohydrate: 39 grams carbohydrates
- Fiber: 1 grams fiber

27. Raspberry Red Velvet Cake

Serving: Cuts into 8 slices | Prep: 25mins | Cook: 30mins | Ready in:

Ingredients

- 280g golden caster sugar
- 175g butter, softened
- 3 large eggs
- 280g self-raising flour
- 75g cocoa powder
- 150ml buttermilk
- 1 tsp white wine vinegar
- 85g full-fat cream cheese
- 75g puréed raspberry, sieved to remove seeds
- ¼ tsp red food gel
- 150g punnet raspberry, optional
- For the cream cheese frosting
- 200g icing sugar
- 50g butter, softened
- 140g cream cheese

Direction

- Heat oven to 180C/160C fan/gas 4. Grease and line the bases of 2 x 20cm sandwich tins with baking parchment. Using an electric hand whisk, beat together the caster sugar and butter until light and fluffy. Add the eggs one at a time, beating well between each addition.
- Sieve the flour and cocoa powder into a bowl. Add half to the egg mixture and fold in carefully. Mix together the buttermilk, vinegar, cream cheese, raspberry purée and food gel. Fold half the buttermilk mixture into the cake batter and repeat the process with both the flour mixture and buttermilk mixture.
- Spoon the combined mixtures into your prepared tins and cook for about 25-30 mins, until an inserted skewer comes out clean. Leave to cool for 10 mins before turning out onto a wire rack.
- For the frosting, mix together the icing sugar and butter until soft and creamy, then stir in the cream cheese. Sandwich the cooled cakes together with half of the frosting, adding 150g fresh raspberries if you like, then spread the remaining frosting over the top. Will keep for up to 3 days in a cool place.

Nutrition Information

- Calories: 750 calories
- Fiber: 3 grams fiber
- Sugar: 62 grams sugar
- Protein: 9 grams protein
- Total Fat: 41 grams fat
- Saturated Fat: 25 grams saturated fat
- Sodium: 1.2 milligram of sodium
- Total Carbohydrate: 86 grams carbohydrates

28. Rhubarb & Custard Blondies

Serving: 12 | Prep: 15mins | Cook: 55mins | Ready in:

Ingredients

- 225g salted butter (or unsalted with a pinch of salt), plus extra for the tin
- 200g light brown soft sugar

- 100g caster sugar
- 150g plain flour
- 50g custard powder
- ½ tsp baking powder
- 3 medium eggs
- 250g white chocolate chips or white chocolate finely chopped
- 2 tsp vanilla extract
- For the rhubarb & custard swirl
- 200g rhubarb (frozen, or canned and drained is fine)
- 75g caster sugar
- pink or red food colouring (optional)
- 4 tbsp ready-made custard (from a carton is fine, or made up from powder)

Direction

- For the rhubarb & custard swirl, put the rhubarb and sugar in a wide pan with 2 tbsp water (omit the water if using canned rhubarb). Cook over a medium heat, stirring frequently for about 10 mins, until the rhubarb breaks down and turns jammy. Add a few drops of food colouring if you want a pink rhubarb swirl, but the flavour will still be great if you're using green-tinged rhubarb. Leave to cool.
- Heat the oven to 180C/160C fan/gas 4. Put the butter and both sugars into a pan and put over a low heat. Melt together until smooth and shiny, then remove from the heat, and leave to cool for 10 mins while you sieve the flour, custard powder and baking powder in a bowl. Butter a 20 x 30cm baking tin and line with baking parchment.
- Beat the eggs into the cooled sugar and butter mixture, then fold in the dry ingredients until you have a smooth batter. Stir in 150g of the chocolate chips and the vanilla. Pour into the brownie tin, then use a teaspoon to swirl rhubarb compote on top of the batter. Add dollops of the custard, then swirl a skewer or cocktail stick through the compote to create a marbled pattern.
- Bake for 35-40 mins until set and the edges are coming away from the sides of the tin, then

leave in the tin to cool. Melt the remaining 100g chocolate in short blasts in the microwave or in a bowl set over a pan of simmering water. Use a spoon to drizzle the chocolate over the blondie in a zig-zag pattern. Cut into squares to serve. Will keep for three days in an airtight container, or freeze the squares individually.

Nutrition Information

- Calories: 464 calories
- Protein: 5 grams protein
- Sodium: 0.6 milligram of sodium
- Sugar: 44 grams sugar
- Fiber: 1 grams fiber
- Total Fat: 24 grams fat
- Total Carbohydrate: 57 grams carbohydrates
- Saturated Fat: 14 grams saturated fat

29. Rhubarb & Custard Tart

Serving: 8 | Prep: 40mins | Cook: 1hours | Ready in:

Ingredients

- For the pastry
- 225g plain flour, plus extra for dusting
- 3 tbsp icing sugar
- 140g unsalted butter, diced and chilled
- 1 medium egg yolk, plus 1 medium egg yolk beaten, for glazing (save the whites for meringues)
- 1 tsp vanilla bean paste
- For the vanilla custard
- ½ vanilla pod or 1 tsp vanilla bean paste
- 250ml whole milk
- 1 large egg, plus 2 large egg yolks
- 100g golden caster sugar
- 25g cornflour
- 1 tbsp unsalted butter
- For the roasted rhubarb

- 700g thin forced rhubarb (about 5 stalks), trimmed, rinsed and cut into 9cm/3 1/2 in-long pieces
- 175g golden caster sugar
- 1 vanilla pod, seeds scraped out, or 1 tsp vanilla paste
- juice 2 oranges
- 1 tbsp pistachio, chopped, to serve

Direction

- Put the flour, icing sugar and a pinch of salt in a large bowl and mix together. Add the butter and rub together until the mixture resembles breadcrumbs. Add 1 egg yolk, the vanilla and 1 tbsp cold water, and mix together until it just starts to come together as a dough. Tip the mixture onto a clean work surface and gently bring together with your hands. Wrap the pastry in cling film and chill for at least 1 hr before rolling out. Can be made 3 days ahead, or frozen for 2 months.
- Put the vanilla beans scraped from the pod (or the paste) in a pan over a medium-high heat, add the milk and bring to the boil. Meanwhile, tip the egg, yolks, sugar and cornflour into a bowl and whisk together until smooth. Pour the milk over the egg mixture, whisking to combine. Pour the custard back into the pan and cook, whisking constantly, for 2-3 mins until thickened. Scrape into a bowl and add the butter, mixing until melted and combined. Press a sheet of cling film onto the surface of the custard to stop a skin forming, and chill for 3 hrs. Can be made and chilled 3 days ahead.
- On a lightly floured surface, roll out the pastry into a large rectangle big enough to line a 30 x 20cm fluted rectangular tart tin. Roll the pastry onto the rolling pin and carefully drape it into the tin, carefully lifting and pressing into the corners and edges. Roll your rolling pin over the tart tin, cutting off the excess. Chill for 30 mins or until the pastry is firm.
- Heat oven to 180C/160C fan/gas 4. Line the tart with a piece of crumpled baking parchment and fill with baking beans or rice and place on a baking tray. Bake for about 30 mins, then remove the parchment and the beans, and return to the oven for another 5 mins or until the base is golden brown. Brush the inside of the tart with the remaining beaten egg yolk and return to the oven for 1 min to set (this creates a seal, meaning the pastry won't become soggy as quickly). Set aside to cool.
- Heat oven to 190C/170C fan/gas 5. Put the rhubarb batons in a small roasting tin (so that they are in one flat layer) and sprinkle over the sugar, the vanilla pod and its scraped out seeds, and the orange juice. Roast for 15-20 mins, or until the rhubarb has softened but is still holding its shape and a vibrant pink syrup has formed. Remove from the oven, discard the vanilla pod and allow to cool.
- Remove the custard from the fridge, beat to loosen, then pour over the pastry and smooth with a spatula. Top with the roasted rhubarb, brushing a little of the syrup on top, then sprinkle over the pistachios. Best eaten on the day its made.

Nutrition Information

- Calories: 515 calories
- Protein: 8 grams protein
- Total Fat: 22 grams fat
- Fiber: 3 grams fiber
- Sodium: 0.2 milligram of sodium
- Saturated Fat: 12 grams saturated fat
- Sugar: 44 grams sugar
- Total Carbohydrate: 68 grams carbohydrates

30. Rhubarb Buckle

Serving: 8 | Prep: 40mins | Cook: 1hours10mins | Ready in:

Ingredients

- For the crumble topping
- 50g plain flour

- 50g golden caster sugar
- ½ tsp ground ginger
- 50g unsalted butter, chilled
- 25g rolled oat
- For the rhubarb filling
- 225g thin, forced rhubarb, trimmed, rinsed and cut into 2.5cm/1in-long pieces
- 50g golden caster sugar
- zest 1 orange
- For the vanilla cake
- 100g unsalted butter, room temperature, plus extra for greasing
- 200g golden caster sugar
- zest 1 orange
- 2 large eggs
- 200g plain flour
- 2 tsp baking powder
- 1 tsp vanilla bean paste
- 125ml soured cream

Direction

- Heat oven to 180C/160C fan/gas 4. Grease a deep 20cm round cake tin and line the base with baking parchment.
- To make the crumble topping, put the flour, sugar and ginger in a bowl and mix together. Add the butter and rub together until the mixture resembles breadcrumbs. Stir in the oats and, using your hands, bring the mixture together into a dough, wrap in cling film and chill until needed.
- Put the rhubarb pieces in a bowl with the sugar and orange zest, and mix together. Set aside while you make the cake batter.
- Put the butter, sugar and orange zest in a large bowl and, using an electric whisk, beat together until light and fluffy, about 5 mins. Add the eggs, one at a time, beating together until combined before adding the next.
- In a separate bowl, mix the flour, baking powder, vanilla paste and a pinch of salt together and, in two additions, fold into the butter mixture, alternating with the soured cream. Tip into your cake tin and level out with a spatula. Top with the rhubarb mixture and finish by breaking the chilled crumble into

irregular-sized pieces and scattering over the rhubarb. Bake in the oven for about 1 hr 10 mins or until the crumble is golden and a skewer inserted into the middle of the cake comes out clean. Check the cake after 1 hr – if it is colouring too quickly, cover lightly with foil for the final 10 mins.
- Allow to cool in the tin for 10 mins before carefully transferring onto a wire rack to cool completely. Will keep in an airtight container for up to 3 days, but the crumble will lose some of its texture after the first day.

Nutrition Information

- Calories: 472 calories
- Total Carbohydrate: 65 grams carbohydrates
- Total Fat: 20 grams fat
- Fiber: 2 grams fiber
- Sugar: 39 grams sugar
- Protein: 6 grams protein
- Saturated Fat: 12 grams saturated fat
- Sodium: 0.4 milligram of sodium

31. Simnel Battenberg Cake

Serving: Cuts into 11 slices | Prep: 50mins | Cook: 25mins | Ready in:

Ingredients

- 200g softened butter, plus extra for greasing
- 200g golden caster sugar
- 3 large eggs
- 175g self-raising flour
- 50g ground almonds
- ½ tsp baking powder
- ¼ tsp almond extract
- 2 tbsp milk
- 3 tsp red food colouring
- ½ tsp yellow food colouring
- To assemble
- 200g apricot jam
- 2 x 500g blocks of marzipan

Direction

- Grease a 20cm square baking tin. Measure a double layer of foil long enough to line the base and 2 sides of the tin with 20cm excess. Fold a 10cm pleat in the centre (step 1). Push the foil into the tin, making sure the pleat is in the centre and the corners are nice and sharp (step 2). Line the 2 halves of the tin by putting a long strip of baking parchment in lengthways over the foil (step 3). Criss-cross another strip widthways to completely cover the foil (step 4). Repeat to line the other compartment. You now have two compartments for the different colours.
- Heat oven to 180C/160C fan/gas 4. Put the butter and sugar into a bowl and, using an electric whisk, beat until light and fluffy. Beat in the eggs, one at a time, then beat in the flour, baking powder and almond extract. The batter needs to be dropping consistency (it should fall off a wooden spoon). If it is a little thick, add a drop of milk and continue to beat.
- Halve the batter by weighing and dividing equally into separate bowls. Fold the red colouring through one and the yellow colouring through the other.
- Tip the batters into each side of the prepared tin and bake for about 25 mins, until the sponges have risen and a skewer inserted into each sponge comes out clean. Leave them to cool in the tin, then remove to a rack to cool completely.
- To assemble, neatly trim each sponge, then sit one on top of the other and trim again so they are both the same size. Cut each sponge in half lengthways so you have 4 long rectangles. Warm the jam in a small pan, then brush along a long side of each sponge. Stick the jam sides together to create the chequerboard effect, then brush the sides and top with more jam.
- Dust a work surface with icing sugar. Roll out one of the blocks of marzipan until it is 20cm long, then roll it so it is wide enough to wrap around the sponge. Brush the loaf all over with more apricot jam, then tightly wrap the marzipan around the sponge, trimming it where the edges meet. Smooth the marzipan over the sponge. Sit the loaf on its seam.
- To make the Apostles, roll the remaining marzipan into 11 small balls (you might not need all the marzipan for this, but any excess can be frozen) and sit on the loaf at even intervals. To give the cake a contrast of colour and a classic simnel cake finish, lightly blowtorch the balls on the top of cake. The cake will now keep for up to 3 days in an airtight container.

Nutrition Information

- Calories: 724 calories
- Protein: 10 grams protein
- Fiber: 1 grams fiber
- Total Fat: 31 grams fat
- Saturated Fat: 11 grams saturated fat
- Sodium: 0.6 milligram of sodium
- Total Carbohydrate: 101 grams carbohydrates
- Sugar: 89 grams sugar

32. Simnel Cake

Serving: Serves 10-12 | Prep: 30mins | Cook: 2hours30mins | Ready in:

Ingredients

- 225g sultanas
- 100g currants
- 50g mixed peel
- 2 lemons, 1 juiced and 2 zested
- 50ml orange juice
- 50ml brandy (optional)
- 225g butter, softened
- 225g light muscovado sugar
- 4 medium eggs
- 225g self-raising flour
- 100g glacé cherries, quartered
- 2 tsp mixed spice
- For the topping
- 500g yellow marzipan

- 1 tbsp apricot jam

Direction

- Put the sultanas, currants and mixed peel in a bowl with the lemon juice, orange juice, and brandy, if using. Mix well, cover and leave to soak overnight.
- Heat the oven to 150C/130C fan/gas 2. Line the base and sides of a 20cm round cake tin with baking parchment.
- Add the rest of the cake ingredients to the soaked fruit and stir until well combined. Spoon half of this mixture into the bottom of the cake tin and level it off so it's as flat as possible. Roll a third of the marzipan into a circle 20cm diameter and put it on the top. Gently add the rest of the mixture, levelling the surface again.
- Bake for approximately 2½ hours until brown, well-risen and firm to the touch. A metal skewer should come out clean when inserted. Allow to cool for 20 mins in the tin and then turn out to cool on a wire rack.
- Warm the apricot jam in a small saucepan and brush on the top of the cake. Roll out half of the remaining marzipan to the size of the top of the cake. Press it down firmly and push the edges down with your thumb to crimp it round the sides.
- Roll the rest of the marzipan into 11 balls (these represent the Apostles). Place the balls evenly on top of the cake in a circle, sticking them down with a little dab of the jam. Gently blow torch the top of the cake until the balls are a light golden brown, alternatively put the whole cake under a hot grill until the marzipan turns a light golden colour.

Nutrition Information

- Calories: 580 calories
- Total Fat: 22 grams fat
- Total Carbohydrate: 86 grams carbohydrates
- Protein: 7 grams protein
- Sodium: 0.7 milligram of sodium
- Saturated Fat: 11 grams saturated fat

- Sugar: 64 grams sugar
- Fiber: 3 grams fiber

33. Simnel Cherry Tart

Serving: Cuts into 15 squares | Prep: 50mins | Cook: 1hours | Ready in:

Ingredients

- 75g self-raising flour, plus extra for dusting
- 375g pack sweet shortcrust pastry
- 140g butter, softened
- 140g golden caster sugar
- 2 large eggs
- 75g ground almond
- 175g mixed dried fruit
- 50g glacé cherry, halved
- zest and juice 1 orange
- 1 tsp mixed spice
- 1 tsp cinnamon
- 6 tbsp cherry jam
- 350g marzipan, ½ cut into small cubes, ½ rolled into 11 balls to represent the apostles
- 50g icing sugar, to decorate
- 25g flaked toasted almond

Direction

- On a floured work surface, roll out the pastry to the thickness of a £1 coin. Lift the pastry over your rolling pin and use to line a 20 x 30cm rectangular fluted tart tin, leaving a rim of overhanging pastry. Chill for at least 30 mins.
- Heat oven to 200C/180C fan/gas 6. Line your pastry case with baking parchment, then fill with baking beans. Blind-bake for 15 mins, remove the beans and parchment, and bake for a further 10 mins until the pastry is pale golden and biscuity. Leave to cool.
- Reduce oven to 170C/150C fan/gas 3. In a bowl, cream the butter and sugar until pale and creamy. Add the eggs, one at a time, whisking well between each addition. Stir in

the flour, almonds, dried fruit, cherries, half the orange zest, and the spices. Spread the jam over the base of the tart case, then dot the cubes of marzipan over the top. Pour over the cake mixture and smooth with a spatula. Bake for 35 mins until golden and risen. Leave to cool in the tin.

- If you want to brown the tops of your marzipan balls, heat the grill to medium. Put the marzipan balls on a baking tray lined with baking parchment and place under the grill for 1-2 mins until golden – make sure you keep an eye on them, as they will burn easily. Let cool. To make the icing, mix the icing sugar with enough orange juice to make a thick, smooth icing. Drizzle the icing over the tart, top with the toasted marzipan balls, flaked almonds and the remaining orange zest. Cut into squares to serve. Will keep for 5 days in a sealed container.

Nutrition Information

- Calories: 448 calories
- Protein: 6 grams protein
- Total Fat: 22 grams fat
- Sugar: 42 grams sugar
- Total Carbohydrate: 56 grams carbohydrates
- Fiber: 1 grams fiber
- Sodium: 0.5 milligram of sodium
- Saturated Fat: 8 grams saturated fat

34. Simnel Loaf Cake

Serving: 8 | Prep: 20mins | Cook: 1hours | Ready in:

Ingredients

- 125g mixed dried fruit (a mixture of sultanas, currants, raisins and candied mixed peel)
- ½ small orange, zested and juiced
- vegetable or sunflower oil, for the tin
- 125g marzipan
- 125g butter, softened
- 100g light brown soft sugar
- 2 eggs
- 90g plain flour
- 50g ground almonds
- ½ tsp baking powder
- ½ lemon, zested and juiced
- 1 tsp mixed spice
- 1 tsp vanilla extract
- 50g glacé cherries, halved, plus 6-8 left whole, to serve
- 100g icing sugar

Direction

- Put the mixed dried fruit in a bowl with the orange juice and zest and 1 tbsp water. Cover and microwave for 2 mins, then leave to cool completely. Alternatively, heat gently in a pan, stirring now and then until the liquid has been absorbed and leave to cool.

- Heat oven to 180C/160C fan/gas 4 and oil a 900g loaf tin before lining the base and sides with baking parchment. Roll out 50g of the marzipan into a sausage that is as long as the loaf tin. Wrap the remaining the marzipan and set aside for later. Beat the butter and sugar together until creamy. Add the eggs, flour, almonds, baking powder, lemon zest, mixed spice and vanilla (all in one go) and mix until well combined. Stir in the cooled, soaked dried fruit, then fold in the cherries.

- Pour the cake batter into the tin until it is halfway full. Lay the sausage of marzipan down the middle, then scrape in the remaining cake mixture, making sure the marzipan is covered. Bake for 40-50 mins. Check it's cooked by inserting a skewer into the cake, if any wet mixture clings to the skewer, return to the oven for another 10 mins, then check again. Cool in the tin for 15 mins, then turn out onto a wire rack and leave to cool completely.

- Mix the icing sugar with the juice from the lemon and enough water (about 1 tbsp) to make a thick but pourable icing. Roll the remaining marzipan into 6-8 equal-sized balls, and caramelise, if you like (see tip below). Drizzle the icing over the top of the cake, letting it stream down the sides a little. Top with the marzipan balls, alternating each one with a cherry. Will keep in an airtight container for up to a week.

Nutrition Information

- Calories: 447 calories
- Protein: 6 grams protein
- Fiber: 1 grams fiber
- Total Fat: 20 grams fat
- Saturated Fat: 9 grams saturated fat
- Total Carbohydrate: 59 grams carbohydrates
- Sodium: 0.5 milligram of sodium
- Sugar: 45 grams sugar

35. Sticky Banoffee Loaf With Toffee Sauce

Serving: 6 | Prep: 10mins | Cook: 50mins | Ready in:

Ingredients

- 100ml dark rum (optional)
- 2 tsp bicarbonate of soda
- 200g chopped dates
- 100g vegetable suet
- 250g plain flour
- 1 tsp vanilla extract
- 100g golden caster sugar
- 2 ripe bananas, chopped
- crème fraîche or vanilla ice cream, to serve (optional)
- For the toffee sauce
- 150ml double cream
- 100g dark brown sugar
- 75g butter

Direction

- Pour the rum and 200ml water into a saucepan (if you're not using the rum, add an extra 100ml water). Bring to the boil, add the bicarb

and dates, then leave to cool, allowing the dates to soak up the boozy liquid.

- Heat oven to 180C/160C fan/gas 4. Pour the dates and the liquid into a bowl and add the suet, flour, vanilla and sugar. Beat until completely mixed, then fold in the banana and spoon into a lined 900g loaf tin. Bake for 40-45 mins until an inserted skewer comes out clean. Leave to cool.
- While the cake is cooling, put the cream, sugar, butter and a small pinch of salt in a saucepan. Bring to the boil and cook until you have a bubbling sauce. Slice the banoffee loaf, pour over some sauce and serve with crème fraîche or vanilla ice cream, if you like.

Nutrition Information

- Calories: 732 calories
- Fiber: 4 grams fiber
- Protein: 6 grams protein
- Saturated Fat: 20 grams saturated fat
- Total Carbohydrate: 95 grams carbohydrates
- Total Fat: 35 grams fat
- Sugar: 61 grams sugar
- Sodium: 1.2 milligram of sodium

36. Sticky Chocolate Cake

Serving: 8 | Prep: 10mins | Cook: 55mins | Ready in:

Ingredients

- 125g butter
- 100g dark chocolate chips or a bar
- 340g jar of marmalade
- 150g caster sugar
- 2 eggs
- 150g self-raising flour

Direction

- Heat oven to 180C/160C fan/gas 4 and line a loose-based 20cm cake tin with baking parchment. Put the butter and chocolate in a medium saucepan and heat gently, stirring all the time, until melted.

- Put 2-3 tbsp of the marmalade in a small bowl and set aside. Off the heat, stir the rest of the marmalade and the sugar into the buttery melted chocolate, and mix well, then break in the eggs and mix again. Finally, stir in the flour in three batches, folding lightly until combined. Scrape into the tin and smooth the top.
- Bake for 45-55 mins, rotating the tin halfway through so it bakes evenly. Keep an eye on it in the later stages as (depending on your marmalade) there may be a tendency for the top to scorch. After about 30 mins, cover loosely with foil. If it starts to get a little dark, tent loosely with a sheet of foil.
- The cake is cooked when the centre is firm when gently touched, and a skewer inserted in the centre comes out with a very few crumbs attached, like a brownie.
- Allow to cool for 10 mins, then turn out and leave to cool right-side-up on a wire rack. Heat the reserved marmalade in the microwave until runny, then brush all over the cake to glaze. Leave to cool before serving.

Nutrition Information

- Calories: 462 calories
- Sodium: 0.6 milligram of sodium
- Saturated Fat: 12 grams saturated fat
- Total Fat: 20 grams fat
- Sugar: 50 grams sugar
- Total Carbohydrate: 66 grams carbohydrates
- Protein: 5 grams protein
- Fiber: 2 grams fiber

37. Tonka Bean Panna Cotta With Roasted Rhubarb

Serving: 4 | Prep: 20mins | Cook: 25mins | Ready in:

Ingredients

- For the panna cotta
- 3 sheets gelatine
- 1 tonka bean (see tip)
- zest ½ orange
- 300ml pot double cream
- 200ml whole milk
- 50g soft light brown sugar
- For the roasted rhubarb
- 200g thin forced rhubarb, trimmed, rinsed and cut into 5cm/2in-long batons
- 50g golden caster sugar
- juice 1 orange

Direction

- To make the panna cotta, put the gelatine in a bowl of ice-cold water and set aside. Grate the tonka bean into a medium saucepan and add the orange zest, cream, milk and sugar. Bring to the boil, stirring occasionally. Remove from the heat and leave to cool for a few mins. Remove the gelatine from the water, squeezing out any excess water, and add to the cream mixture, stirring until fully melted. Pour the panna cotta mixture into a jug and divide between four dariole moulds. Carefully press a piece of cling film onto the surface of each pudding and chill for at least 4 hrs or until fully set.
- Heat oven to 190C/170C fan/gas 5. Put the rhubarb, sugar and orange juice in a small roasting tin and cook in the oven for 15-20 mins or until the rhubarb has softened but is still holding its shape.
- To serve, remove the panna cotta from the fridge and carefully peel off the cling film. Fill a bowl with hot water and dip each dariole mould into the water for about 10 secs to loosen the puddings. Invert onto a plate, tapping the mould firmly if it doesn't release easily. Serve with the rhubarb and a little of the syrup (this can be warm or cold).

Nutrition Information

- Calories: 518 calories
- Fiber: 1 grams fiber
- Sodium: 0.1 milligram of sodium
- Sugar: 29 grams sugar
- Total Fat: 42 grams fat
- Saturated Fat: 26 grams saturated fat
- Protein: 4 grams protein
- Total Carbohydrate: 29 grams carbohydrates

38. Vanilla Chick Biscuit Pops

Serving: Makes 15-18 biscuits | Prep: 15mins | Cook: 7mins | Ready in:

Ingredients

- 200g unsalted butter, at room temperature
- 100g golden caster sugar
- 1 medium egg, beaten
- 1 tsp vanilla extract
- 200g plain flour, plus extra for dusting
- 200g icing sugar
- 2 tbsp milk
- few drops yellow food colouring
- 75g unsweetened desiccated coconut
- 50g small chocolate chips
- 25g orange or white fondant icing, plus a few drops orange food colouring
- You will need
- 15-18 lolly sticks (see tip)
- ribbon, to decorate (optional)

Direction

- Put half the butter and all the sugar in a bowl. Using an electric whisk or wooden spoon, beat together until smooth and creamy. Beat in the egg and half the vanilla extract until thoroughly combined.
- Tip the flour into the mixture and mix on a low speed until it comes together to form a dough. Gather up into a ball, wrap in cling film and chill in the fridge for 20 mins.
- Heat oven to 180C/160C fan/gas 4. Line 2 baking trays with baking parchment. Put the biscuit dough on a lightly floured surface and roll out until about 5mm thick. Cut out the biscuits using a 6cm round cutter. Transfer the biscuits to the prepared trays and insert the lolly sticks into the sides, just a quarter of the way through. Bake for 6-7 mins until the edges are golden brown, then carefully transfer to a wire rack and allow to cool completely before decorating.
- Meanwhile, make some buttercream frosting. Place the remaining softened butter in a bowl and beat with a wooden spoon. Slowly add the icing sugar, 1 tbsp at a time, until thoroughly incorporated and you have a smooth, creamy mixture. Add a little milk and the remaining vanilla extract with a few drops of food colouring to give a pale yellow colour. Chill for 5 mins.
- Put the desiccated coconut in a small bowl, add a few drops of yellow food colouring and mix well until the coconut is coloured pale yellow.
- Spread the buttercream frosting over one side of the biscuit and sprinkle with the coconut. Add 2 chocolate chip eyes to each. Pinch a little orange fondant icing and shape into a beak and press into the mixture. Decorate with a ribbon, if you like, and serve. Will keep for 2 days in an airtight container.

Nutrition Information

- Calories: 240 calories
- Fiber: 1 grams fiber
- Protein: 2 grams protein
- Total Fat: 13 grams fat
- Saturated Fat: 9 grams saturated fat
- Total Carbohydrate: 28 grams carbohydrates
- Sugar: 20 grams sugar

39. Vegan Hot Cross Buns

Serving: Makes 12 | Prep: 35mins | Cook: 20mins | Ready in:

Ingredients

- 300ml unsweetened almond milk
- 50g dairy-free spread
- 500g strong white bread flour
- 7g sachet fast action yeast
- 70g golden caster sugar
- ½ tsp salt
- 2 heaped tsp ground cinnamon
- 2 heaped tsp mixed spice
- 1 large orange, zested
- 70g sultanas
- 50g mixed peel
- For the cross
- 70g plain flour
- For the glaze
- 50g apricot jam

Direction

- Put the almond milk in a saucepan over a medium heat. Once simmering, add the spread, remove from the heat and allow to melt. Set aside to cool to hand temperature.
- Mix the flour, yeast, sugar, salt and spices in a large mixing bowl. Make a well in the centre and pour in the milk mixture, swiftly combining with a wooden spoon to create a sticky dough. Tip out of the bowl onto a lightly floured surface.
- Knead the dough by stretching it back and forth on the surface for 5 - 7 mins or until smooth, springy and elastic. Shape into a ball and put into a lightly oiled mixing bowl. Cover and leave in a warm spot to rise, for 1hr or until doubled in size.
- Turn the dough back onto the surface and flatten into a round. Spread the orange zest, sultanas and mixed peel onto the dough and knead again until everything is well distributed. Form into a ball, return to the bowl, cover and leave to rise for another hour.
- Line a large baking sheet with baking parchment. Knock the dough back by turning it out onto your surface and gently punching out the air. Divide the dough into 12 even-sized pieces, weighing for accuracy if you like.

Roll each one into a ball. Arrange the buns on the baking sheet, leaving a 2cm space between each one. Cover with lightly oiled cling film and leave to rise for 45 mins.

- Heat the oven to 220C/ 200 fan/ gas 7. To make the cross, in a small bowl, mix together the flour with 1 tbsp of water at a time to create a thick, pipeable paste. Spoon it into a piping bag fitted with a small round nozzle and pipe crosses on the buns. Transfer to the middle shelf of the oven and bake for 15-20 mins or until deep golden brown.
- Meanwhile, gently heat the jam in a small saucepan over a low heat to loosen. Pass through a sieve to remove any lumps. Once cooked, brush the warm jam over the tops of the buns. Set aside to cool a little before eating.

Nutrition Information

- Calories: 268 calories
- Total Carbohydrate: 51 grams carbohydrates
- Total Fat: 3 grams fat
- Sugar: 15 grams sugar
- Fiber: 3 grams fiber
- Sodium: 0.34 milligram of sodium
- Saturated Fat: 1 grams saturated fat
- Protein: 6 grams protein

---

40. White Rabbit Biscuits

Serving: Makes 30-35 biscuits or 15 bunnies | Prep: 1hours10mins | Cook: 45mins |Ready in:

Ingredients

- 200g unsalted butter, at room temperature
- 400g plain flour
- 280g caster sugar
- 1 egg
- ¼ tsp vanilla extract
- a pinch of salt
- ½ tsp cream of tartar
- For the icing:

- 600g icing sugar
- pink food colouring gel
- 170g pack of desiccated coconut
- 15 mini marshmallows
- You will also need:
- 1 x rabbit head-shaped cookie cutter
- 1 x 7cm round cookie cutter
- 1 x 3cm round cookie cutter

Direction

- Heat oven to 180C/160C fan/gas 4. Lightly rub the butter and flour together with your fingertips until the mixture looks like fresh breadcrumbs.
- Mix the sugar and egg together in another in a bowl with a whisk and when it is really well combined and runny add it to the flour mixture.
- Add all the other ingredients and squish it together with your hands, keep working the dough until it's smooth, soft and comes together in one piece.
- Roll the dough out on a lightly floured surface with a rolling pin until it is about half a centimetre thick. Cut into shapes. We did 15 rabbit heads, 15 large circles and 30 mini circles.
- Place your biscuits on baking sheets lined with baking paper and bake in batches for about 15 mins (or until they are lightly golden at the edges).
- Let them cool in the tin for a few minutes before carefully transferring them to a wire rack to cool completely and become crisp.
- While the biscuits cool mix enough cold water with the icing sugar to create a thick icing. Place a quarter of the icing in another bowl and add a very small amout of pink gel food colouring. Transfer both the white icing and the pink icing into disposable piping bags and snip off the end to make a very small nozzle on the pink icing and a wider one on the white icing.
- Pipe white icing over the small round biscuits and leave to dry. Then pipe white icing to cover all of the large circular biscuits and the

rabbit biscuits (be fairly sparing and spread it out with the back of a spoon – it doesn't have to be neat on these ones). Once you've iced each one sprinkle generously with dessicated coconut before the icing dries.

- Take the pink icing and use to create paws on the smaller circles then stick 2 of them onto each of the large circles using icing like glue. With the icing you have left, coat the marshmallows and cover those in coconut too before sticking them onto the middle of the larger circles to create a fluffy tail. Leave to set completely for about 15-20 mins then serve.

Nutrition Information

- Calories: 219 calories
- Sugar: 25 grams sugar
- Fiber: 2 grams fiber
- Protein: 1 grams protein
- Total Fat: 8 grams fat
- Saturated Fat: 6 grams saturated fat
- Total Carbohydrate: 34 grams carbohydrates

Chapter 2: Valentine'S Baking Recipes

***

41. Champagne & Raspberry Possets

Serving: 2 | Prep: 10mins | Cook: 5mins | Ready in:

Ingredients

- 140g frozen raspberries, defrosted

- 2 tbsp champagne (buy a mini bottle and treat yourself to a glass while you prepare dinner!)
- 200ml double cream
- 4 tbsp golden caster sugar
- 2 tsp freeze-dried raspberry pieces
- shortbread biscuits, to serve

Direction

- Put the raspberries and Champagne in a mini food processor or blender (or use a jug and a hand blender). Whizz until the purée is as smooth as you can get it, then use a wooden spoon or spatula to push as much of it through a sieve as you can. Discard the seeds left behind.
- Put the cream and sugar in a saucepan and warm gently until the sugar melts. Increase the heat until just boiling, then boil vigorously for 2 1/2 mins, stirring constantly. Turn off the heat and stir in the raspberry-Champagne purée. Cool for 15 mins before dividing between 2 small pots or glasses. Chill for 30 mins, then sprinkle over the freeze-dried raspberry pieces and chill for at least 2 hrs more until set (or overnight if you're making ahead).
- To serve, remove the possets from the fridge and add some shortbread biscuits (shop-bought or find shortbread recipes here on bbcgoodfood.com).

Nutrition Information

- Calories: 698 calories
- Sugar: 46 grams sugar
- Fiber: 3 grams fiber
- Sodium: 0.1 milligram of sodium
- Total Fat: 54 grams fat
- Total Carbohydrate: 46 grams carbohydrates
- Protein: 3 grams protein
- Saturated Fat: 33 grams saturated fat

42. Cherry Shortbread Hearts

Serving: Makes 14-16, depending on cutter | Prep: 15mins | Cook: 15mins | Ready in:

Ingredients

- 100g icing sugar, plus extra for dusting
- 200g plain flour, plus extra for dusting
- 50g cornflour
- 50g ground almonds
- 250g pack cold butter, cut into cubes
- 50g glacé cherries, finely chopped
- ½ tsp almond extract
- 8 tbsp cherry jam, sieved

Direction

- Heat oven to 180C/160C fan/gas 4. Sift the icing sugar, flour and cornflour together into a bowl. Stir in the ground almonds and butter, then rub in the butter until smooth. Stir in the chopped glacé cherries and almond extract, and bring together to form a dough.
- Roll out on a lightly floured surface, then stamp out biscuits using a heartshaped cutter. Keep re-rolling the trimmings until all the dough is used. Carefully transfer the biscuits to baking trays lined with parchment and bake for just 8-10 mins until just pale golden.
- Using an upturned bottle top or similar, press gently into the centre of each biscuit to make a round indent. Spoon in a little jam and return to the oven for 2 mins. Remove and cool on a wire rack, before dusting with icing sugar to serve.

Nutrition Information

- Calories: 242 calories
- Sodium: 0.21 milligram of sodium
- Fiber: 1 grams fiber
- Saturated Fat: 8 grams saturated fat
- Protein: 2 grams protein
- Total Carbohydrate: 27 grams carbohydrates
- Total Fat: 15 grams fat
- Sugar: 14 grams sugar

43. Chocolate Brownie Cake

Serving: 8 | Prep: | Cook: |Ready in:

Ingredients

- 100g butter
- 125g caster sugar
- 75g light brown or muscovado sugar
- 125g plain chocolate (plain or milk)
- 1 tbsp golden syrup
- 2 eggs
- 1 tsp vanilla extract/essence
- 100g plain flour
- ½ tsp baking powder
- 2 tbsp cocoa powder

Direction

- Heat oven to 180C/fan 160C/gas 4. Grease and line a 20cm cake tin.
- Place the butter, caster sugar, brown sugar, chocolate and golden syrup in the pan and melt gently on a low heat until it is smooth and lump-free.
- Remove the pan from the heat.
- Break the eggs into the bowl and whisk with the fork until light and frothy. 5 Add the eggs, vanilla extract or essence, flour, baking powder and cocoa powder to the chocolate mixture and mix thoroughly.
- Put the mixture into the greased and lined cake tin and place on the middle shelf of the oven. Bake for 25-30 mins.
- Remove and allow to cool for 20-30 mins before cutting into wedges and serving.
- Serve with cream or ice cream and plenty of fresh fruit.

Nutrition Information

- Calories: 500 calories
- Sodium: 0.5 milligram of sodium
- Protein: 5 grams protein
- Fiber: 1 grams fiber
- Total Fat: 23 grams fat
- Sugar: 59 grams sugar
- Saturated Fat: 13 grams saturated fat
- Total Carbohydrate: 73 grams carbohydrates

44. Chocolate Caramel Cake

Serving: 12 | Prep: 20mins | Cook: 30mins |Ready in:

Ingredients

- 300g butter, plus extra for greasing
- 300g light muscovado sugar
- 3 large eggs
- 1½ tsp baking powder
- 85g cocoa powder
- 225g plain flour
- 225ml soured cream
- 300ml pot double cream
- 5 tbsp dulce de leche or caramel sauce
- 25g caramel flavoured chocolate, finely chopped (we used Lindt)

Direction

- Heat oven to 180C/160C fan/gas 4. Lightly grease 2 x 23cm loose-bottom cake tins and line with a circle of baking parchment. Beat together the butter and sugar until pale and creamy. Add the eggs, one at a time, beating well between each addition, then add the baking powder, cocoa and a third of the flour. Mix well to combine, then stir in half the soured cream. Alternating between adding the flour and soured cream, mix everything until just combined. Spoon into the prepared tins, then smooth over the surface with a spoon.
- Bake for 30 mins or until the cakes are firm to touch and a skewer inserted into the centres comes out clean. Leave to cool in the tins for 5 mins, then turn out onto a rack and cool completely.

- When you're ready to serve, whip the double cream with 2 tbsp Dulce de leche until soft peaks form. Place 1 cake on a serving plate and spread with half the cream, then drizzle over the remaining Dulce de leche. Top with the other cake, then spread the remaining cream on top. Sprinkle with the chocolate. Chill until ready to serve.

Nutrition Information

- Calories: 597 calories
- Sugar: 32 grams sugar
- Fiber: 1 grams fiber
- Protein: 5 grams protein
- Saturated Fat: 25 grams saturated fat
- Total Fat: 43 grams fat
- Total Carbohydrate: 51 grams carbohydrates
- Sodium: 0.74 milligram of sodium

45. Chocolate, Raspberry & Rose Battenberg Gateau

Serving: Cuts into 16 slices | Prep: 1hours20mins | Cook: 1hours10mins |Ready in:

Ingredients

- For the chocolate sponges
- 225g very soft salted butter, plus a little extra for greasing
- 225g golden caster sugar
- 175g self-raising flour
- 85g ground almond
- 50g cocoa powder
- 3 large eggs
- 1 tsp vanilla extract
- 140g natural yogurt
- For the raspberry-rose sponges
- 25g freeze-dried raspberries, plus extra for decorating (optional)
- 200g self-raising flour
- 225g very soft butter, plus a little extra for greasing
- 225g golden caster sugar
- 3 large eggs
- 85g ground almond
- 1 ½ tbsp rose water
- 100g natural yogurt
- artificial pink food colouring
- To assemble and ice
- jar of raspberry jam
- 200g bar of dark chocolate
- 200ml pot double cream
- 25g butter

Direction

- Heat oven to 160C/140C fan/gas 3. Grease and line the base of 2 x 18cm round sandwich tins.
- Start with the chocolate sponges. Put all the ingredients in a bowl and beat with an electric whisk until the mixture comes together smoothly. Working quickly, weigh the batter, then spread exactly half in each tin. Bake for 30 mins – when you poke a skewer into the middle, it should come out clean. Cool in the tins for 15 mins, then carefully turn out onto wire racks to finish cooling while you make the raspberry-rose sponges.
- Clean the tins, then grease and line as above. Whizz the freeze-dried raspberries and flour together until no lumps of raspberry remain. Tip into a mixing bowl, add the butter, sugar, eggs, almonds, rose water and yogurt, and beat together as above. When smooth, beat in a little pink food colouring bit by bit until you get a nice colour – it will fade a bit during baking. Weigh, divide between the tins and bake and cool as above.
- Once cool, gently cover and chill the sponges for 30 mins – this will make cutting them easier and neater.
- Unwrap the sponges and, if they have domed in the centre, trim to flatten. Cut a 12cm-diameter circle out of the centre of each sponge using a biscuit cutter or paper template. Then cut a 6cm-diameter circle from the centre of your 12cm sponge. From each sponge, you should end up with a 6cm circle, a

12cm ring and an 18cm ring. Swap the middle rings of the chocolate sponges with the middle rings from the raspberry-rose sponges, and fit the cut pieces back together. Handle the sponges very gently to avoid cracking the edges too much.

- Heat the jam to melt, then sieve to remove the seeds. Generously brush some over one of the sponges and top with an alternating sponge. Repeat to stack up all the layers. Sit the cake on a serving plate or cake stand.

- Break the chocolate into a heatproof bowl with the cream and butter. Set over a pan of barely simmering water so the bottom of the bowl doesn't touch the water, and very gently melt together. Cool until slightly thickened and more spreadable, then spread all over the cake to finish. Don't return to the fridge – this cake keeps for two days at room temperature – and tastes better the day after assembling.

Nutrition Information

- Calories: 697 calories
- Saturated Fat: 25 grams saturated fat
- Sugar: 42 grams sugar
- Total Fat: 46 grams fat
- Fiber: 3 grams fiber
- Total Carbohydrate: 61 grams carbohydrates
- Sodium: 0.9 milligram of sodium
- Protein: 10 grams protein

---

46. Coconut & Raspberry Cupcakes

Serving: Makes 12-15 | Prep: 25mins | Cook: 20mins | Ready in:

Ingredients

- 175g self-raising flour
- 140g caster sugar
- 50g desiccated coconut
- 140g butter, softened
- ½ tsp vanilla extract

- 2 large eggs
- 4 tbsp milk
- 140g raspberry, fresh or frozen
- For the frosting
- 280g icing sugar
- 85g butter, softened
- 4 tbsp raspberry coulis, from a bottle or fresh
- a little desiccated or shredded coconut, to decorate

Direction

- Heat oven to 190C/170C fan/gas 5. Line a 12-hole muffin tin with deep paper cases or a 15-hole bun tin with cake cases. Tip all the cake ingredients except the raspberries into a bowl and beat for 1-2 mins until light and fluffy. Gently fold in the raspberries.

- Divide the mixture between the cases and bake for 18-20 mins (add a couple of extra mins for deep cases), until golden brown and firm to the touch. Leave to cool.

- Beat together the icing sugar, butter and raspberry coulis to make a light, fluffy icing. Spoon or pipe onto the cakes and sprinkle with coconut.

Nutrition Information

- Calories: 314 calories
- Total Fat: 17 grams fat
- Saturated Fat: 11 grams saturated fat
- Total Carbohydrate: 37 grams carbohydrates
- Fiber: 2 grams fiber
- Sugar: 28 grams sugar
- Sodium: 0.4 milligram of sodium
- Protein: 3 grams protein

---

47. Custard Kisses

Serving: Makes 15-25 | Prep: 30mins | Cook: 10mins | Ready in:

Ingredients

- 175g softened butter
- 50g golden caster sugar
- 50g icing sugar
- 2 egg yolks
- 2 tsp vanilla extract
- 300g plain flour, plus extra for dusting
- For the custard filling
- 100g softened butter
- 140g icing sugar, sifted, plus a little extra
- 2 tbsp custard powder
- few drops yellow food colouring, if you have any

Direction

- Heat oven to 200C/180C fan/gas 6. Mix the butter, sugars, egg yolks and vanilla with a wooden spoon until creamy, then mix in the flour in 2 batches. Roll out thinly on a floured surface, then use a standard 30cm ruler as a template to cut the dough into small, even squares. Do this by starting with the ruler flush with one side and cutting along the length of it. Repeat across the width of the dough, then do the same from the top down. Transfer to baking sheets and bake for 8-10 mins until golden.
- While the biscuits cool, mix the butter, icing sugar, custard powder and food colouring, if you have any. Pipe or spread a little icing onto a biscuit, then sandwich with 1 or 2 more biscuits. Repeat until all the biscuits are used, then dust with a little more icing sugar.

Nutrition Information

- Calories: 220 calories
- Total Carbohydrate: 20 grams carbohydrates
- Sugar: 18 grams sugar
- Protein: 1 grams protein
- Sodium: 0.24 milligram of sodium
- Total Fat: 16 grams fat
- Saturated Fat: 10 grams saturated fat

48. Dark Chocolate & Orange Cake

Serving: Cuts into 10 slices | Prep: 40mins | Cook: 1hours30mins | Ready in:

Ingredients

- 1 Seville orange
- a little melted butter, for greasing
- 100g plain chocolate, broken into pieces
- 3 eggs
- 280g caster sugar
- 240ml sunflower oil
- 25g cocoa powder
- 250g plain flour
- 1½ tsp baking powder
- orange candied peel, to decorate
- For the chocolate ganache
- 200g plain chocolate, broken into pieces
- 225ml double cream

Direction

- Pierce the orange with a skewer (right through). Cook in boiling water for 30 minutes until soft. Whizz the whole orange in a food processor until smooth; let cool.
- Preheat the oven to 180C/gas 4/fan 160C. Grease and line the base of a 23cm/9in round cake tin. Melt the chocolate in a heatproof bowl set over a pan of simmering water or in the microwave for 2 minutes on High, stirring after 1 minute. Let cool.
- In a large bowl, lightly beat the eggs, sugar and oil. Gradually beat in the puréed orange, discarding any pips, then stir in the cooled melted chocolate. Sift in the cocoa, flour and baking powder. Mix well and pour into the tin. Bake in the centre of the oven for 55 minutes, or until the cake springs back when lightly pressed in the middle. (Check after 45 minutes and cover with foil if it is browning too much.) Allow to cool for 10 minutes in the tin, then turn out on to a wire rack to cool completely.
- Make the chocolate ganache: put the chocolate into a heatproof bowl. Bring the cream to the boil and pour over the chocolate. Leave for 2

minutes, then stir until smooth. Set aside until firm enough to spread over the cake – up to 1½ hours.

- Transfer the cake to a serving plate. Using a palette knife, swirl the ganache over the top. Decorate with strips of candied orange peel.

49. Easy Chocolate Cupcakes

Serving: Makes 10 | Prep: 20mins | Cook: 20mins | Ready in:

Ingredients

- 300g dark chocolate, broken into chunks - don't use one with a high cocoa content
- 200g self-raising flour
- 200g light muscovado sugar, plus 3 tbsp extra
- 6 tbsp cocoa
- 150ml sunflower oil, plus a little extra for greasing
- 284ml pot soured cream
- 2 eggs
- 1 tsp vanilla extract

Direction

- Heat oven to 180C/fan 160C/gas 4 and line a 10-hole muffin tin with paper cases. Whizz the chocolate into small pieces in a food processor. In the largest mixing bowl you have, tip in the flour, sugar, cocoa, oil, 100ml soured cream, eggs, vanilla and 100ml water. Whisk everything together with electric beaters until smooth, then quickly stir in 100g of the whizzed-up chocolate bits. Divide between the 10 cases, then bake for 20 mins until a skewer inserted comes out clean (make sure you don't poke it into a chocolate chip bit). Cool on a wire rack.
- To make the icing, put the remaining chocolate bits, soured cream and 3 tbsp sugar in a small saucepan. Heat gently, stirring, until the chocolate is melted and you have a smooth

icing. Chill in the fridge until firm enough to swirl on top of the muffins, then tuck in.

Nutrition Information

- Calories: 534 calories
- Total Carbohydrate: 62 grams carbohydrates
- Sugar: 46 grams sugar
- Protein: 6 grams protein
- Sodium: 0.3 milligram of sodium
- Total Fat: 31 grams fat
- Saturated Fat: 11 grams saturated fat

50. Fortune Cookies

Serving: Makes about 15 | Prep: 10mins | Cook: 10mins | Ready in:

Ingredients

- 2 egg whites
- 1 tsp vanilla extract
- 1 tsp almond extract
- 3 tbsp sunflower oil
- 100g plain flour
- 2 tsp cornflour
- 100g caster sugar
- 1 ½ tbsp black sesame seeds

Direction

- Preheat the oven to 180C/160 fan/gas 4 and line a large baking sheet with baking parchment, or use a silicone baking sheet. Write or print fortunes on paper measuring 6cm long by 1cm wide.
- Put the egg whites, vanilla, almond extract, oil and 2 tsp cold water into a bowl and whisk with an electric hand whisk until frothy, 20-30 secs. Measure the flour, cornflour, sugar and a good pinch of salt into a bowl, then sift into the egg white mixture. Whisk everything together until you have a smooth batter-like consistency. Chill the mixture for 1 hr.

- Next, put a tbsp of mixture onto the prepared baking sheet. Oil a metal spoon, then use the back of it to swirl the mixture out into a 8-10cm circle. Repeat with another tablespoon of the mixture, to create 2 cookies. Make sure there is space between each cookie as they will spread in the oven. It is best to only bake 2-3 cookies at a time, as you will need to shape them whilst they are hot. Sprinkle 1 of the cookies with black sesame seeds, then bake for 10-12 mins until the edges of the cookies turn golden.
- One at a time remove the cookies with a palette knife once they are out the oven. You want them to still be soft so you can shape them so work quickly. Turn the cookie over so that the sesame seeds are face down and put the fortune in the middle of the circle. Fold the circle in half to secure the fortune and pinch the 2 edges together to seal. Pop the cookie on the rim of a mug or cup and very gently pull the 2 corners down to get the fortune cookie shape. Hold for 10 secs, then transfer the cookies to muffin tins so that they hold their shape whilst cooling completely. Repeat with the remaining cookie mixture.

Nutrition Information

- Calories: 81 calories
- Total Fat: 3 grams fat
- Saturated Fat: 0.4 grams saturated fat
- Fiber: 0.4 grams fiber
- Sodium: 0.1 milligram of sodium
- Protein: 1 grams protein
- Sugar: 7 grams sugar
- Total Carbohydrate: 12 grams carbohydrates

51. Glamorous Fairy Cakes

Serving: Makes 24 cakes | Prep: 15mins | Cook: 15mins | Ready in:

Ingredients

- For the cakes
- 140g butter, very well softened
- 140g golden caster sugar
- 3 medium eggs
- 100g self-raising flour
- 25g custard powder or cornflour
- For decorating
- 600g icing sugar, sifted
- 6 tbsp water, or half water and half lemon juice, strained
- edible green and pink food colourings
- crystallised violets
- crystallised roses or rose petals
- edible wafer flowers

Direction

- Heat the oven to 190C/fan 170C/gas 5. Arrange paper cases in bun tins. Put all the cake ingredients in a large bowl and beat for about 2 mins until smooth. Divide the mixture between the cases so they are half filled and bake for 12-15 mins, until risen and golden. Cool on a wire rack.
- Mix the icing sugar and water until smooth and use a third on eight of the cakes. Divide the rest in half, and colour one half pale green and the other half pale pink. Decorate the white ones with crystallised violets, the pink ones with the roses and the green ones with the wafer flowers. Leave to set. Will keep for up to 2-3 days stored in an airtight container in a cool place.

Nutrition Information

- Calories: 193 calories
- Total Fat: 6 grams fat
- Saturated Fat: 3 grams saturated fat
- Total Carbohydrate: 36 grams carbohydrates
- Sugar: 31 grams sugar
- Protein: 2 grams protein
- Sodium: 0.2 milligram of sodium

52. Hidden Heart Cake

Serving: Cuts into 8-10 slices | Prep: 50mins | Cook: 2hours20mins | Ready in:

Ingredients

- For the cake
- 2 x 175g unsalted butter, softened
- 2 x 175g golden caster sugar
- 6 large eggs
- 2 x 140g self-raising flour, sifted
- 2 x ½ tsp baking powder
- 3 tbsp cocoa powder
- 2 x 85g ground almond
- 2 x 100ml milk
- 3 tsp vanilla extract
- 28ml bottle red food colouring or ½ tsp red food colouring gel
- For the icing
- 100ml double cream
- 200g dark chocolate, finely chopped
- 50g unsalted butter
- pink sprinkles (optional)

Direction

- Heat oven to 160C/140C fan/gas 3. Grease a 900g loaf tin and line with a long strip of baking parchment. Cream 175g butter and 175g sugar until light and fluffy. Beat 3 of the eggs and pour in, a little at a time, mixing after each addition. Sift together 140g flour, 1/2 tsp baking powder and the cocoa, then fold into the butter mixture along with the almonds. Combine 100ml milk, 11/2 tsp vanilla and all the food colouring and add to the batter, then mix until evenly coloured.
- Pour into the prepared loaf tin and bake for 1 hr 10 mins until a skewer comes out clean. Cool for 10 mins in the tin, then transfer to a wire rack. When cool, cut the cake into 4cm slices. Using a 5cm cutter, stamp out the hearts (save any remaining cake for another treat).
- Repeat step 1 to make a second cake mixture – you won't have cocoa or food colour in this batch. Pour 3/4 of the mixture into the prepared loaf tin. Push the bottoms of the hearts into the batter in a tightly packed row. Spoon over the remaining cake mixture, covering as much of the hearts as possible. bake for 1 hr or until a skewer comes out clean. Cool for 10 mins in the tin, then transfer to a wire rack to cool completely.
- For the icing, gently heat all the ingredients over a low heat until combined. Leave to cool, then chill until needed. Spread over the cooled cake and decorate with the sprinkles, if using. Will keep for 3 days stored in a cake tin.

Nutrition Information

- Calories: 858 calories
- Total Carbohydrate: 65 grams carbohydrates
- Total Fat: 60 grams fat
- Fiber: 4 grams fiber
- Sodium: 0.6 milligram of sodium
- Saturated Fat: 31 grams saturated fat
- Sugar: 42 grams sugar
- Protein: 13 grams protein

53. Lemon Kisses

Serving: Makes 20 | Prep: 30mins | Cook: 12mins | Ready in:

Ingredients

- 200g soft butter
- 140g caster sugar
- 1 egg yolk
- 1 tsp vanilla extract
- zest 2 lemons, juice 1
- 280g plain flour, plus a little extra for rolling
- ½ jar good lemon curd(we used Tiptree)
- 140g icing sugar, sifted

Direction

- Stir together the butter, sugar, egg yolk, vanilla and zest from 1 lemon using a wooden spoon. Stir in the flour – you might need to get your hands in at the end. Tip onto a floured surface, bring together into a smooth dough, then roll out, half at a time, and stamp out 5-6cm rounds. Keep re-rolling trimmings, you should get about 40 biscuits. Arrange on trays lined with baking parchment, cover with cling film and chill for 30 mins.

- Heat oven to 200C/180C fan/gas 6. Bake the biscuits for 8-12 mins until pale golden, then cool. Once cool, spread half the biscuits with a little lemon curd and top with a second biscuit. Arrange the biscuits on wire racks over trays. Mix enough lemon juice into the icing sugar to give a runny consistency, then drizzle over the biscuits. Scatter over a bit more lemon zest and leave to set.

Nutrition Information

- Calories: 202 calories
- Total Carbohydrate: 31 grams carbohydrates
- Total Fat: 8 grams fat
- Saturated Fat: 5 grams saturated fat
- Fiber: 1 grams fiber
- Protein: 1 grams protein
- Sodium: 0.14 milligram of sodium
- Sugar: 18 grams sugar

54. Love Bug Biscuits

Serving: Makes 20 | Prep: 30mins | Cook: 12mins | Ready in:

Ingredients

- 175g plain flour
- 100g chilled butter, cubed
- 85g icing sugar
- 1 tsp vanilla extract
- 1 egg yolk
- To decorate
- 500g ready-to-roll fondant icing
- red food colouring
- 100g icing sugar
- black food colouring
- edible pearly ball decorations
- You will also need
- 8cm heart-shaped cutter
- 6cm heart-shaped cutter

Direction

- Put the flour, butter, sugar, vanilla and egg yolk in a food processor. Dribble in 1 tbsp water and blitz until the mixture comes together to form a dough. Tip onto a work surface and knead briefly to bring together, then wrap in cling film and chill for 20 mins.
- Heat oven to 180C/160C fan/gas 4. Roll out the dough to the thickness of a £1 coin. Use your 8cm heart cutter to stamp out heart shapes – you'll have to re-roll the trimmings to make 20 biscuits. Put the hearts on 2 baking trays and bake for 12 mins, swapping the trays over halfway through, until pale golden and crisp. Leave to cool on a wire rack.
- Dye your lump of icing with red food colouring and wrap in cling film until ready to roll. Mix the icing sugar with enough water to make a thick icing. Dye the icing with the black food colouring. Pour the icing into a piping bag with a small plain nozzle attached (or use a small sandwich bag and snip off the corner). Roll out the red icing to 3mm thick and use your 6cm cutter to stamp out hearts. Stick onto the biscuits with a little of the black icing.
- Use the black icing to give your love bug a head at the pointy end, draw a line down the centre to give it wings, then add spots. Stick 2 pearly balls onto each love bug's head, then leave to set on a wire rack. You can pack your love bugs into boxes or cellophane bags to give as gifts for Valentine's Day.

Nutrition Information

- Calories: 166 calories
- Total Carbohydrate: 29 grams carbohydrates
- Sugar: 22 grams sugar

- Protein: 1 grams protein
- Sodium: 0.1 milligram of sodium
- Total Fat: 5 grams fat
- Saturated Fat: 3 grams saturated fat

- Total Fat: 7 grams fat
- Saturated Fat: 4 grams saturated fat
- Total Carbohydrate: 26 grams carbohydrates

55. Microwave Boozy Fudge

Serving: Makes about 24 pieces | Prep: 5mins | Cook: 12mins | Ready in:

Ingredients

- 400g golden caster sugar
- 397g can condensed milk
- 140g salted butter, chopped into pieces
- 1 tsp vanilla bean paste
- 2 tbsp coffee liqueur (or another alcohol of your choice - amaretto or brandy works well)

Direction

- Grease and line a 20cm square baking tin with baking parchment. Put the sugar, condensed milk and butter in a large heatproof bowl (the mixture will bubble up as it cooks to roughly double its size), add a good pinch of salt and stir together.
- Heat the mixture in the microwave on High for 10 mins, stirring every 2-3 mins. Keep an eye on the mixture, as it will bubble up and may go over the sides of the bowl.
- Add the vanilla and liqueur to the mixture, whisk together and heat on High for another 2 mins. The mixture should be caramel-coloured and thickened. Scrape into the tin and set aside for 45 mins to 1 hr until cool and firm before cutting. Pack into a box and eat within 3 weeks.

Nutrition Information

- Calories: 170 calories
- Sugar: 26 grams sugar
- Protein: 1 grams protein
- Sodium: 0.2 milligram of sodium

56. Mini Eclairs

Serving: Makes about 30 | Prep: 45mins | Cook: 1hours | Ready in:

Ingredients

- 150ml milk
- 100g butter, diced
- 200g plain flour, sieved
- 4 large eggs, beaten
- 200ml milk
- 1 tsp vanillapaste, or 1 vanilla pod, split down the middle
- 2 large egg yolks
- 4 tbsp caster sugar
- 1 tbsp plain flour
- 1 tsp cornflour
- 200ml double cream
- 2 tbsp berry liqueur, such as cassis, framboise or sloe gin (optional)
- 500g pack fondant icing sugar, sifted
- food colouring(use pinks and purples if you flavour with a berry liqueur)
- sprinkles and edible cake decoration(we used Smarties and Mini Smarties)

Direction

- To make the buns, heat the milk, butter and 150ml water very gently in a medium-sized saucepan until all the butter has melted. Get the flour and some salt ready, then increase the heat and bring the liquid to the boil. As soon as it is boiling, remove from the heat and beat in the flour and a pinch of salt with a wooden spoon. Keep beating until the mixture is smooth and comes away from the sides of the pan. Cool for 5 mins.
- Gradually add the eggs, mixing well between each addition until the mixture reluctantly

drops off the spoon. Don't add all the egg unless you need to. Spoon into a piping bag with a 1.5-2cm star or round nozzle and set aside until ready to bake.

- To make the filling, bring the milk just to the boil in a saucepan with the vanilla paste or split pod. Meanwhile, whisk together the egg yolks, sugar and flours in a mixing bowl. Pour on the hot milk while continuously whisking the egg mixture. Discard the pod (if using) and return the mix to a wiped-out saucepan. Cook over a gentle heat, stirring, until the mix is thicker than a custard – it will get lumpy, but just carry on stirring and beat out the lumps. Transfer to another mixing bowl and lay cling film directly on the surface. Leave to cool, then chill.

- Heat oven to 220C/200C fan/gas 7. Line a couple of baking sheets with baking parchment. Pipe on 8-10cm long lengths of the dough, about 2cm wide – leaving space to expand between each one. Put in the oven for 5 mins, then reduce heat to 200C/200C fan/gas 6 and bake for 10 mins more until golden, puffed and crisp. Using a skewer, poke 3 small holes along the base of each bun. Put back on the baking sheets, base up, and return to the oven for a further 8-10 mins until slightly crisper. Cool. Can be frozen for up to a month, or stored in an airtight container for up to 3 days – just crisp up in a hot oven again when ready to fill.

- Add the cream to the thick custard filling and beat with an electric whisk until it holds its own shape again. Put into a piping bag with a tiny nozzle, then pipe some filling into the bottom of the buns using the skewer holes you made before (see Secrets of success, below). When it squirts back out, that bit is probably full.

- Stir the liqueur, if using, into the icing sugar, plus just enough water to make a pretty thick icing. Divide among as many bowls as you want colours, and colour each batch as you like. (Depending on your colouring, you may need to add a drop more water to icings so that they are thick but runny.)

- Dip the top of each eclair in icing to cover, or use a teaspoon to spread a little on – use less at first and wait for it to spread and settle. Add sprinkles and decorations, then gently sit on wire racks to set. Eclairs are best eaten on the day they are filled and decorated, before they go soggy.

Nutrition Information

- Calories: 182 calories
- Sugar: 20 grams sugar
- Protein: 2 grams protein
- Sodium: 0.1 milligram of sodium
- Total Fat: 8 grams fat
- Saturated Fat: 4 grams saturated fat
- Total Carbohydrate: 25 grams carbohydrates

57. Passion Cake

Serving: 10 | Prep: 1hours | Cook: 25mins | Ready in:

Ingredients

- 150ml sunflower oil, plus a little extra for the tin
- 300g self-raising flour
- 1 tsp ground cinnamon
- 1 tsp baking powder
- 300g caster sugar
- 50g desiccated coconut
- 2 eggs, plus 2 egg whites, whole eggs beaten
- 2 over-ripe bananas, mashed
- 140g carrots, grated
- 432g can crushed pineapple in juice, drained in a sieve, reserving the juice (or briefly whizz a can of pineapple chunks, then sieve)
- 100ml milk
- For the drizzle & icing
- 4 ripe passion fruits, halved
- 25g caster sugar
- 200g tub soft cheese
- 100g softened butter
- 85g icing sugar

- 1 tsp vanilla extract

Direction

- Heat oven to 180C/160C fan/gas 4. Oil and line the bases of 3 x 20cm sandwich tins with baking parchment. Mix the flour, cinnamon, baking powder, half the sugar and the coconut in a large mixing bowl. In another bowl mix the beaten whole eggs, mashed bananas, grated carrot, drained crushed pineapple, milk and oil. Beat the egg whites until stiff, then add the remaining sugar and beat until stiff and shiny again.
- Stir the wet mixture into the dry until smooth and lump-free, then using a large metal spoon or spatula, fold in the egg white mixture. Divide evenly between the tins and bake for 25 mins until risen and a skewer comes out clean. You might need to swap the position of the tins after 20 mins.
- For the drizzle, scoop out the passion fruit pulp into a small pan. Add the pineapple juice and caster sugar and heat until bubbling, then bubble until syrupy. For the icing, beat the cheese and butter until lump-free, then beat in icing sugar and vanilla. Chill until ready to assemble.
- Poke the cakes all over with a skewer, drizzle over most of the passion syrup, then cool. Once cool, spread the icing over two of the sponges. Sandwich together and top with the third, un-iced, sponge. Drizzle over the remaining syrup.

Nutrition Information

- Calories: 611 calories
- Total Fat: 32 grams fat
- Total Carbohydrate: 80 grams carbohydrates
- Sugar: 56 grams sugar
- Protein: 7 grams protein
- Saturated Fat: 13 grams saturated fat
- Fiber: 3 grams fiber
- Sodium: 0.83 milligram of sodium

58. Passion Fruit Soufflés With Passion Fruit Sauce

Serving: 4 | Prep: 15mins | Cook: 15mins | Ready in:

Ingredients

- knob of butter, plus extra for greasing
- 75g caster sugar, plus extra for dusting
- 4 medium egg whites
- 6 ripe passion fruits, halved
- 150ml ready-made custard

Direction

- Heat oven to 180C/160C fan/gas 4. Put a baking tray on the top shelf to heat up. Grease 4 x 150ml ramekins with butter and dust the insides with caster sugar to coat.
- Whisk the egg whites in a bowl until stiff. Add 1 tbsp of the sugar and whisk for 30 secs more until thick and glossy. In a separate bowl, scoop the pulp from 1 passion fruit into the custard, then fold in the whisked egg white. Spoon the mixture into the prepared ramekins and put on the hot baking tray. Bake for 15 mins until risen and golden on top.
- While the soufflés are cooking, make the sauce. Scoop the remaining passion fruit pulp into a saucepan, add the remaining sugar and simmer gently for 5 mins. Finally add a knob of butter and stir until melted. Pass through a sieve and serve in a jug with the hot soufflés as soon as they come out of the oven. Let your guests break a hole in the centre of their soufflé, then pour in the sauce.

Nutrition Information

- Calories: 226 calories
- Total Fat: 8 grams fat
- Total Carbohydrate: 29 grams carbohydrates
- Fiber: 2 grams fiber
- Sodium: 0.3 milligram of sodium
- Saturated Fat: 3 grams saturated fat

- Sugar: 27 grams sugar
- Protein: 7 grams protein

59. Passion Layer Torte

Serving: 12 | Prep: 1hours | Cook: 25mins | Ready in:

Ingredients

- 225g softened butter, cubed, plus extra for greasing
- 225g caster sugar
- 4 large eggs
- 225g self-raising flour
- 50g desiccated coconut
- finely grated zest 1 orange
- 1 tsp baking powder
- For the frosting
- 5 large passion fruits
- 225g softened butter, cubed
- 375g icing sugar, sifted
- 280g full-fat cream cheese
- 75g white chocolate

Direction

- Heat oven to 190C/170C fan/gas 5. Grease 2 x 20cm loose-based sandwich tins and line the bases with discs of baking parchment. Put the butter, sugar, eggs, flour, coconut, orange zest and baking powder in a food processor or food mixer and blend or beat until well combined, thick and creamy. Do not over-blend or the cake will be tough rather than light. If you don't have a food mixer, put all the ingredients in a bowl and beat hard with a wooden spoon until soft and creamy.
- Spoon the mixture evenly into the prepared tins and smooth the surface. Bake on the same shelf in the centre of the oven for 25 mins or until well risen and just beginning to shrink back from the sides of the tin. Remove the tins from the oven and leave to cool for 5 mins before running a knife around the edge of the cakes and turning out onto a wire rack. Peel off the parchment and leave to cool completely.
- When the cakes are completely cold, very carefully cut horizontally through each one with a serrated knife to make 4 thin sponges. To make the frosting, cut the passion fruits in half and scoop into a sieve. Press through the sieve to strain the juice – you should have 4 tbsp. Set aside and reserve the seeds. Put the butter, icing sugar and cheese in a food processor or mixer and blend until smooth. Do not overbeat or it will become runny. Slowly add the passion fruit juice and blend until just combined.
- Place one of the sponges, cut-side down, on the metal base of the sandwich tin and put on an upturned bowl on a tray. This will help make frosting the cake easier. Spread with roughly a fifth of the frosting – just enough to cover the sponge. Use a paddling motion with a palette knife or soft spatula for the best result, trying to keep contact with the cake to prevent the sponge from lifting.
- Cover with a second cake, spread with frosting and repeat the layers once more, ending with the last sponge, cut-side down. By this stage, you should have layered 4 cakes with passion fruit frosting between 3 of them. Use the remaining frosting to spread over the top and sides of the cakes to cover completely. Don't worry if the sides are a little messy, as the grated chocolate should cover any imperfections.
- Put the cake in the fridge for 30-60 mins to allow the icing to set a little. Coarsely grate the chocolate. Working your way slowly around the cake, scoop grated chocolate onto a palette knife and sweep up the sides of the cake, pressing into the soft icing.
- Take the cake off the bowl, slide the palette knife between the cake and the metal base, and gently transfer to a plate or cake stand. (If the icing is too soft to do this, pop the cake in the freezer for 30 mins and then try again.) Chill until ready to serve. Before serving, drizzle over 1 tsp of the reserved passion fruit seeds over the top of the cake. If making a day

ahead, cover with a cake tin or a bowl large enough to cover the cake without touching it, so the cake doesn't get damaged in the fridge.

Nutrition Information

- Calories: 705 calories
- Fiber: 2 grams fiber
- Sugar: 54 grams sugar
- Saturated Fat: 28 grams saturated fat
- Sodium: 1.1 milligram of sodium
- Total Fat: 45 grams fat
- Total Carbohydrate: 68 grams carbohydrates
- Protein: 7 grams protein

60. Peek A Boo Battenberg Cake

Serving: Makes a tall 18cm cake | Prep: 1hours20mins | Cook: 1hours | Ready in:

Ingredients

- For the almond sponge
- 225g very soft salted butter, plus a little extra for greasing
- 225g golden caster sugar
- 225g self-raising flour
- 85g ground almond
- 3 large eggs
- ½ tsp vanilla extract
- ½ tsp almond extract
- 1 tbsp milk
- For the rose sponge
- 225g very soft salted butter
- 225g golden caster sugar
- 225g self-raising flour
- 85g ground almond
- 3 large eggs
- ½ tsp vanilla extract
- 1 tsp rosewater
- 1 tbsp milk
- a little artificial pink food colouring (see tip, below)
- To assemble and ice

- jar of apricot jam
- 1 tsp rosewater
- a little icing sugar, for dusting
- 2 x 500g packs white marzipan (you'll have trimmings, but better to have leftovers than leave yourself short)

Direction

- Heat oven to 160C/140C fan/gas 3. Grease and line the base of 2 x 18cm round sandwich tins with baking parchment.
- Start with the almond sponge: put all the ingredients in a bowl and beat with an electric whisk until the mix comes together smoothly. Weigh the mixture and spread exactly half into each tin. Bake for 30 mins – when you poke a skewer into the middle, it should come out clean. Cool in the tins for 15 mins, then carefully turn out onto wire racks to finish cooling while you make the second sponge.
- Clean the tins, then grease and line as above. Beat together the butter, sugar, flour, ground almonds, eggs, vanilla, rose water and milk as above. When smooth, beat in a little pink food colouring, bit by bit, until you get a nice colour – it will fade a little during baking, so you can go slightly stronger than you want the finished sponge. Weigh, divide between the tins and bake as above. Cool in the same way.
- Once the sponges are cool, cover gently and chill for 30 mins – this will make cutting them easier and neater.
- Unwrap the sponges and, if they have domed in the centre, trim to flatten. Cut a 6cm diameter circle out of the centre of each sponge (a 6cm biscuit cutter is ideal, or make yourself a paper template) and set aside. Then cut a 12cm diameter circle from the centre of each sponge by tracing a knife around a plate of the same diameter (or use another paper template). So from each sponge you should end up with a 6cm circle, a 12cm ring and an 18cm ring.
- Swap the middle rings of the almond sponges with the middle rings from the rose sponges, and fit the cut pieces back together. Handle the

sponges very gently, to avoid cracking or crumbling up the edges too much. You should end up with 4 sponges that look like targets.

- Heat the apricot jam to melt, then sieve and stir in the rose water. Brush some over the top of one of the sponges and top with an alternating sponge. Repeat to stack up all the layers. Sit the cake on a serving plate or cake stand.

- Dust your work surface with a little icing sugar and roll out your marzipan until big enough to cover the cake (use a piece of string to measure the cake; see tip below). Brush some more jam all over the top and sides of the cake. Use your rolling pin to lift up the marzipan onto the cake, then ease it down the sides, pressing to stick. Trim the marzipan from the base, then decorate the cake as you like. Cut into wedges and serve with tea. Will keep for three days in an airtight container.

Nutrition Information

- Calories: 964 calories
- Total Fat: 51 grams fat
- Saturated Fat: 22 grams saturated fat
- Fiber: 2 grams fiber
- Protein: 13 grams protein
- Total Carbohydrate: 113 grams carbohydrates
- Sodium: 1.1 milligram of sodium
- Sugar: 89 grams sugar

61. Peppermint Candy Biscuits

Serving: Makes about 20 | Prep: 25mins | Cook: 12mins | Ready in:

Ingredients

- 175g plain flour, plus a little extra for dusting
- 100g butter, cut into small cubes
- 85g caster sugar
- 1 egg yolk
- about 5 peppermint candy canes

Direction

- Before you start, read the tips at the bottom of the recipe.
- Tip the flour and butter into a bowl. Use your fingers to squash the lumps of butter into the flour, then rub together until the mixture resembles wet sand. Add the sugar and egg yolk and 1-2 tbsp cold water. Mix together with a blunt cutlery knife, then your hands, until it becomes a soft dough. (Or, get an adult to help you to do this in a food processor.) Wrap the dough in cling film and pop in the fridge for 20 mins to chill.
- Heat oven to 200C/180C fan/gas 6. Line 2 baking trays with baking parchment. Put the candy canes in a resealable plastic bag, then wrap in a tea towel. Use a rolling pin to bash them to a chunky rubble. Set to one side.
- Dust your work surface with a little flour, then use a rolling pin to roll out the dough. Cut out heart shapes with your big cookie cutter. Put them on the baking trays, spaced a little apart. Use your small cutter to cut out a little heart in the centre of each big heart. Re-roll your cuttings to make about 20 hearts in total.
- Bake for 8 mins. Carefully remove the trays from the oven, then fill each small heart with a little of the crushed candy cane. Return to the oven for 4 mins more, until the biscuits are just starting to turn golden and the candy cane has melted.
- Once out of the oven, quickly sprinkle the gooey centre of each heart with a little extra crushed candy cane. Leave to set and cool completely on the trays. Once cool, the biscuits will peel straight off the trays. Wrap them in pretty boxes to give as a gift.

Nutrition Information

- Calories: 99 calories
- Total Carbohydrate: 14 grams carbohydrates
- Sugar: 7 grams sugar
- Protein: 1 grams protein
- Sodium: 0.1 milligram of sodium
- Total Fat: 5 grams fat

- Saturated Fat: 3 grams saturated fat

62. Raspberry Religieuse

Serving: Makes 4 | Prep: 1hours | Cook: 35mins | Ready in:

Ingredients

- For the choux pastry
- flavourless oil for greasing, such as sunflower oil
- 50g butter
- 75g strong white flour
- 1 tsp golden caster sugar
- 2 large eggs, beaten
- For the filling
- 150ml double cream
- 75g icing sugar
- 1 tsp vanilla extract or vanilla bean paste
- 100g crème fraîche
- 200g raspberries
- For the icing
- 50g raspberries
- 100g icing sugar
- For the buttercream
- 50g butter, softened
- 1 tbsp milk
- ¼ tsp vanilla extract or vanilla bean paste
- 100g icing sugar

Direction

- Heat oven to 220C/200C fan/gas 7. Line a large baking tray with baking parchment and grease lightly with oil. Sprinkle 1-2 tsp of water over the surface of the parchment with your fingers.
- To make the choux buns, pour 100ml water into a small saucepan and add the butter. Heat until the butter has completely melted and the mixture starts to simmer. Take the pan off the heat and quickly add the flour and the caster sugar, stirring vigorously with a wooden spoon to remove any lumps. Working quickly,

add the egg, bit by bit, beating continuously until you have a smooth, thick and glossy batter. Allow to cool for 5 mins, then transfer the mixture to a disposable piping bag and snip off the end.

- Pipe 4 large buns onto your prepared tray (approximately 8cm in diameter) and 4 mini ones (approximately 4cm in diameter). Leave space between each bun, as they will spread as they cook. Bake for 18-20 mins or until well risen and golden brown. Take the tray out of the oven, transfer the smaller buns to a wire rack (as they will have cooked slightly quicker) and pop the larger buns back in the oven for a further 2-3 mins.
- Split all the choux buns in half as soon as they come out of the oven, then lay them, cut-side up, on a baking tray and return to the oven for a further 2 mins. This will allow the steam to escape and crisp up the pastry inside. Leave to cool, cut-side up, on the tray or a wire rack.
- While the pastry is cooling, make the filling. Whip the cream together with the icing sugar and vanilla until just starting to thicken (try not to overwhip the mixture as it will continue to thicken when it is piped). Fold in the crème fraîche. Spoon into a disposable piping bag and chill until needed.
- To make the icing, mash the raspberries with a fork, then push the juice and pulp through a sieve using the back of a spoon. Discard the seeds. Stir the icing sugar into the sieved pulp to create a thick pink icing – if the mixture is too runny, add a little more icing sugar. Use to decorate the top halves of all of the choux buns, then leave to set.
- For the buttercream, use an electric whisk to beat the butter, milk, vanilla extract and icing sugar together until pale and fluffy. Scoop into a piping bag fitted with a star nozzle.
- To assemble, place the bases of all the choux buns on a serving platter and fill with the cream mixture and the remaining raspberries, reserving 4 for decoration. Top the choux buns with their pink lids, then pipe a small amount of buttercream at the centre of the top of the 4 large filled buns. Place a small choux bun on

top of the buttercream and press gently so that it sticks. Use the rest of the buttercream to pipe short blobs starting on the large choux bun and ending halfway up the small bun. Finally, pipe a tiny amount of buttercream into the cavity of the 4 remaining raspberries and use this to fix it in place on the very top of each bun. Serve immediately.

Nutrition Information

- Calories: 871 calories
- Sodium: 0.5 milligram of sodium
- Total Fat: 54 grams fat
- Saturated Fat: 33 grams saturated fat
- Fiber: 3 grams fiber
- Total Carbohydrate: 87 grams carbohydrates
- Protein: 8 grams protein
- Sugar: 73 grams sugar

63. Red Velvet Cake

Serving: 20 | Prep: 1hours5mins | Cook: 1hours | Ready in:

Ingredients

- For the sponges
- 300ml vegetable oil, plus extra for the tins
- 500g plain flour
- 2 tbsp cocoa powder
- 4 tsp baking powder
- 2 tsp bicarbonate of soda
- 560g light brown soft sugar
- 1 tsp fine salt
- 400ml buttermilk
- 4 tsp vanilla extract
- 30ml red food colouring gel or about ¼ tsp food colouring paste, (use a professional food colouring paste if you can, a natural liquid colouring won't work and may turn the sponge green)
- 4 large eggs
- For the icing

- 250g slightly salted butter, at room temperature
- 750g icing sugar
- 350g tub full-fat soft cheese
- 1 tsp vanilla extract

Direction

- Heat the oven to 180C/160C fan/gas 4. Oil and line the base and sides of two 20cm cake tins with baking parchment – if your cake tins are quite shallow, line the sides to a depth of at least 5cm.
- Put half each of the flour, cocoa powder, baking powder, bicarb, sugar and salt in a bowl and mix well. If there are any lumps in the sugar, squeeze these through your fingers to break them up.
- Mix half each of the buttermilk, oil, vanilla extract, food colouring and 100ml water in a jug. Add 2 eggs and whisk until smooth. Pour the wet ingredients into the dry and whisk until well combined. The cake mixture should be bright red, it will get a little darker as it cooks. If it's not as vivid as you'd like, add a touch more colouring. Pour the cake mixture evenly into the two tins, and bake for 25-30 mins, or until risen and a skewer inserted into the centre comes out clean. Cool in the tins for 10 mins, then turn out onto a wire rack, peel off the baking parchment and leave to cool.
- Repeat steps 1 and 2 with the remaining ingredients, so you have four sponge cakes in total. Can be made up to three days ahead and will stay moist if wrapped in cling film, or you can wrap well and freeze for up to two months.
- To make the icing, put the butter in a large bowl and sieve in half the icing sugar. Roughly mash together with a spatula, then whizz with a hand mixer until smooth. Add the soft cheese and vanilla, sieve in the remaining icing sugar, mash together again, then blend once more with the hand mixer.
- To assemble the cake, stick one of the sponges to a cake stand or board with a little of the soft cheese icing. Use roughly half the icing to

stack the remaining cakes on top, spreading a generous amount between each layer. Pile the remaining icing on top of the assembled cake, and use a palette knife to ease it over the edges, covering the entire surface of the cake. Tidy the plate with a piece of kitchen paper. Store leftovers in the fridge for up to 2 days, but bring back to room temperature for an hour or so before eating.This recipe was refreshed in July 2018 based on user feedback. For the original recipe, see our beetroot cake.

Nutrition Information

- Calories: 656 calories
- Fiber: 1 grams fiber
- Protein: 6 grams protein
- Total Fat: 31 grams fat
- Saturated Fat: 11 grams saturated fat
- Sugar: 66 grams sugar
- Sodium: 1.5 milligram of sodium
- Total Carbohydrate: 86 grams carbohydrates

64. Romantic Rose Cupcakes

Serving: Makes 12 deep cupcakes | Prep: | Cook: 20mins | Ready in:

Ingredients

- 150ml pot natural yogurt
- 3 eggs, beaten
- 1 tsp vanilla extract
- 175g golden caster sugar
- 140g self-raising flour
- 1 tsp baking powder
- 100g ground almond
- 175g unsalted butter, melted
- For the white chocolate frosting
- 100g white chocolate
- 140g unsalted butter
- 140g icing sugar

Direction

- Line a 12-hole muffin tin with paper cases and heat oven to 190C/fan 170C/gas 5. In a jug, mix the yogurt, eggs and vanilla extract. Put the dry ingredients, plus a pinch of salt, into a large bowl and make a well in the middle.
- Add the yogurty mix and melted butter, and quickly fold in with a spatula or metal spoon – don't overwork it. Spoon into the cases (they will be quite full) and bake for 18-20 mins or until golden, risen and springy to the touch. Cool for a few mins, then lift the cakes onto a wire rack to cool completely. Keep in an airtight container for up to 3 days or freeze as soon as possible.
- White chocolate frosting: Melt the chocolate in the microwave on High for 1½ mins, stirring halfway. Leave to cool. Beat the butter and icing sugar in a large bowl until creamy. Beat in the chocolate. Cover and chill for up to one month.
- Up to 48 hrs before serving (or the day before if it's really hot), bring the frosting back to room temperature, then spread over the cakes. Put the ribbon around the cakes now if you like, tying or glueing in place. Keep cool, out of direct sunlight.

Nutrition Information

- Calories: 525 calories
- Saturated Fat: 16 grams saturated fat
- Total Carbohydrate: 57 grams carbohydrates
- Protein: 6 grams protein
- Sugar: 47 grams sugar
- Sodium: 0.36 milligram of sodium
- Fiber: 1 grams fiber
- Total Fat: 32 grams fat

65. Squidgy Chocolate & Pomegranate Torte

Serving: Cuts into 12 slices | Prep: 20mins | Cook: 35mins | Ready in:

Ingredients

- 225g unsalted butter, plus extra for greasing
- 250g dark chocolate (70% cocoa), broken into squares
- 5 large eggs
- 225g light muscovado sugar, squished through your fingers to remove any lumps
- 85g ground almond
- 50g plain flour, plus an extra 1 tbsp
- For the topping
- 150ml double cream
- 100g bar dark chocolate (70% cocoa), roughly chopped
- 1 tbsp icing sugar, sifted
- handful pomegranate seeds

Direction

- Generously grease a 23cm springform tin, then line the base with parchment. Heat oven to 180C/160C fan/gas 4. Put the butter and chocolate in a medium bowl and gently melt together, either over a pan of simmering water or in the microwave. Stir until smooth, then set aside.
- Crack the eggs into a large bowl, add the sugar, then whisk for 5-8 mins with electric hand beaters until thick, mousse-like and doubled in volume. Pour the chocolate mix around the edge of the bowl, then fold together using a large metal spoon until the batter is evenly brown with the odd ribbon of chocolate appearing. Don't rush this bit, it's important to preserve the bubbles you've so carefully made. Sift over the almonds, flour and ¼ tsp salt, then fold in until even. Slowly pour the batter into the tin, then use a spatula to get every last bit from the bowl. Bake on a middle shelf for 30-35 mins, or until the cake is risen and set on top. Cool the cake in its tin on a rack. The torte may sink and crack a little, which is fine.
- For the topping, bring the cream to the boil. Put the chocolate in a bowl with the icing sugar, then tip the hot cream over it. Leave for a few mins, stir until smooth, then let it cool

and thicken for 10 mins. Carefully remove the torte from its tin onto a plate, then spread the icing over the top, letting it drip down the sides. Leave to set for a few mins, then scatter with the pomegranate seeds and either chill for a few hours, or serve straight away.

Nutrition Information

- Calories: 544 calories
- Fiber: 3 grams fiber
- Protein: 7 grams protein
- Sodium: 0.2 milligram of sodium
- Saturated Fat: 22 grams saturated fat
- Total Fat: 40 grams fat
- Total Carbohydrate: 35 grams carbohydrates
- Sugar: 28 grams sugar

66. Strawberry & White Chocolate Choux Buns

Serving: 8 | Prep: 30mins | Cook: 35mins | Ready in:

Ingredients

- For the choux pastry
- 50g butter
- 75g plain flour
- 2 large eggs
- 1 tbsp flaked almonds (optional)
- For the filling
- 2 tbsp custard powder
- 300ml milk
- ½ tsp sugar free vanilla extract
- 150ml Greek yogurt
- 15g coarsely grated white chocolate
- 125g small strawberries, halved
- dusting of icing sugar (optional)

Direction

- Line a large baking tray with baking paper. Heat oven to 200C, 180C fan gas 6. Heat the butter in a nonstick pan with 125ml water until melted. Increase the heat until boiling then remove from the heat and quickly beat in the flour until the mixture comes together as a ball. Cool 5 mins then beat the eggs with 1 tbsp water then beat into the pastry a little as a time to make a thick glossy mix.

- Spoon onto the baking tray in 8 equal size blobs then add the almonds if using poking them into the mixture. Bake for 25-30 mins until well risen and golden. Take from the oven make a slash in the sides and return to the oven for 5 mins more to dry out.
- While baking make the filling. Mix the custard powder with a little of the milk then, with the remaining milk and vanilla put in a non stick pan and cook, stirring over the heat until thickened. Stand for 5 mins then beat in the yogurt and set aside to cool, stirring frequently to make sure a skin doesn't form. When cold, stir in the grated chocolate.
- Reserve 1 tbsp of the custard mix then use the rest to fill the buns. Distribute all but 8 halves of strawberries between the buns, then blob a little of the remaining custard filling on top and add the reserved strawberries. Lightly dust with the icing sugar before serving if you like.

Nutrition Information

- Calories: 177 calories
- Sodium: 0.3 milligram of sodium
- Total Fat: 11 grams fat
- Fiber: 1 grams fiber
- Saturated Fat: 6 grams saturated fat
- Protein: 5 grams protein
- Total Carbohydrate: 15 grams carbohydrates
- Sugar: 5 grams sugar

67. Sugared Scones

Serving: Makes about 8 | Prep: 20mins | Cook: 12mins | Ready in:

Ingredients

- 85g diced butter
- 350g self-raising flour
- ¼ tsp salt
- 1 ½ tsp bicarbonate of soda
- 4 tbsp caster sugar
- 200ml milk, warmed to room temperature, plus a splash extra
- crushed sugar cubes, to decorate

Direction

- Heat oven to 200C/180C fan/gas 6. Whizz butter into flour. Tip into a bowl and stir in salt with bicarbonate of soda and sugar. Using a cutlery knife, quickly stir in milk – don't over-mix.
- Tip out onto a lightly floured surface and turn over a couple of times to very gently bring together with your hands. Gently pat to about 1in thick, then stamp out rounds with a floured cutter. Pat together trimmings to stamp out more. Brush the tops with a splash more milk, then scatter with crushed sugar cubes. Bake on a baking sheet for 10-12 mins until risen and golden.

Nutrition Information

- Calories: 283 calories
- Total Fat: 10 grams fat
- Sugar: 14 grams sugar
- Total Carbohydrate: 44 grams carbohydrates
- Protein: 5 grams protein
- Saturated Fat: 6 grams saturated fat
- Fiber: 1 grams fiber
- Sodium: 1.1 milligram of sodium

68. Tia Maria Cheesecake

Serving: 16 | Prep: | Cook: 35mins | Ready in:

Ingredients

- For the biscuit crust
- 85g hot melted butter, plus extra butter for greasing
- 14 plain chocolate digestive biscuits, finely crushed
- For the cheesecake
- 3 x 300g packs full-fat Philadelphia cheese
- 200g golden caster sugar
- 4 tbsp plain flour
- 2 tsp vanilla extract
- 2 tbsp Tia Maria
- 3 large eggs
- 285ml carton soured cream
- For the topping
- 142ml carton soured cream
- 2 tbsp Tia Maria
- cocoa, for dusting
- 8 Ferrero Rocher chocolates, unwrapped

Direction

- Heat oven to 180C/fan 160C/gas 4. Line the base of a 25cm springform tin with baking parchment. Blend butter and biscuit crumbs. Press onto the base of the tin, bake for 10 mins, then cool.
- Increase the oven temperature to 240C/fan 200C/gas 9. Beat the cheese and sugar with an electric whisk until smooth, then whisk in the flour, vanilla, 2 tbsp Tia Maria, eggs and 285ml soured cream.
- Grease sides of the cake tin with butter. Pour in the mixture and smooth. Bake for 10 mins, then turn oven down to 110C/fan 90C/ gas ¼ for 25 mins. Turn off the oven, then open the door and leave to cool inside the oven for 2 hrs. Don't worry if it cracks a little.
- Mix 142ml soured cream and Tia Maria, then smooth on top of the cheesecake. Chill.

Nutrition Information

- Calories: 410 calories
- Fiber: 1 grams fiber
- Protein: 7 grams protein
- Saturated Fat: 17 grams saturated fat
- Total Fat: 29 grams fat
- Total Carbohydrate: 32 grams carbohydrates
- Sugar: 24 grams sugar
- Sodium: 0.89 milligram of sodium

69. Valentine's Day Cupcakes

Serving: makes 8 | Prep: 40mins | Cook: 20mins | Ready in:

Ingredients

- For the muffins
- 175g butter
- 200g light muscovado sugar
- 50g cocoa
- 140g self-raising flour
- 2 large eggs
- 8 white truffles
- For the decorations
- 150g butter, softened
- 300g icing sugar
- 1 tsp vanilla extract
- 2 tbsp cocoa
- 8 white chocolate hearts (we used Dr Oetker)

Direction

- Heat oven to 180C/160C fan/ gas 4 and line a muffin tin with eight paper cases. Melt the butter in a small pan, then leave to cool for 5 mins. Tip the sugar, cocoa and flour into a food processor and whizz to get rid of any little clusters of sugar that are sticking together. Tip in the melted butter and eggs, and blitz to make a smooth batter.
- Scoop a little of the mixture into each muffin case, then lightly press a white chocolate truffle in the centre. Spoon over the remaining mixture, making sure that the truffles are covered. Bake for 15-20 mins until the mixture has firmed up. Leave to cool.
- To decorate the muffins, tip the butter and sugar into a large bowl, add the vanilla and beat with an electric hand whisk until really

smooth. Thinly spread a little of the vanilla mixture over the top of the cakes to cover them, taking the icing down the sides to meet the paper case. Beat the cocoa powder into the rest of the icing, then put in a piping bag fitted with a large star nozzle and pipe hearts onto the top of each cake. Add a chocolate heart to decorate for the final flourish.

Nutrition Information

- Calories: 758 calories
- Sugar: 69 grams sugar
- Protein: 6 grams protein
- Saturated Fat: 27 grams saturated fat
- Total Fat: 43 grams fat
- Fiber: 2 grams fiber
- Total Carbohydrate: 84 grams carbohydrates
- Sodium: 1 milligram of sodium

Chapter 3: Chocolate Baking Recipes

***

70. Amazing Chocolate Cupcakes

Serving: Makes 12 | Prep: 15mins | Cook: 25mins | Ready in:

Ingredients

- 100g plain flour
- 20g cocoa powder
- 140g caster sugar
- 1½ tsp baking powder
- 40g unsalted butter (at room temperature)
- 120ml whole milk
- 1 egg
- ¼ tsp vanilla extract

- To decorate
- buttercream
- chocolate vermicelli (optional)

Direction

- Heat oven to 180C/160C fan/gas 4. Put the flour, cocoa powder, sugar, baking powder, a pinch of salt and the butter in a free-standing electric mixer with a paddle attachment (or use a handheld electric whisk). Beat on a slow speed until you get a sandy consistency and everything is combined.
- Whisk the milk, egg and vanilla extract together in a jug, then slowly pour about half into the flour mixture. Beat to combine and turn the mixer up to high speed, scraping any mixture from the side of the bowl with a rubber spatula. Pour in the remaining liquid and continue mixing for a couple more minutes until the mixture is smooth. Do not overmix.
- Spoon the mixture into the paper cases until approximately two-thirds full. Bake in a preheated oven for 20-25 minutes, or until the sponge bounces back when touched and a skewer inserted into the centre comes out clean.
- Leave the cupcakes to cool slightly in the tray before turning out onto a wire cooling rack to cool completely. Meanwhile, make chocolate buttercream or plain buttercream and spread it over the cakes with a palette knife, or use a piping bag. Scatter over chocolate vermicelli, if you like.

Nutrition Information

- Calories: 122 calories
- Saturated Fat: 2 grams saturated fat
- Total Fat: 4 grams fat
- Total Carbohydrate: 19 grams carbohydrates
- Sugar: 12 grams sugar
- Fiber: 1 grams fiber
- Sodium: 0.2 milligram of sodium
- Protein: 2 grams protein

71. Beetroot Brownies

Serving: Makes 15-20 | Prep: 15mins | Cook: 40mins | Ready in:

Ingredients

- 500g whole raw beetroot (3-4 medium beets)
- 100g unsalted butter, plus extra for the tin
- 200g bar plain chocolate (70% cocoa)
- 1 tsp vanilla extract
- 250g golden caster sugar
- 3 eggs
- 100g plain flour
- 25g cocoa powder

Direction

- Wear a pair of rubber gloves to stop your hands from staining, then top, tail and peel the beetroot – you'll need about 400g flesh. Roughly chop and put into a large bowl. Add a splash of water, cover with cling film, then microwave on High for 12 mins or until tender.
- Heat oven to 180C/160C fan/gas 4. While the beetroot cooks, butter then line a 20 x 30cm traybake or small roasting tin. Roughly chop the chocolate and cut the butter into cubes. Tip the cooked beetroot into a sieve, drain off any excess liquid, then put into a food processor or blender with the chocolate, butter and vanilla. Whizz until the mix is as smooth as you can get it. The chocolate and butter will melt as you do this.
- Put the sugar and eggs into a large bowl, then beat using an electric hand whisk until thick, pale and foamy, about 2 mins. Spoon the beetroot mix into the bowl (it won't look too pretty at this stage, but bear with me), then use a large metal spoon to fold it into the whisked eggs. Try to conserve as much air in the mixture as you can. Sift in the flour and cocoa powder, then gently fold these in to make a smooth batter.
- Pour into the prepared tin and bake for 25 mins or until risen all over, with just the merest quiver under the centre of the crust when you shake the pan. Cool completely in the tin, then cut into squares.

Nutrition Information

- Calories: 255 calories
- Total Carbohydrate: 32 grams carbohydrates
- Protein: 4 grams protein
- Sodium: 0.11 milligram of sodium
- Sugar: 24 grams sugar
- Fiber: 2 grams fiber
- Total Fat: 13 grams fat
- Saturated Fat: 7 grams saturated fat

72. Best Ever Chocolate Raspberry Brownies

Serving: Cuts into 15 squares | Prep: 10mins | Cook: 40mins | Ready in:

Ingredients

- 200g dark chocolate, broken into chunks
- 100g milk chocolate, broken into chunks
- 250g pack salted butter
- 400g soft light brown sugar
- 4 large eggs
- 140g plain flour
- 50g cocoa powder
- 200g raspberries

Direction

- Heat oven to 180C/160C fan/gas 4. Line a 20 x 30cm baking tray tin with baking parchment. Put the chocolate, butter and sugar in a pan and gently melt, stirring occasionally with a wooden spoon. Remove from the heat.
- Stir the eggs, one by one, into the melted chocolate mixture. Sieve over the flour and cocoa, and stir in. Stir in half the raspberries,

scrape into the tray, then scatter over the remaining raspberries. Bake on the middle shelf for 30 mins or, if you prefer a firmer texture, for 5 mins more. Cool before slicing into squares. Store in an airtight container for up to 3 days.

Nutrition Information

- Calories: 389 calories
- Saturated Fat: 13 grams saturated fat
- Sugar: 38 grams sugar
- Fiber: 2 grams fiber
- Protein: 5 grams protein
- Sodium: 0.4 milligram of sodium
- Total Fat: 22 grams fat
- Total Carbohydrate: 44 grams carbohydrates

73. Cherry Oat Squares With Chocolate Drizzle

Serving: Makes 16 | Prep: 20mins | Cook: 25mins | Ready in:

Ingredients

- 140g butter, melted, plus extra butter for the tin
- 100g self-raising flour
- 175g caster sugar
- 175g porridge oat
- 1 egg, beaten
- 100g glacé cherry, halved
- 50g dark chocolate

Direction

- Heat oven to 180C/160C fan/gas 4. Butter and line the base and sides of a 22cm square cake tin: cut 2 strips of baking parchment the width of the tin and longer than the base and sides, and fit into the tin each way and up the sides. This will make lifting it out easier.

- Mix together the flour, sugar and oats in a bowl. Add the egg, melted butter and cherries, and mix well. Tip into the tin and spread evenly with a fork.
- Bake for 20-25 mins until golden brown. Cool in the tin for 10 mins, then carefully lift out using the paper and place on a board. Mark, but don't cut, 4 lines each way to make 16 squares. Melt the chocolate in the microwave for 1 min, then drizzle over the squares. When the chocolate has set, cut the squares down the marked lines.

Nutrition Information

- Calories: 208 calories
- Total Carbohydrate: 27 grams carbohydrates
- Protein: 3 grams protein
- Sugar: 17 grams sugar
- Sodium: 0.2 milligram of sodium
- Saturated Fat: 5 grams saturated fat
- Total Fat: 9 grams fat
- Fiber: 2 grams fiber

74. Chocolate & Caramel Flapjacks

Serving: Cuts into 12 mini squares | Prep: 10mins | Cook: 55mins | Ready in:

Ingredients

- 200g soft brown sugar
- 200g butter, plus extra for greasing
- 2 tbsp golden syrup
- 350g whole oats
- 397g can caramel (we used Carnation Caramel)
- 200g plain chocolate
- 1 tbsp unflavoured oil, like sunflower

Direction

- Heat oven to 150C/130C fan/gas 2. Place the sugar, butter and golden syrup together in a saucepan and gently heat until the butter has melted, stirring occasionally. Take the saucepan off the heat and stir in the oats, mixing thoroughly. Pour the mixture into a lined and lightly greased 22cm square tin, pressing it out evenly using the back of a wooden spoon. Bake in the centre of the oven for 40-45 mins.

- Allow the mixture to cool in the tin for 10 mins (or for best results, leave to cool completely overnight), then evenly spread over the caramel. There can be discrepancies between the thickness of caramel, and the more you stir the runnier it gets. If it looks too thin pop it into a pan and boil for a few minutes, stirring. Then leave to cool - it should be thicker. Chill until firm.
- Melt the chocolate in a heatproof bowl over a pan of barely simmering water, then stir in the oil and pour over the chilled caramel flapjack base. Let the chocolate set, then cut into squares. Setting chocolate on top of something squidgy can make it difficult to cut, this is why the oil is added.

Nutrition Information

- Calories: 492 calories
- Fiber: 4 grams fiber
- Protein: 8 grams protein
- Saturated Fat: 13 grams saturated fat
- Total Carbohydrate: 67 grams carbohydrates
- Sodium: 0.37 milligram of sodium
- Total Fat: 23 grams fat
- Sugar: 48 grams sugar

75. Chocolate Cookies

Serving: Makes 12 big cookies | Prep: | Cook: | Ready in:

Ingredients

- 300g plain chocolate (about 55% cocoa solids)
- 100g bar milk chocolate
- 100g light muscovado sugar
- 85g butter, at room temperature
- 100g peanut butter, crunchy is best
- 1 medium egg
- ½ tsp vanilla extract
- 100g self-raising flour
- 100g large salted roasted peanuts

Direction

- Preheat the oven to 180C/gas 4/fan 160C.Gather together and weigh all the ingredients.
- Chop 200g/7oz of the plain chocolate into rough, irregular chunks. Chop the milk chocolate in the same way, but keep separate.
- Break the remaining plain chocolate into a large heatproof mixing bowl. Melt in the microwave on medium for about 1½ minutes (or over a pan of simmering water).
- Stir the chocolate until melted, then tip in the sugar, butter, peanut butter, egg and vanilla and beat with a wooden spoon until well mixed. Stir in the flour, all the milk chocolate chunks, the nuts (no need to chop) and half the plain chocolate chunks. The mixture will feel quite soft, and drop easily from the spoon if you shake it.
- Drop big spoonfuls in 12 piles on to 2 or 3 baking sheets, leaving room for them to spread (you may need to bake in batches). Stick the remaining chunks into the cookies (2-3 pieces in each).
- Bake for 10-12 minutes until they are tinged very slightly darker around the edges. The smell will let you know they are ready. They will be soft in the middle, but will crisp up as they cool. (Cook for longer and you'll have crisper cookies.) Let them cool and firm up for a few minutes on the baking sheet (they'll break if you move them while still hot), then lift off with a wide spatula on to a cooling rack. They will keep crisp in an airtight tin for 3-4 days.

Nutrition Information

- Calories: 381 calories
- Fiber: 2 grams fiber
- Saturated Fat: 10 grams saturated fat
- Sugar: 27 grams sugar
- Total Carbohydrate: 36 grams carbohydrates
- Protein: 7 grams protein
- Sodium: 0.42 milligram of sodium
- Total Fat: 24 grams fat

76. Chocolate Fudge Cake

Serving: Cuts into 12 | Prep: 20mins | Cook: 1hours | Ready in:

Ingredients

- 200g plain chocolate, broken into chunks (use one with a low cocoa content - we used Waitrose plain Belgian chocolate)
- 200g butter
- 200g light brown muscovado sugar
- 100ml soured cream
- 2 eggs, beaten
- 200g self-raising flour
- 5 tbsp cocoa powder
- hundreds and thousands, to decorate
- For the icing
- 100g plain chocolate
- 170g can condensed milk
- 100g butter

Direction

- Heat oven to 160C/140C fan/gas 3. Line a 22 x 22cm square tin with baking parchment. Put the chocolate, butter and sugar into a large pan with 100ml hot water and gently melt together. Set aside for 2 mins, then stir in the soured cream followed by the eggs. Finally, stir or whisk in the flour and cocoa until lump-free, then pour into the prepared tin. Bake for 50-55 mins until a skewer comes out clean. Sit the tin on a wire rack to cool.
- Meanwhile, make the icing. Gently melt together icing ingredients in a heatproof bowl

set over a pan of barely simmering water, then chill or cool until spreadable.
- To decorate, carefully turn out the cooled cake and peel off the baking parchment. Spread the icing over the top and scatter with hundreds and thousands, then cut the cake into triangles or fingers before serving.

Nutrition Information

- Calories: 502 calories
- Protein: 6 grams protein
- Saturated Fat: 20 grams saturated fat
- Total Carbohydrate: 49 grams carbohydrates
- Total Fat: 33 grams fat
- Sugar: 35 grams sugar
- Sodium: 0.66 milligram of sodium
- Fiber: 1 grams fiber

77. Chocolate Macarons

Serving: Makes 12 filled macarons | Prep: 25mins | Cook: 20mins | Ready in:

Ingredients

- 125g icing sugar
- 1 tbsp cocoa
- 100g ground almonds
- 2 medium egg whites
- For the filling
- 50g milk or dark chocolate, chopped
- 2 tsp skimmed milk, warmed a little

Direction

- Heat oven to 180C/ 160C fan/gas 4. Line a large baking sheet with baking paper. Sift the icing sugar and cocoa into a bowl, then stir in the ground almonds. Whisk the egg whites until stiff, then fold them into the dry ingredients.
- Fill an icing bag fitted with a plain nozzle with the mixture (or put in a large food bag and

snip off the corner). Pipe 24 small blobs, about 3cm across, onto the baking sheet, leaving a little space between each. Smooth the surface with a wet finger, then leave for 15 mins to dry out. Bake for 15-20 mins until macaroons feel firm to the touch and peel easily off the paper. Cool on the paper, then peel off and store in a tin for up to 1 week.

- To make the filling, put chocolate into a heatproof bowl and gently melt over a pan of barely simmering water. Stir in the warm milk until smooth. Leave to cool and thicken a little, then use to sandwich the macarons together

Nutrition Information

- Calories: 119 calories
- Total Carbohydrate: 14 grams carbohydrates
- Protein: 3 grams protein
- Sodium: 0.04 milligram of sodium
- Total Fat: 6 grams fat
- Sugar: 14 grams sugar
- Fiber: 1 grams fiber
- Saturated Fat: 1 grams saturated fat

78. Chocolate Orange Marble Cake

Serving: Cuts into 10 slices | Prep: 15mins | Cook: 55mins | Ready in:

Ingredients

- 225g very soft butter, plus extra for greasing
- 225g caster sugar
- 225g self-raising flour
- 4 large eggs, beaten
- 2 tbsp milk
- 3 tbsp cocoa powder, sifted
- 1 large orange, zest and 1 tbsp orange juice
- a few drops orange food colouring (optional)
- 50g orange chocolate (we used Green & Black's Maya Gold), broken into pieces

Direction

- Heat oven to 180C/fan 160C/gas 4. Grease and line the base of a loaf tin (8 x 21cm/ 2lb) with baking parchment. Beat the butter, sugar, eggs and flour together in a large bowl with an electric whisk or in a food processor until lump free.
- Split the mixture into two bowls, beat the milk, followed by the cocoa powder into one. Beat the orange juice, zest and orange food colouring, if using, into the other.
- Spoon alternate dollops of the mixture into the cake tin, then use a skewer to create a marble pattern by dragging it through the mixture in swirls. Make sure you don't overmix or you won't see the pattern. Smooth the surface if necessary.
- Bake the cake for 45 - 55 mins until golden and risen, and a skewer poked in comes out clean.
- Leave the cake in the tin to cool, then turn out. Melt the chocolate in a bowl over barely simmering water or gently in the microwave. Use a spoon to drizzle the chocolate over the cake.

Nutrition Information

- Calories: 397 calories
- Total Fat: 23.1 grams fat
- Total Carbohydrate: 41.5 grams carbohydrates
- Sugar: 26.1 grams sugar
- Sodium: 0.7 milligram of sodium
- Saturated Fat: 13.7 grams saturated fat
- Fiber: 1.6 grams fiber
- Protein: 5.6 grams protein

79. Cinnamon Nutella Cake

Serving: Cuts into about 12 slices | Prep: 20mins | Cook: 1hours10mins | Ready in:

Ingredients

- 175g softened butter
- 175g golden caster sugar

- 3 eggs
- 200g self-raising flour
- 1 tsp baking powder
- 2 tsp ground cinnamon
- 4 tbsp milk
- 4 rounded tbsp Nutella or own-brand chocolate hazelnut spread
- 50g hazelnuts, roughly chopped

Direction

- Preheat the oven to 180C/gas 4/ fan 160C. Butter and line the base of a 20cm round cake tin.
- Put the butter, sugar, eggs, flour, baking powder, cinnamon and milk into a bowl. Beat with a wooden spoon for 2-3 minutes, or with an electric hand mixer for 1-2 minutes, until light and fluffy.
- Tip three quarters of the mixture into the tin, spread it level, then spoon the Nutella on in four blobs. Top with the remaining mixture, swirl a few times with a skewer, then smooth to cover the Nutella.
- Sprinkle with the nuts. Bake for 1 hour to 1 hour 10 minutes, until risen, nicely browned, feels firm to touch and springs back when lightly pressed (cover with foil if it starts to brown too quickly). Cool in the tin for 10 minutes, then turn out, peel off the paper and cool on a wire rack. Wrap tightly in double thick foil to keep fresh for up to a week.

Nutrition Information

- Calories: 320 calories
- Sodium: 0.63 milligram of sodium
- Saturated Fat: 8 grams saturated fat
- Total Fat: 19 grams fat
- Total Carbohydrate: 34 grams carbohydrates
- Fiber: 1 grams fiber
- Sugar: 20 grams sugar
- Protein: 5 grams protein

80. Custard & White Chocolate Biscuits

Serving: Makes about 25 | Prep: 15mins | Cook: 15mins | Ready in:

Ingredients

- 140g butter, softened
- 175g caster sugar
- 1 egg
- ½ tsp vanilla extract
- 225g self-raising flour
- 85g custard powder
- 85g white chocolate, chopped into small chunks

Direction

- Heat oven to 180C/160C fan/gas 4. Line 2-3 baking sheets with baking parchment. Put the butter and sugar in a food processor and whizz until light and fluffy. Add the egg and vanilla, and mix well. Sift together the flour and custard powder, then tip into the bowl and pulse to mix into a dough. Scrape out the food processor and work the chocolate in by hand.
- Roll the dough into balls a little smaller than a walnut, then place on the baking sheets, a little apart to allow for spreading. Press each biscuit down lightly with your fingers.
- Bake for 12-15 mins until lightly golden. Remove and cool on a wire rack.

Nutrition Information

- Calories: 132 calories
- Saturated Fat: 4 grams saturated fat
- Total Carbohydrate: 18 grams carbohydrates
- Sugar: 9 grams sugar
- Protein: 1 grams protein
- Sodium: 0.2 milligram of sodium
- Total Fat: 6 grams fat

81. Double Chocolate Loaf Cake

Serving: Cuts into 8-10 slices | Prep: 25mins | Cook: 55mins | Ready in:

Ingredients

- 175g softened butter, plus extra for greasing
- 175g golden caster sugar
- 3 eggs
- 140g self-raising flour
- 85g ground almonds
- ½ tsp baking powder
- 100ml milk
- 4 tbsp cocoa powder
- 50g plain chocolate chip or chunks
- few extra chunks white, plain and milk chocolate, for decorating

Direction

- Heat oven to 160C/140C fan/gas 3. Grease and line a 2lb/900g loaf tin with a long strip of baking parchment. To make the loaf cake batter, beat the butter and sugar with an electric whisk until light and fluffy. Beat in the eggs, flour, almonds, baking powder, milk and cocoa until smooth. Stir in the chocolate chips, then scrape into the tin. Bake for 45-50 mins until golden, risen and a skewer poked in the centre comes out clean.
- Cool in the tin, then lift out onto a wire rack over some kitchen paper. Melt the extra chocolate chunks separately in pans over barely simmering water, or in bowls in the microwave, then use a spoon to drizzle each in turn over the cake. Leave to set before slicing.

Nutrition Information

- Calories: 504 calories
- Sodium: 0.64 milligram of sodium
- Saturated Fat: 16 grams saturated fat
- Total Fat: 32 grams fat
- Total Carbohydrate: 48 grams carbohydrates
- Sugar: 33 grams sugar
- Fiber: 2 grams fiber

- Protein: 8 grams protein

82. Easter Brownie Bites

Serving: Makes 24 mini brownies | Prep: 15mins | Cook: 15mins | Ready in:

Ingredients

- 175g butter, chopped
- 150g dark chocolate
- 250g light brown soft sugar
- 85g self-raising flour
- 50g cocoa powder
- 3 large eggs, beaten
- 100g milk chocolate chips
- 24 mini chocolate eggs, plus extra to decorate

Direction

- Heat oven to 180C/160C fan/gas 4. Line 24 holes of a mini muffin tray with paper cases. Put the butter, dark chocolate and sugar in a pan and heat it very gently, stirring all the time until the butter and chocolate have melted. Remove from the heat and leave to cool for a few mins.
- Meanwhile, sift the flour, cocoa and a good pinch of salt into a large bowl. Stir in the warm, melted chocolate mixture and the beaten eggs, then add half the chocolate chips and mix until just combined.
- Divide the mixture between the cases and place a mini egg into the middle of each muffin, pushing down gently. Bake for 12-15 mins until cooked but still gooey in the centre – they will continue cooking a little as they cool down. Leave to cool for 10 mins in the tin before transferring to a wire rack to cool completely.
- Melt the rest of the chocolate chips in short bursts in the microwave, or in a bowl set over a pan of simmering water, stirring frequently. Leave to cool until it is quite thick, then dot a

small amount on each cake and stick on some more mini eggs.

Nutrition Information

- Calories: 194 calories
- Sodium: 0.2 milligram of sodium
- Total Carbohydrate: 19 grams carbohydrates
- Sugar: 15 grams sugar
- Protein: 3 grams protein
- Total Fat: 12 grams fat
- Saturated Fat: 7 grams saturated fat
- Fiber: 1 grams fiber

83. Easter Nest Cake

Serving: 15 | Prep: 45mins | Cook: 30mins | Ready in:

Ingredients

- For the chocolate sponges
- 200ml vegetable oil, plus extra for the tin
- 250g plain flour
- 6 tbsp cocoa powder
- 2 tsp baking powder
- 1 tsp bicarbonate of soda
- 280g soft light brown sugar
- 250ml buttermilk
- 2 tsp vanilla extract
- 3 large eggs
- For the nest
- 200g marshmallows
- 100g butter, chopped into chunks
- 2 tbsp cocoa powder
- 75g salted pretzels, crushed
- 4 shredded wheat biscuits, crushed
- chocolate eggs, to decorate
- For the icing
- 150g slightly salted butter, softened
- 2 tbsp cocoa powder
- 300g icing sugar
- 4 tbsp milk

Direction

- Heat oven to 180C/160C fan/gas 4. Oil and line two 20cm round cake tins. Add the flour, cocoa powder, baking powder, bicarb, sugar and a large pinch of salt to a bowl. Mix with a whisk, squeezing any large lumps of sugar through your fingers, until you have a fine, sandy mix.
- Whisk the oil with the buttermilk in a jug. Stir in the vanilla and eggs, then pour the wet ingredients into the dry and mix until there are no more streaks of flour. Divide the mixture between the tins and bake for 25 mins. Test the cakes by inserting a skewer into the centre – if there is any wet mixture on the skewer, return the cakes to the oven for 5 mins more, then check again. Leave the cakes to cool in the tins for 15 mins, then transfer to wire racks to cool fully.
- Next, make the nest. Clean one tin and line it with some oiled baking parchment. Put the marshmallows and butter in a heatproof bowl and microwave on high for 1 min, stirring halfway through (or heat gently in a pan on the hob). Continue microwaving in 20-second blasts until you get a runny mixture. Stir in the cocoa, pretzels and shredded wheat until well combined. Tip the mixture into your lined tin and use the back of your spoon to create a nest shape. Leave to cool at room temperature for a few hrs, or chill in the fridge if you need it to set faster.
- To make the icing, beat the butter, cocoa, icing sugar and milk together until smooth, adding a splash more milk if the mixture is too stiff. Assemble the cake by stacking the sponges with icing in between, topping with more icing and the nest. Fill your nest with as many chocolate eggs as it will hold, then serve. It may be easier to cut the cake if you remove the nest – you can then chop the nest into chunks and serve alongside the cake.

Nutrition Information

- Calories: 606 calories
- Sugar: 47 grams sugar

- Sodium: 1 milligram of sodium
- Total Carbohydrate: 72 grams carbohydrates
- Fiber: 3 grams fiber
- Protein: 8 grams protein
- Total Fat: 31 grams fat
- Saturated Fat: 11 grams saturated fat

84. Easy Chocolate Biscuits

Serving: Makes 25 biscuits | Prep: 25mins | Cook: 15mins | Ready in:

Ingredients

- 250g butter, softened
- 350g light soft brown sugar
- 2 large eggs
- 350g self-raising flour
- 100g cocoa powder
- 200g chocolate chips or chopped chocolate chunks, or 400g for optional dipping (choose your favourite type)

Direction

- Beat the butter and sugar together with an optional pinch of sea salt in a bowl until light and fluffy, then beat in the eggs one at a time. Sift over the flour and cocoa powder and beat into the butter mix, then fold through the chocolate chips. The mix can be made up to 2 days ahead and chilled or frozen for a month, or used straight away.
- To bake, heat oven to 190C/170C fan/gas 5. If the mix is at room temperature, place evenly spaced spoonfuls on parchment-lined baking sheets, allowing 2 tbsp for each cookie. If the mix is fridge cold, you can roll it into 40g balls before baking. The balls can be frozen and the biscuits baked from frozen, but they'll need a few minutes more. Bake for 12-15 mins until spread out and crusty around the outside. Leave to cool slightly and enjoy warm, or leave to cool completely and eat

cold. The biscuits will keep in a tin for three days.
- As an optional extra, the biscuits can be dipped in chocolate. To do this, melt your chosen type of chocolate in a bowl over a pan of simmering water or in the microwave. Leave to cool a little, then dip half of each biscuit in the chocolate and leave them on parchment-lined trays somewhere cool to set. Again, the dipped biscuits will keep for up to three days in a tin or lidded plastic container.

Nutrition Information

- Calories: 243 calories
- Sodium: 0.35 milligram of sodium
- Total Carbohydrate: 29 grams carbohydrates
- Total Fat: 12 grams fat
- Protein: 4 grams protein
- Fiber: 1 grams fiber
- Saturated Fat: 7 grams saturated fat
- Sugar: 18 grams sugar

85. Easy Chocolate Brownie Cake

Serving: 10 | Prep: 20mins | Cook: 45mins | Ready in:

Ingredients

- 175g unsalted butter, plus extra for greasing
- 225g dark chocolate, broken into pieces
- 200g caster sugar
- 3 medium eggs, separated
- 65g plain flour
- 50g chopped pecan nuts

Direction

- Heat oven to 180C/fan 160C/gas 4. Butter a 20-25cm cake tin and line with greaseproof paper.
- Place 175g/6oz of the chocolate, plus the butter and sugar in a heavy-based pan and

heat gently until melted, stirring occasionally. Leave to cool.

- Whisk the egg yolks into the chocolate mixture, then add the flour, nuts and the remaining chocolate.
- Whisk the egg whites until they form soft peaks, then gently, but thoroughly, fold into the chocolate mixture.
- Pour into the prepared tin and bake in the centre of the oven for about 35-40 mins until crusty on top. Leave to cool, then run a knife around the sides and remove from the tin. Dust with icing sugar and serve warm with custard or ice cream or cold with cream.

Nutrition Information

- Calories: 405 calories
- Sugar: 34 grams sugar
- Fiber: 0.44 grams fiber
- Protein: 4 grams protein
- Saturated Fat: 14 grams saturated fat
- Total Carbohydrate: 41 grams carbohydrates
- Sodium: 0.06 milligram of sodium
- Total Fat: 26 grams fat

86. Easy Chocolate Chip Cookies

Serving: Makes 10 | Prep: 20mins | Cook: 12mins | Ready in:

Ingredients

- 120g butter, softened
- 75g light brown sugar
- 75g golden caster sugar
- 1 medium egg
- 1 tsp vanilla extract
- 180g plain flour
- ½ tsp bicarbonate of soda
- 150g dark chocolate, cut into chunks

Direction

- Heat oven to 180C/160C fan/gas 4 and line two baking sheets with parchment. Cream the butter and sugars together until very light and fluffy, then beat in the egg and vanilla. Once combined, stir in the flour, bicarb, chocolate and ¼ tsp salt.
- Scoop 10 large tbsps of the mixture onto the trays, leaving enough space between each to allow for spreading. Bake for 10-12 mins or until firm at the edges but still soft in the middle – they will harden a little as they cool. Leave to cool on the tray for a few mins before eating warm, or transfer to a wire rack to cool completely. Will keep for three days in an airtight container.

Nutrition Information

- Calories: 308 calories
- Sodium: 0.5 milligram of sodium
- Total Fat: 16 grams fat
- Total Carbohydrate: 35 grams carbohydrates
- Sugar: 21 grams sugar
- Protein: 3 grams protein
- Fiber: 2 grams fiber
- Saturated Fat: 10 grams saturated fat

87. Easy Chocolate Fudge Cake

Serving: 8 | Prep: 25mins | Cook: 30mins | Ready in:

Ingredients

- 150ml sunflower oil, plus extra for the tin
- 175g self-raising flour
- 2 tbsp cocoa powder
- 1 tsp bicarbonate of soda
- 150g caster sugar
- 2 tbsp golden syrup
- 2 large eggs, lightly beaten
- 150ml semi-skimmed milk
- For the icing
- 100g unsalted butter
- 225g icing sugar

- 40g cocoa powder
- 2½ tbsp milk (a little more if needed)

Direction

- Heat the oven to 180C/160C fan/gas 4. Oil and line the base of two 18cm sandwich tins. Sieve the flour, cocoa powder and bicarbonate of soda into a bowl. Add the caster sugar and mix well.
- Make a well in the centre and add the golden syrup, eggs, sunflower oil and milk. Beat well with an electric whisk until smooth.
- Pour the mixture into the two tins and bake for 25-30 mins until risen and firm to the touch. Remove from oven, leave to cool for 10 mins before turning out onto a cooling rack.
- To make the icing, beat the unsalted butter in a bowl until soft. Gradually sieve and beat in the icing sugar and cocoa powder, then add enough of the milk to make the icing fluffy and spreadable.
- Sandwich the two cakes together with the butter icing and cover the sides and the top of the cake with more icing.

Nutrition Information

- Calories: 608 calories
- Fiber: 2 grams fiber
- Total Carbohydrate: 69 grams carbohydrates
- Protein: 7 grams protein
- Total Fat: 33 grams fat
- Saturated Fat: 11 grams saturated fat
- Sodium: 0.7 milligram of sodium
- Sugar: 52 grams sugar

88. Easy Chocolate Molten Cakes

Serving: Makes 6 | Prep: 15mins | Cook: 20mins | Ready in:

Ingredients

- 100g butter, plus extra to grease
- 100g dark chocolate, chopped
- 150g light brown soft sugar
- 3 large eggs
- ½ tsp vanilla extract
- 50g plain flour
- single cream, to serve

Direction

- Heat oven to 200C/180C fan/gas 6. Butter 6 dariole moulds or basins well and place on a baking tray.
- Put 100g butter and 100g chopped dark chocolate in a heatproof bowl and set over a pan of hot water (or alternatively put in the microwave and melt in 30 second bursts on a low setting) and stir until smooth. Set aside to cool slightly for 15 mins.
- Using an electric hand whisk, mix in 150g light brown soft sugar, then 3 large eggs, one at a time, followed by ½ tsp vanilla extract and finally 50g plain flour. Divide the mixture among the darioles or basins.
- You can now either put the mixture in the fridge, or freezer until you're ready to bake them. Can be cooked straight from frozen for 16 mins, or bake now for 10-12 mins until the tops are firm to the touch but the middles still feel squidgy.
- Carefully run a knife around the edge of each pudding, then turn out onto serving plates and serve with single cream.

Nutrition Information

- Calories: 391 calories
- Total Carbohydrate: 36 grams carbohydrates
- Protein: 6 grams protein
- Saturated Fat: 14 grams saturated fat
- Total Fat: 24 grams fat
- Sugar: 28 grams sugar
- Fiber: 2 grams fiber
- Sodium: 0.5 milligram of sodium

89. Easy Millionaire's Shortbread

Serving: Makes up to 24 squares | Prep: 25mins | Cook: 35mins | Ready in:

Ingredients

- For the shortbread
- 250g plain flour
- 75g caster sugar
- 175g butter, softened
- For the caramel
- 100g butter or margarine
- 100g light muscovado sugar
- 397g can condensed milk
- For the topping
- 200g plain or milk chocolate, broken into pieces

Direction

- Heat the oven to 180C/160C fan/gas 4. Lightly grease and line a 20-22cm square or rectangular baking tin with a lip of at least 3cm.
- To make the shortbread, mix 250g plain flour and 75g caster sugar in a bowl. Rub in 175g softened butter until the mixture resembles fine breadcrumbs.
- Knead the mixture together until it forms a dough, then press into the base of the prepared tin.
- Prick the shortbread lightly with a fork and bake for 20 minutes or until firm to the touch and very lightly browned. Leave to cool in the tin.
- To make the caramel, place 100g butter or margarine, 100g light muscovado sugar and the can of condensed milk in a pan and heat gently until the sugar has dissolved. Continually stir with a spatula to make sure no sugar sticks to the bottom of the pan. (This can leave brown specks in the caramel but won't affect the flavour.)
- Turn up the heat to medium high, stirring all the time, and bring to the boil, then lower the heat back to low and stirring continuously, for about 5-10 minutes or until the mixture has

thickened slightly. Pour over the shortbread and leave to cool.

- For the topping, melt 200g plain or milk chocolate slowly in a bowl over a pan of hot water. Pour over the cold caramel and leave to set. Cut into squares or bars with a hot knife.

Nutrition Information

- Calories: 248 calories
- Fiber: 1 grams fiber
- Protein: 3 grams protein
- Total Fat: 13 grams fat
- Saturated Fat: 8 grams saturated fat
- Total Carbohydrate: 29 grams carbohydrates
- Sugar: 21 grams sugar
- Sodium: 0.3 milligram of sodium

90. Flourless Chocolate & Pear Cake

Serving: 8 | Prep: 20mins | Cook: 40mins | Ready in:

Ingredients

- 85g butter, plus 1 tbsp extra for tin
- 85g golden caster sugar, plus extra for tin
- 85g gluten-free dark chocolate, broken into pieces
- 1 tbsp brandy
- 3 eggs, separated
- 85g hazelnut, toasted and ground in a food processor
- 4 very ripe pears, peeled, halved and cored
- icing sugar, for dusting

Direction

- Cut a circle of baking parchment to fit the base of a 25cm loose-bottomed tin. Melt 1 tbsp butter and brush the inside of the tin, then line the base with the parchment and brush again with more butter. Spoon in 2 tbsp caster sugar,

- swirl it around to coat the base and sides, then tip out any excess.
- Heat oven to 180C/fan 160C/gas 4. Melt the chocolate and butter in a bowl over a pan of hot water, remove from the heat, stir in the brandy and leave to cool. Whisk the egg yolks with the sugar in a large bowl until pale and thick; fold into the chocolate with the hazelnuts.
- In a separate bowl, with a clean whisk, beat the whites until they reach a soft peak (try not to whisk them too stiffly or you'll have trouble folding them in). Stir a spoonful of the whites into the chocolate mix, then carefully fold in the rest of them in 2 additions. Spoon into the prepared tin. Level, then arrange the pears over the mixture, cut-side down. Bake for 40 mins until the pears are soft and the cake is cooked all the way through. Leave to cool in the tin slightly before releasing it, then place on a rack to cool completely. Dust with icing sugar and serve with crème fraîche.

Nutrition Information

- Calories: 334 calories
- Saturated Fat: 9 grams saturated fat
- Total Carbohydrate: 28 grams carbohydrates
- Sugar: 28 grams sugar
- Protein: 5 grams protein
- Sodium: 0.28 milligram of sodium
- Total Fat: 23 grams fat

91. Frosted White Chocolate Easter Cake

Serving: 10 | Prep: 10mins | Cook: 1hours | Ready in:

Ingredients

- 250g butter, plus a little extra for greasing
- 140g white chocolate, broken into pieces
- 250ml milk
- 1 tsp vanilla extract
- 250g self-raising flour
- ¼ tsp bicarbonate of soda
- 300g caster sugar
- 2 large eggs, lightly beaten
- For the frosting
- 300g tub Philadelphia cheese
- 85g butter, softened
- 100g icing sugar, sifted
- mini eggs, to decorate (or use 50g/2oz chopped hazelnuts)

Direction

- Heat oven to 160C/fan 140C/gas 3. Grease a deep 23cm cake tin and line the base with greaseproof paper. Place the butter, white chocolate, milk and vanilla extract in a small saucepan, then heat gently, stirring, until melted. Combine the flour, bicarb and sugar in a large bowl with a pinch of salt, then stir in the melted ingredients and eggs until smooth. Pour the batter into the tin, then bake for 1 hr, or until the cake is golden and a skewer inserted into the centre comes out clean. Cool in the tin. Once cool, the cake can be wrapped in cling film and foil, then frozen for up to 1 month.
- To make the frosting, beat together the Philadelphia, butter and icing sugar until smooth. Spread over the cake, then decorate with mini eggs.

Nutrition Information

- Calories: 770 calories
- Total Fat: 50 grams fat
- Saturated Fat: 29 grams saturated fat
- Fiber: 1 grams fiber
- Sugar: 58 grams sugar
- Protein: 7 grams protein
- Sodium: 1.04 milligram of sodium
- Total Carbohydrate: 76 grams carbohydrates

92. Fudgy Coconut Brownies

Serving: Cuts into 16 squares | Prep: 10mins | Cook: 50mins | Ready in:

Ingredients

- 100g cocoa
- 250g butter
- 500g golden caster sugar
- 4 eggs, beaten
- 100g self-raising flour
- 100g desiccated coconut
- icing sugar, to dust (optional)

Direction

- Heat oven to 180C/160C fan/gas 4. Line the base of a 21cm square tin with baking parchment. Put the cocoa, butter and sugar in your largest saucepan and gently melt, stirring so the mixture doesn't catch. When the cocoa mixture is melted and combined, cool slightly, then stir in the eggs, little by little, followed by the flour and coconut.
- Tip into the tin and bake for 45 mins on a middle shelf – check after 30 mins and cover with another piece of baking parchment if the crust is browning too much. Cool in the tin, then carefully lift out and cut into squares.

Nutrition Information

- Calories: 358 calories
- Total Carbohydrate: 43 grams carbohydrates
- Fiber: 2 grams fiber
- Protein: 3 grams protein
- Saturated Fat: 13 grams saturated fat
- Sugar: 35 grams sugar
- Total Fat: 21 grams fat
- Sodium: 0.39 milligram of sodium

93. Gooey Chocolate Cherry Cookies

Serving: Makes 20 large cookies | Prep: 15mins | Cook: 14mins | Ready in:

Ingredients

- 200g unsalted butter, at room temperature
- 85g light muscovado sugar
- 85g golden caster sugar
- 1 egg
- 225g self-raising flour
- 50g plain chocolate, 50-70% cocoa, roughly chopped
- 50g white chocolate, roughly chopped
- 85g natural colour glacé cherry, roughly chopped

Direction

- Heat oven to 190C/fan 170C/gas 5. Beat the butter, sugars and egg until smooth, then mix in the flour, chocolates and cherry pieces and ½ tsp salt. Spoon onto non-stick baking sheets in large rough blobs – you'll get 20 out of this mix. Make sure they are well spaced as the cookies grow substantially as they bake. The raw dough can be frozen.
- Bake for 12-14 mins until just golden, but still quite pale and soft in the middle. If baking from frozen, give them a few mins more. Cool on the sheets for 5 mins, then lift onto racks with a fish slice and leave to cool completely.

Nutrition Information

- Calories: 186 calories
- Fiber: 1 grams fiber
- Total Fat: 11 grams fat
- Sugar: 14 grams sugar
- Saturated Fat: 6 grams saturated fat
- Protein: 2 grams protein
- Sodium: 0.13 milligram of sodium
- Total Carbohydrate: 23 grams carbohydrates

94. John Whaite's Chocolate Chiffon Cake With Salted Caramel Butter Cream

Serving: Cuts into 12 slices | Prep: 45mins | Cook: 1hours15mins | Ready in:

Ingredients

- 125ml sunflower oil, plus extra for greasing
- 7 large eggs, separated
- 2 tsp vanilla bean paste
- 375g golden caster sugar
- 50g cocoa powder
- 300g plain flour
- 1 tsp bicarbonate of soda
- For the salted caramel icing
- 250g light soft brown sugar
- 150ml double cream
- 140g butter, softened
- ½ tsp salt
- For the ganache
- 250ml double cream
- 250g dark chocolate, finely chopped or grated
- sea salt crystals, to decorate

Direction

- Heat oven to 160C/140C fan/gas 3. Grease and line a 25cm round deep cake tin with baking parchment. In a large bowl, mix the oil, egg yolks, vanilla paste, caster sugar and 200ml water until well combined. Sift in the cocoa powder and whisk until smooth.
- Sift in the flour, bicarb and 1 tsp salt. In a separate bowl, whisk the egg whites to stiff peaks. Fold into the batter with a large metal spoon and mix until everything is well combined.
- Gently pour the mixture into your cake tin, then bang it on the work surface twice to expel any large air pockets. Bake for 1 hr 10 mins or until the cake springs back when gently prodded and an inserted skewer comes out clean. (Cover with foil after 1 hr if the cake starts to get too dark.) Remove from the oven, cool in the tin for 10 mins, then transfer to a large wire rack and peel off the parchment. Leave until the cake is completely cool.
- Make the salted caramel icing while the cake bakes. Heat the brown sugar, ½ tsp salt and cream in a saucepan until the sugar has dissolved. Bubble for a few mins, then leave to cool completely. Beat the butter until smooth, pour in the cooled cream mixture and continue mixing until softly whipped. Chill until needed.
- To make the ganache, heat the cream until just boiling. Remove from the heat and pour over the chocolate. Leave to stand for a few mins until the chocolate has melted and you have a smooth sauce consistency. Leave to cool at room temperature until the ganache is a pipeable thickness, then transfer to a piping bag fitted with a star nozzle. To finish the cake, slice in half and fill with the salted caramel buttercream. Pipe tall spikes of chocolate ganache on top and decorate with the sea salt crystals. Will keep for up to 2 days in a cool place.

Nutrition Information

- Calories: 795 calories
- Total Fat: 48 grams fat
- Total Carbohydrate: 82 grams carbohydrates
- Sodium: 0.8 milligram of sodium
- Saturated Fat: 24 grams saturated fat
- Fiber: 2 grams fiber
- Protein: 8 grams protein
- Sugar: 65 grams sugar

95. Microwave Mug Cake

Serving: 1 | Prep: 5mins | Cook: 2mins | Ready in:

Ingredients

- 4 tbsp self-raising flour

- 4 tbsp caster sugar
- 2 tbsp cocoa powder
- 1 medium egg
- 3 tbsp milk
- 3 tbsp vegetable oil or sunflower oil
- a few drops of vanilla essence or other essence (orange or peppermint work well)
- 2 tbsp chocolate chips, nuts, or raisins etc (optional)

Direction

- Add 4 tbsp self-raising flour, 4 tbsp caster sugar and 2 tbsp cocoa powder to the largest mug you have (to stop it overflowing in the microwave) and mix.
- Add 1 medium egg and mix in as much as you can, but don't worry if there's still dry mix left.
- Add the 3 tbsp milk, 3 tbsp vegetable or sunflower oil and a few drops of vanilla essence and mix until smooth, before adding 2 tbsp chocolate chips, nuts, or raisins, if using, and mix again.
- Centre your mug in the middle of the microwave oven and cook on High for 1½ -2 mins, or until it has stopped rising and is firm to the touch.

Nutrition Information

- Calories: 1117 calories
- Total Fat: 47 grams fat
- Saturated Fat: 9 grams saturated fat
- Sugar: 83 grams sugar
- Sodium: 0.9 milligram of sodium
- Total Carbohydrate: 146 grams carbohydrates
- Fiber: 8 grams fiber
- Protein: 23 grams protein

---

96. Peanut Butter Brownies

Serving: Cuts into 16 squares | Prep: 20mins | Cook: 25mins | Ready in:

Ingredients

- 225g crunchy peanut butter
- 200g bar dark chocolate, broken into pieces
- 280g soft light brown sugar
- 3 medium eggs
- 100g self-raising flour

Direction

- Set aside 50g each of the peanut butter and chocolate. Heat oven to 180C/160C fan/gas 4 and line a 20cm square baking tin with baking parchment. Gently melt remaining peanut butter, chocolate and all the sugar in a pan, stirring occasionally, until the sugar has just about melted. Transfer mix into a bowl to cool down slightly. Turn off heat and use a wooden spoon to beat in the eggs one by one. Stir in the flour and scrape into the tin.
- Melt reserved peanut butter in the microwave on High for 45 secs, or in a pan, until runny, then drizzle over the brownie. Bake for 20-25 mins until it has a crust, but the middle still seems slightly uncooked.
- Melt reserved chocolate, drizzle over the brownie, then cool in the tin before cutting into squares.

Nutrition Information

- Calories: 250 calories
- Total Carbohydrate: 32 grams carbohydrates
- Sodium: 0.24 milligram of sodium
- Fiber: 1 grams fiber
- Saturated Fat: 4 grams saturated fat
- Sugar: 26 grams sugar
- Protein: 6 grams protein
- Total Fat: 12 grams fat

---

97. Salted Caramel Brownies

Serving: Makes 16 larger or 32 bite-sized brownies | Prep: 20mins | Cook: 30mins | Ready in:

Ingredients

- 200g unsalted butter, plus a little extra for greasing
- 100g chocolate, 70% cocoa solids
- 100g chocolate, 50% cocoa solids
- 397g can Carnation caramel
- 1 tsp flaky sea salt, plus a little extra for the top
- 200g golden caster sugar
- 4 medium eggs, at room temperature
- 130g plain flour
- 50g cocoa powder

Direction

- Heat oven to 180C/160C fan/gas 4.
- Grease then line a 23cm square traybake tin with baking parchment.
- Melt 200g unsalted butter in a medium pan, break in 100g chocolate (70% cocoa solids) and 100g chocolate (50% cocoa solids), then remove the pan from the heat and wait for the cubes to melt.
- In a small bowl, mix 175g Carnation caramel from a 397g can with 1 tsp sea salt – it will loosen up.
- Put the rest of the caramel in a large bowl with 200g golden caster sugar and 4 medium eggs, and beat with an electric hand mixer or balloon whisk until even. Whisk in the chocolate and butter.
- In another bowl, combine 130g plain flour, 50g cocoa powder and a good pinch of table salt, then sift this on top of the chocolate mix. Beat briefly until smooth.
- Pour half the brownie batter into the tin and level it with a spatula.
- Using a teaspoon, spoon half of the salted caramel on top of the batter layer in 5 thick, evenly spaced stripes.
- Spoon the rest of the brownie batter on top and smooth it out, trying not to disturb the caramel beneath. Top with the rest of the caramel in the same stripy fashion. Drag a skewer or tip of a knife through the caramel to make a feathered pattern on the top.
- Scatter with a little more sea salt, then bake for 25-30 mins or until risen all the way to the middle with a firm crust on top. When ready, the brownie will jiggle just a little when you shake the tin.
- Let it cool completely in the tin, then cut into squares.

Nutrition Information

- Calories: 345 calories
- Total Carbohydrate: 37 grams carbohydrates
- Sugar: 29 grams sugar
- Protein: 5 grams protein
- Total Fat: 19 grams fat
- Fiber: 2 grams fiber
- Sodium: 0.8 milligram of sodium
- Saturated Fat: 11 grams saturated fat

98. Self Saucing Jaffa Pudding

Serving: 8 | Prep: 35mins | Cook: 30mins | Ready in:

Ingredients

- 100g butter, melted, plus a little extra for the dish
- 250g self-raising flour
- 140g caster sugar
- 50g cocoa
- 1 tsp baking powder
- zest and juice 1 orange
- 3 eggs
- 150ml milk
- 100g orange milk chocolate or milk chocolate, broken into chunks (we used Divine orange milk chocolate)
- single cream or ice cream, to serve
- For the sauce
- 200g light muscovado sugar
- 25g cocoa

Direction

- Butter a 2-litre baking dish and heat oven to 180C/160C fan/gas 4. Put the kettle on. Put the flour, caster sugar, 50g cocoa, baking powder, orange zest and a pinch of salt in a large mixing bowl. Whisk together the orange juice and any pulp left in the juicer, the eggs, melted butter and milk, then pour onto the dry ingredients and mix together until smooth. Stir in the chocolate chunks and scrape everything into the baking dish.
- Mix 300ml boiling water from the kettle with the sugar and cocoa for the sauce, then pour this all over the pudding batter – don't worry, it will look very strange at this stage! Bake on the middle shelf of the oven for 30 mins until the surface looks firm, risen and crisp. As you scoop spoonfuls into serving bowls, you should find a glossy, rich chocolate sauce underneath the sponge. Eat immediately with vanilla ice cream or single cream.

Nutrition Information

- Calories: 522 calories
- Sodium: 0.86 milligram of sodium
- Sugar: 54 grams sugar
- Saturated Fat: 11 grams saturated fat
- Total Carbohydrate: 82 grams carbohydrates
- Fiber: 2 grams fiber
- Protein: 8 grams protein
- Total Fat: 21 grams fat

99. Squidgy Chocolate Pear Pudding

Serving: 8 | Prep: 20mins | Cook: 35mins | Ready in:

Ingredients

- 200g butter, plus extra for greasing
- 300g golden caster sugar
- 4 large eggs
- 75g plain flour
- 50g cocoa powder
- 410g can pear halves in juice, drained
- 100g plain dark chocolate (70% cocoa solids)
- 25g flaked almonds (optional)
- cream or ice cream, to serve

Direction

- Heat oven to 190C/170C fan/gas 5. Lightly grease a roughly 20 x 30cm shallow ovenproof dish. Put the butter in a large saucepan and place over a low heat until just melted. Remove the butter from the heat and stir in the sugar until well combined.
- Whisk the eggs together in a large bowl. Gradually add the eggs to the butter and sugar, beating well with a wooden spoon in between each addition. Sift the flour and cocoa powder on top of the egg mixture, then beat hard with a wooden spoon until thoroughly combined.
- Pour into the prepared tin or dish and nestle the pears into the chocolate batter. Put the chocolate on a board and cut into chunky pieces roughly 1.5cm with a large knife. Scatter the chocolate pieces over the batter and sprinkle with almonds, if you like. Can be frozen at this stage.
- Bake in the centre of the oven for 30 mins or until the mixture is crusty on the surface and lightly cooked inside. Do not allow to overcook, as the cake will become spongy rather than gooey in the centre. Serve warm with cream or ice cream

Nutrition Information

- Calories: 513 calories
- Protein: 6 grams protein
- Sodium: 1 milligram of sodium
- Total Fat: 30 grams fat
- Sugar: 43 grams sugar
- Saturated Fat: 17 grams saturated fat
- Fiber: 4 grams fiber
- Total Carbohydrate: 53 grams carbohydrates

100. Sticky Chocolate Drop Cakes

Serving: 15 | Prep: 10mins | Cook: 35mins | Ready in:

Ingredients

- 250g pack unsalted butter
- 300g golden caster sugar
- 1 tsp vanilla extract
- 3 large eggs
- 200g self-raising flour
- 50g cocoa
- 100g milk chocolate drops
- For the topping
- 85g butter
- 85g caster sugar
- 200g light condensed milk
- 50g milk chocolate drops, plus extra, to scatter

Direction

- Butter and line a traybake or small roasting tin, about 20 x 30cm. Heat oven to 180C/160C fan/gas 4. Gently melt the butter in a large saucepan, cool for 5 mins, add sugar, vanilla and eggs, then beat until smooth with a wooden spoon. Stir in the flour, cocoa and ¼ tsp salt. Stir in the milk chocolate drops and bake for 35 mins until risen all over and a skewer comes out with a few damp crumbs.
- For the top, gently heat 85g butter and 85g caster sugar together until both are melted. Stir in 200g light condensed milk and bring to a boil. Cool for 5 mins, then stir in 50g milk chocolate drops to melt. Spread over the cold cake, scatter with more chocolate drops and cut into squares.

Nutrition Information

- Calories: 433 calories
- Fiber: 1 grams fiber
- Protein: 5 grams protein
- Total Carbohydrate: 54 grams carbohydrates
- Total Fat: 24 grams fat
- Sodium: 0.31 milligram of sodium
- Saturated Fat: 14 grams saturated fat
- Sugar: 42 grams sugar

101. The Ultimate Makeover: Chocolate Chip Cookies

Serving: Makes 22 | Prep: 25mins | Cook: 12mins | Ready in:

Ingredients

- 85g butter
- 1 tbsp cocoa powder
- 1 tsp instant coffee granules
- 85g light muscovado sugar
- 25g golden granulated sugar
- 85g dark chocolate, about 70% cocoa solids (we used Lindt as it keeps its shape when baked)
- 1 medium egg, beaten
- ½ tsp vanilla extract
- 140g plain flour
- ½ tsp bicarbonate of soda

Direction

- Line a couple of baking sheets with baking parchment. Put the butter, cocoa and coffee in a medium saucepan then heat gently until the butter has melted. Remove from the heat, stir in both the sugars, then leave to cool.
- Chop the chocolate into small pieces. Beat the egg and vanilla into the cooled butter mix to make a smooth batter. Stir the flour and bicarbarbonate of soda together. Tip it into the batter mixture with two-thirds of the chocolate, then gently stir together to combine. Don't overmix. Leave for 10-15 mins to firm up slightly, ready for shaping. Heat oven to 180C/160C fan/gas 4.
- Using your hands, shape the mixture into 22 small balls. Lay them on the lined sheets, well apart so they have room to spread (you may have to bake in batches). Press the rest of the chocolate pieces on top of each cookie. Can be

frozen on sheets and then transferred to bags at this stage for up to 1 month. Bake for 12 mins. Leave on the sheets for a couple of mins, then transfer to a cooling rack.

Nutrition Information

- Calories: 97 calories
- Saturated Fat: 3 grams saturated fat
- Sugar: 6 grams sugar
- Sodium: 0.12 milligram of sodium
- Protein: 1 grams protein
- Total Carbohydrate: 12 grams carbohydrates
- Fiber: 1 grams fiber
- Total Fat: 5 grams fat

102. Triple Chocolate Cookies

Serving: Makes 24 | Prep: 15mins | Cook: 10mins | Ready in:

Ingredients

- 100g soft brown sugar
- 100g golden caster sugar
- 100g butter, softened
- 1 egg
- 1 tsp vanilla extract
- 225g plain flour
- 140g milk chocolate, melted
- 85g white chocolate, chips or chopped into chunks
- 85g plain chocolate, chips or chopped into chunks

Direction

- Heat oven to 200C/180C fan/gas 6. Line 1-2 baking sheets with baking parchment. Mix the sugars and butter together with a wooden spoon, then add the egg, vanilla, flour and half the melted milk chocolate and mix together. Stir in the white and plain chocolate chips or chunks, then use an ice-cream scoop or round

tablespoon (like a measuring spoon) to scoop out balls of cookie dough and drop them straight onto the trays.

- Bake in batches for 8-9 mins until pale golden and still soft to touch – they will firm up as they cool. Carefully transfer to a wire rack as soon as they can be lifted up, then drizzle with the remaining melted chocolate.

Nutrition Information

- Calories: 167 calories
- Protein: 2 grams protein
- Sodium: 0.1 milligram of sodium
- Total Fat: 8 grams fat
- Saturated Fat: 5 grams saturated fat
- Total Carbohydrate: 24 grams carbohydrates
- Sugar: 17 grams sugar

103. Vegan Cherry & Almond Brownies

Serving: Makes 12 | Prep: 20mins | Cook: 45mins | Ready in:

Ingredients

- 80g vegan margarine, plus extra for greasing
- 2 tbsp ground flaxseed
- 120g dark chocolate
- ½ tsp coffee granules
- 125g self-raising flour
- 70g ground almond
- 50g cocoa powder
- ¼ tsp baking powder
- 250g golden caster sugar
- 1 ½ tsp vanilla extract
- 70g glacé cherry (rinsed and halved)

Direction

- Heat oven to 170C/150C fan/gas 3½. Grease and line a 20cm square tin with baking parchment. Combine the flaxseed with 6 tbsp water and set aside for at least 5 mins.

- In a saucepan, melt the chocolate, coffee and margarine with 60ml water on a low heat. Allow to cool slightly.
- Put the flour, almonds, cocoa, baking powder and 1/4 tsp salt in a bowl and stir to remove any lumps. Using a hand whisk, mix the sugar into the melted chocolate mixture, and beat well until smooth and glossy, ensuring all the sugar is well dissolved. Stir in the flaxseed mixture and vanilla extract, the cherries and then the flour mixture. It will now be very thick. Stir until combined and spoon into the prepared tin. Bake for 35-45 mins until a skewer inserted in the middle comes out clean with moist crumbs. Allow to cool in the tin completely, then cut into squares. Store in an airtight container and eat within 3 days.

Nutrition Information

- Calories: 296 calories
- Protein: 4 grams protein
- Total Carbohydrate: 36 grams carbohydrates
- Saturated Fat: 5 grams saturated fat
- Sodium: 0.2 milligram of sodium
- Total Fat: 15 grams fat
- Sugar: 27 grams sugar
- Fiber: 3 grams fiber

| 104. | Wedding Cake Rich Dark Chocolate Cake |

Serving: 50 | Prep: | Cook: 2hours30mins | Ready in:

Ingredients

- 650g unsalted butter
- 650g plain chocolate (70% cocoa)
- 100ml very strong coffee- espresso is ideal
- 3 tsp vanilla essence
- 650g plain flour
- 2 tsp baking powder

- 2 tsp bicarbonate of soda
- 950g light soft brown sugar
- 10 eggs
- 2 x 284ml/9.5 fl oz soured cream

Direction

- Heat oven to 160C/fan 140C/gas 3. Butter, double-line and wrap the sides of the 30cm deep-round cake tin as before. Put the butter and chocolate into a medium saucepan, then stir over a low heat until melted and smooth. Stir in the coffee and vanilla.
- Sift the flour, baking powder and bicarbonate of soda into the biggest bowl you have. Add the sugar, breaking down any lumps with your fingertips if necessary. Beat the eggs and soured cream together in a jug or bowl and pour into the flour mix. Pour in the melted chocolate mix as well, then stir with a wooden spoon until you have a thick, even chocolaty batter.
- Pour into the prepared tin and bake for 2½ hrs – don't open the oven door before 2 hrs is up, as this will cause the cake to sink. Once cooked, leave in the tin to cool completely. The unfilled cake will keep for up to four days, wrapped as before, or frozen for a month.

Nutrition Information

- Calories: 274 calories
- Fiber: 1 grams fiber
- Total Carbohydrate: 30 grams carbohydrates
- Saturated Fat: 9 grams saturated fat
- Protein: 3 grams protein
- Total Fat: 16 grams fat
- Sugar: 20 grams sugar
- Sodium: 0.23 milligram of sodium

105. White Chocolate & Raspberry Cake

Serving: Cuts into 8-10 slices | Prep: 20mins | Cook: 25mins |Ready in:

Ingredients

- 200g butter, chopped into small cubes, plus extra for greasing
- 100g white chocolate, broken into pieces
- 4 large eggs
- 200g caster sugar
- 200g self-raising flour
- 175g raspberries, fresh or frozen
- For the ganache
- 200g white chocolate, chopped
- 250ml double cream
- a little icing sugar, for dusting

Direction

- Heat oven to 180C/160C fan/gas 4. Grease and line the base of 2 x 20cm round, loose-bottomed cake tins. Put the butter and chocolate in a heatproof mixing bowl, set over a pan of barely simmering water and allow to melt slowly, stirring occasionally.
- When the butter and chocolate have melted, remove from the heat and allow to cool for 1-2 mins, then beat in the eggs and sugar with an electric whisk. Fold in the flour and raspberries.
- Gently pour the mixture into the tins and bake for 20-25 mins or until golden brown and a skewer inserted into the centre comes out clean (the raspberries may leave a residue on the skewer, so don't be fooled by their juiciness). Remove the cakes from the oven and allow to cool in the tins for 10 mins before turning out onto a wire rack.
- To make the ganache, put the chocolate in a heatproof bowl with 100ml of the cream, set over a pan of barely simmering water. Stir until the chocolate has melted into the cream and you are left with a smooth, glossy ganache. Leave the ganache to cool to room temperature, then beat in the rest of the cream.
- When the cakes have cooled, sandwich them together with the chocolate ganache. Dust with icing sugar just before serving.

Nutrition Information

- Calories: 540 calories
- Sodium: 0.7 milligram of sodium
- Total Carbohydrate: 52 grams carbohydrates
- Fiber: 1 grams fiber
- Protein: 7 grams protein
- Total Fat: 34 grams fat
- Saturated Fat: 20 grams saturated fat
- Sugar: 39 grams sugar

106. White Chocolate Cake

Serving: Cuts into 15 squares | Prep: 20mins | Cook: 30mins |Ready in:

Ingredients

- 250g pack butter, softened
- 300g self-raising flour
- 250g golden caster sugar
- ½ tsp baking powder
- 4 eggs
- 150ml pot natural yogurt
- 3 tbsp milk
- 1 tsp vanilla paste
- 200g bar white chocolate, half chopped
- 300g soft cheese, not fridge cold
- 100g icing sugar, sifted
- sweets, to decorate

Direction

- Heat oven to 180C/160C fan/gas 4. Grease a 20 x 30cm tin, then line with baking parchment. Beat the butter, flour, sugar, baking powder, eggs, yogurt, milk and vanilla until lump-free. Stir in the chopped chocolate.

Spoon into tin; bake for 25-30 mins until golden and risen and a skewer comes out clean. Cool in the tin.

- Melt the rest of the chocolate. Stir icing sugar into soft cheese, then the chocolate until smooth. Chill, spread over the cake, then cut into squares and decorate.

Nutrition Information

- Calories: 489 calories
- Total Fat: 28 grams fat
- Sugar: 40 grams sugar
- Protein: 8 grams protein
- Sodium: 0.73 milligram of sodium
- Saturated Fat: 16 grams saturated fat
- Total Carbohydrate: 55 grams carbohydrates
- Fiber: 1 grams fiber

Chapter 4: Caramel Baking Recipes

***

107. Asian Caramel Chicken Wings

Serving: 4 | Prep: 40mins | Cook: 45mins | Ready in:

Ingredients

- 100g golden caster sugar
- 4 tbsp gluten-free fish sauce
- 1 green chilli, halved (optional)
- small piece cinnamon bark
- small piece ginger, finely chopped
- juice 1 large lime, plus extra for squeezing over
- 1kg chicken wing, tips removed and cut in half
- To garnish
- small bunch spring onion, cut into 1cm lengths
- large piece ginger, cut into matchsticks
- 1 green chilli (seeds removed if you don't like it too hot), cut into rings
- handful coriander sprigs
- boiled white rice, to serve

Direction

- Put the sugar in a medium sauté pan with enough water to make it go sludgy. Place on a low heat and bring to the boil, then cook until you have a dark amber caramel (see tip, below).
- At arms length, add the other ingredients, except for the chicken and garnish, and bring to a simmer – take care as it will spit. Once it has calmed down a little and you have a thick sauce, stir in the wings until well coated. Pour over 100ml water and simmer on a medium heat for about 30 mins, stirring every now and then until the sauce is a thicker consistency – add a splash more water if needed.
- Turn down the heat and continue to cook, covered, for a further 15 mins, stirring occasionally, until the wings are lacquered and tender and the sauce is very thick. Turn off the heat and quickly stir through half the spring onion, ginger and chilli. Tip the wings and sauce onto a platter. Scatter with the remaining garnish and coriander, and serve with extra lime and rice.

Nutrition Information

- Calories: 391 calories
- Sugar: 25 grams sugar
- Protein: 28 grams protein
- Sodium: 3.2 milligram of sodium
- Total Fat: 19 grams fat
- Saturated Fat: 5 grams saturated fat
- Total Carbohydrate: 26 grams carbohydrates

108. BBQ Rum & Caramel Bananas

Serving: 6 | Prep: 10mins | Cook: 15mins | Ready in:

Ingredients

- 50g butter, softened
- 40g light brown muscovado sugar
- 1-2 tsp treacle
- 1-2 tbsp spiced rum
- 6 unpeeled bananas
- ice cream, to serve (we like coconut)

Direction

- Mix the butter with the sugar and treacle, then add the rum. Make a split through the inside curve of each banana skin – be careful not to cut all the way through. Spread a spoonful of the spiced butter inside each skin.
- Place the bananas, curved-side up – so the butter doesn't leak when it melts – onto individual sheets of foil large enough to wrap them completely. Crimp up the foil to make a parcel, then put onto the embers for 15 mins, turning once. The bananas should be sticky and caramelised, but check one and cook for longer if necessary. Serve with a scoop of ice cream.

Nutrition Information

- Calories: 184 calories
- Total Carbohydrate: 27 grams carbohydrates
- Sodium: 0.2 milligram of sodium
- Fiber: 1 grams fiber
- Protein: 1 grams protein
- Total Fat: 7 grams fat
- Saturated Fat: 4 grams saturated fat
- Sugar: 25 grams sugar

109. Banana & Choc Bundt Cake With Peanut Caramel Drizzle

Serving: 12 | Prep: 35mins | Cook: 1hours | Ready in:

Ingredients

- 200g butter, melted, plus a little for greasing
- 3 tbsp cocoa powder
- 3 large ripe bananas
- 150ml full-fat milk, plus 1 tbsp for the icing
- 3 large eggs
- 1 tsp vanilla extract
- 350g self-raising flour
- 1 tsp bicarbonate of soda
- 350g soft light brown sugar
- 150g natural yogurt
- 100g dark chocolate chips or bar of chocolate, chopped into small chunks
- 80g salted peanuts, roughly chopped
- 100g dulce de leche caramel, from a can or jar

Direction

- Heat oven to 180C/160C fan/gas 4. Grease a 2.5-litre bundt tin (ours was 26cm in diameter) with some melted butter, making sure you get in all the crevices. Mix the cocoa with 50ml kettle-hot water and set aside to cool.
- Mash the bananas, then stir in the butter, milk, eggs and vanilla. In another bowl, combine the flour, bicarb, sugar and 1/2 tsp salt. Shake the bowl a few times to encourage any lumps of sugar to come to the surface, squeeze them through your fingers and mix again.
- Stir the banana mixture into the dry ingredients, then transfer half the cake mixture to another bowl. Add the cocoa mix, 50g yogurt and the chocolate chips to one bowl, and the remaining 100g yogurt and 50g peanuts to the other.
- Scrape the peanut mixture into the prepared tin, then spoon over the chocolate mixture. Swirl a skewer through the two cake mixtures to create a marbled effect. Bake on the middle shelf for 1 hr. Check the cake is cooked by

inserting a skewer into the centre of the sponge – if it comes out coated in any wet mixture, return to the oven for 10 mins more, then check again. Cool for 15 mins in the tin, then transfer to a wire rack to cool completely.

- Mix the caramel with 1 tbsp milk to create a drizzly icing. Once the cake is cool, drizzle over the icing and scatter with the remaining peanuts. Will keep in a tin for four days.

Nutrition Information

- Calories: 530 calories
- Fiber: 4 grams fiber
- Protein: 10 grams protein
- Sodium: 1 milligram of sodium
- Total Fat: 25 grams fat
- Saturated Fat: 13 grams saturated fat
- Total Carbohydrate: 65 grams carbohydrates
- Sugar: 41 grams sugar

| 110. | Boozy Caramel Mini Shakes |

Serving: 6 | Prep: 15mins | Cook: |Ready in:

Ingredients

- 50ml double cream
- 50ml Irish cream liqueur (we used Baileys)
- 2 tbsp caramel (we used dulce de leche)
- 150ml milk
- 25ml vodka
- 2 scoops vanilla ice cream
- To serve
- 6rolled chocolate wafers
- 2pieces of fudge, chopped small

Direction

- In a small bowl whisk the double cream until thick, then add 1 tbsp of the cream liqueur and whisk again until the mixture just holds its

shape then transfer to a disposable piping bag and set aside until needed.

- In a small jug stir together the caramel and 2 tsp of the cream liqueur until smooth then pour into the base of 6 x 60ml tall shot glasses, reserving 1-2 tsp of the mixture to decorate. Put the rest of the cream liqueur into a blender with the milk, vodka and ice cream. Blitz until smooth then pour into the prepared glasses.
- Pipe the boozy cream on top, drizzle with the reserved caramel sauce and decorate with chocolate wafers and tiny pieces of fudge. Serve immediately.

Nutrition Information

- Calories: 142 calories
- Total Fat: 8 grams fat
- Saturated Fat: 5 grams saturated fat
- Total Carbohydrate: 11 grams carbohydrates
- Sugar: 10 grams sugar
- Protein: 2 grams protein
- Sodium: 0.1 milligram of sodium

| 111. | Caramel Apple Loaf Cake |

Serving: Cuts into 8-10 slices | Prep: 20mins | Cook: 1hours30mins | Ready in:

Ingredients

- 175g soft butter, plus extra for greasing
- 175g golden caster sugar
- 1 tsp vanilla extract
- 2 eggs
- 225g self-raising flour
- ½ tsp cinnamon
- 4 rounded tbsp Greek yogurt
- 2 eating apples
- 50g walnuts, very roughly chopped, plus 1 tbsp extra, chopped
- 50g soft toffee (we used Werther's chewy toffees)
- 2 tbsp double cream

Direction

- Heat oven to 160C/140C fan/gas 3. Grease a 2lb loaf tin and line the base and ends with a long strip of baking paper.
- Beat together the butter, sugar and vanilla until pale, then beat in the eggs, one by one. Tip in the flour, cinnamon and yogurt. Peel, core and chop apples into small chunks, then add to the bowl and mix everything together with a wooden spoon.
- Scrape into the tin, smooth the top and scatter the walnuts down the middle. Bake on a middle shelf for 1 hr 20-30 mins until a skewer poked in comes out clean. Cool in the tin.
- To decorate, put the toffees in a small saucepan with the double cream. Gently heat, stirring, until toffees have melted into a smooth caramel sauce. Cool for about 1 min while you gently turn out the cake. Slowly drizzle the toffee sauce over the top of the cake. Scatter immediately with the extra walnuts – they should stick where they hit toffee. Leave for 10 mins before serving. Best fresh but will keep in an airtight tin for 3-4 days.

Nutrition Information

- Calories: 490 calories
- Sodium: 0.64 milligram of sodium
- Total Fat: 29 grams fat
- Sugar: 30 grams sugar
- Fiber: 2 grams fiber
- Protein: 7 grams protein
- Saturated Fat: 15 grams saturated fat
- Total Carbohydrate: 53 grams carbohydrates

---

112.   Caramel Button Cupcakes

Serving: Makes 12 cupcakes | Prep: 30mins | Cook: 20mins | Ready in:

Ingredients

- 175g butter, softened
- 175g light muscovado sugar
- 2 large eggs
- 175g self-raising flour
- 2 tbsp milk
- homemade caramel buttons (see recipe in tips, below)
- For the icing
- 397g can Nestlé Carnation Caramel
- 200g tub full-fat cream cheese
- 100g salted butter, softened
- 450g golden icing sugar

Direction

- Heat oven to 180C/160C fan/gas 4 and line a 12-hole muffin tin with cases. Put the butter and sugar into a mixing bowl, cream with an electric whisk until smooth and pale. Add the eggs and whisk again, then add the flour and milk, and mix with a spatula until well combined. Divide the mixture between the muffin cases. Bake for 18-20 mins until springy and a skewer comes out clean. Leave to cool.
- Mix 140g of the Carnation Caramel with the cream cheese, butter and icing sugar with an electric hand whisk, until smooth. Chill for 10 mins. Cut a hole in the centre of each cupcake (we used an apple corer) and fill with remaining Carnation Caramel. Transfer the icing to a piping bag fitted with a round nozzle and swirl over the cupcakes. Will keep for 3 days if kept in the fridge.

Nutrition Information

- Calories: 667 calories
- Sugar: 76 grams sugar
- Fiber: 1 grams fiber
- Protein: 5 grams protein
- Saturated Fat: 21 grams saturated fat
- Sodium: 0.8 milligram of sodium
- Total Fat: 33 grams fat
- Total Carbohydrate: 87 grams carbohydrates

113. Caramel Cheesecake

Serving: 8 | Prep: 25mins | Cook: | Ready in:

Ingredients

- 50g unsalted butter
- 140g plain digestive biscuit
- For the filling
- 4 gelatine leaves (I used Supercook), cut into wide strips (or 1 x 11g sachet, see Know-how, below)
- 400g crème fraîche
- 100g light muscovado sugar
- 50g dark muscovado sugar
- 1 tsp vanilla extract
- 400g ricotta
- 50g fudge, finely sliced
- icing sugar, for dusting

Direction

- Gently melt the butter in a small pan over a low heat. Place the digestives in a plastic bag and crush to fine crumbs using a rolling pin; you can also do this in a food processor. Tip them into the pan with the melted butter, stir to coat, then transfer to a 20cm springform cake tin (9cm deep). Using the back of a spoon, press them into the base, making sure you seal the edges. Place in the fridge while you prepare the next stage.
- If using leaf gelatine, place in a bowl, cover with cold water, soak for 5 mins, then drain. Pour 3 tbsp boiling water over the soaked gelatine and stir to dissolve. If using a sachet, see Know-how, below.
- Place the crème fraîche in a small pan with the muscovado sugars and a pinch of sea salt, then gently heat, stirring constantly with a wooden spoon until the mixture liquefies and the sugar has dissolved. Give the mixture a quick whisk to get rid of any lumps. It should be warm, roughly the same temperature as the gelatine solution. Stir the gelatine and vanilla extract

into the crème fraîche mixture, transfer to a bowl and cool.
- Place the ricotta in a food processor and whizz until smooth, then add the crème fraîche mixture and whizz again. Pour this on top of the cheesecake base. Cover with cling film and chill overnight.
- Run a knife around the sides of the tin, then undo the clip and remove it. Transfer to a plate or leave the cheesecake on the base for ease of serving. Pile the fudge flakes in the centre and dust with icing sugar. Cover and chill until required.

Nutrition Information

- Calories: 498 calories
- Sugar: 30 grams sugar
- Protein: 8 grams protein
- Sodium: 0.59 milligram of sodium
- Total Fat: 35 grams fat
- Saturated Fat: 22 grams saturated fat
- Total Carbohydrate: 40 grams carbohydrates

114. Caramel Passion Fruit Slice

Serving: makes 16 | Prep: 15mins | Cook: 20mins | Ready in:

Ingredients

- For the shortbread
- 150g plain flour
- 100g desiccated coconut
- 170g cold butter, cubed, plus a little for the tin
- 75g golden caster sugar
- For the caramel
- 90g butter
- 397g can of condensed milk
- 2 tbsp golden syrup
- 2 tbsp dark brown sugar
- 3 passion fruits, pulp only
- For the topping

- 200g dark chocolate
- 30g coconut shavings, toasted

Direction

- Heat oven to 180C/160C fan/gas 4 and butter a 23 x 23cm brownie tin. First, make the shortbread by stirring the flour and coconut together in a bowl, then rub in the butter with your fingers until the mixture looks like breadcrumbs. Stir through the sugar, then bring the dough together with your hands. Pat into the tin, pricking the top all over with a fork. Bake for 15-18 mins until lightly golden and crisp.
- For the caramel, put the butter, condensed milk, sugar and syrup in a pan with a large pinch of salt. Heat gently until simmering, then whisk for 6 mins until thick and fudgy. Take off the heat and stir in the passion fruit pulp. Pour over the shortbread, smooth over with a palette knife and leave to set.
- Once set, melt the chocolate in the microwave in 30-second bursts until glossy and smooth. Smooth over the caramel shortbread, then scatter over the coconut shavings. Leave to set, then cut into 16 squares. Will keep for five days in an airtight container.

Nutrition Information

- Calories: 395 calories
- Total Fat: 26 grams fat
- Sodium: 0.4 milligram of sodium
- Saturated Fat: 17 grams saturated fat
- Sugar: 26 grams sugar
- Total Carbohydrate: 34 grams carbohydrates
- Protein: 4 grams protein
- Fiber: 3 grams fiber

---

115. Caramel Ripple Cheesecake Cups

Serving: 4 | Prep: 10mins | Cook: | Ready in:

Ingredients

- 100g amaretti biscuit (about 20)
- 400g soft cheese
- 50g golden caster sugar
- ¼ tsp vanilla extract
- 6 tbsp caramel sauce, we used Carnation, beaten until smooth

Direction

- Crush the biscuits into large crumbs and divide between 4 ramekins or small glasses.
- In a bowl, beat the cheese with the sugar and vanilla then add 4 tbsp of the sauce and beat until mostly incorporated but still streaked slightly. Carefully spoon over the biscuits and smooth the top.
- Spoon the rest of the caramel over the top and use a teaspoon to swirl the top of the cheese layer with the caramel. Set in the fridge for at least 2 hours but up to 2 days before serving.

Nutrition Information

- Calories: 462 calories
- Total Fat: 33.2 grams fat
- Saturated Fat: 21.4 grams saturated fat
- Sugar: 30.9 grams sugar
- Protein: 9.2 grams protein
- Total Carbohydrate: 31.3 grams carbohydrates
- Fiber: 0.2 grams fiber
- Sodium: 0.8 milligram of sodium

---

116. Caramel Sauce

Serving: 10 | Prep: 2mins | Cook: 10mins | Ready in:

Ingredients

- 250g caster sugar
- 142ml pot double cream
- 50g butter

Direction

- Tip the sugar into a heavy-based frying pan, stir in 4 tbsp water, then place over a medium heat until the sugar has dissolved. Turn up the heat and bubble for 4-5 mins until you have caramel. Take off the heat, then carefully stir in the cream and butter. Leave the sauce to cool, then tip into a squeezy bottle.

Nutrition Information

- Calories: 206 calories
- Sodium: 0.09 milligram of sodium
- Total Fat: 12 grams fat
- Saturated Fat: 7 grams saturated fat
- Total Carbohydrate: 27 grams carbohydrates
- Sugar: 27 grams sugar

---

117. Caramel Soufflés With Caramel Sauce

Serving: Makes 5 (to serve 4, with a spare for testing) | Prep: 30mins | Cook: 30mins | Ready in:

Ingredients

- 100g unsalted butter, plus extra for greasing
- 200g light, soft brown sugar, plus 4 tbsp extra
- 200ml whipping cream
- 1 tsp vanilla extract
- 2 egg yolks
- 1 tbsp plain flour
- 3 egg whites

Direction

- Heat oven to 200C/180C fan/gas 6. Butter 5 x 150ml individual soufflé dishes or ramekins and sprinkle all over with 2 tbsp soft brown sugar. Place on a baking sheet. Melt the butter in a saucepan, then add sugar, cream, vanilla and a good pinch salt. When sugar is melted, bubble for 1 min until it looks like a sauce. Pour 200ml into a jug for serving.

- Stir egg yolks and flour into remaining caramel in the saucepan. Whisk constantly over medium heat until mixture thickens, about 3 mins. Sieve into a bowl and cool for 15 mins. Beat egg whites in large bowl until foamy, then gradually beat in remaining 2 tbsp sugar until whites are stiff but not dry. Fold one-third of whites into caramel mixture in the pan, then fold that back into the whites. Divide among dishes, and use a palette knife to scrape top level. Bake until soufflés are puffed and golden – about 11 mins. The soufflés should still be a little unset in the middle, but not runny, so if you're serving four, break into your tester to check. Return the rest to oven for 2 mins if underdone. Serve immediately with caramel sauce, warmed a little while soufflés are baking.

Nutrition Information

- Calories: 545 calories
- Sodium: 0.49 milligram of sodium
- Total Fat: 35 grams fat
- Saturated Fat: 21 grams saturated fat
- Sugar: 54 grams sugar
- Fiber: 1 grams fiber
- Total Carbohydrate: 6 grams carbohydrates
- Protein: 4 grams protein

---

118. Caramelised Apple Cake With Streusel Topping

Serving: 8 | Prep: 25mins | Cook: 1hours10mins | Ready in:

Ingredients

- 100g butter, plus 1 tbsp
- 175g light brown muscovado sugar, plus 1 tbsp
- 2 dessert apples, peeled and cut into 1.5cm pieces
- 2 eggs

- 1 tsp vanilla extract
- 200g plain flour
- 1 tsp baking powder
- ½ tsp ground cinnamon
- 100ml milk
- For the streusel topping
- 25g flour
- 85g demerara sugar, plus 1 tbsp
- ½ tsp ground cinnamon
- 50g cold butter
- 3 tbsp toasted, chopped hazelnuts

Direction

- Heat 1 tbsp butter and 1 tbsp sugar in a large frying pan over medium heat until the sugar starts to melt. Add apples, then cook for about 5 mins, until nicely browned and the sauce is a rich caramel. Leave to cool.
- While the apples cool, make the topping. In a food processor or using the tips of your fingers, rub together flour, 85g sugar, cinnamon and cold butter until the mixture is crumbly and only pea-size pieces of butter remain. Stir in 2 tbsp of hazelnuts. Set aside in a cool place.
- Heat oven to 180C/160C fan/gas 4. To make the cake, place the remaining butter and sugar in a bowl or food mixer and beat until light and creamy. Add the eggs one at a time, followed by the vanilla extract. Add the flour, baking powder, cinnamon and milk in two goes, alternating between dry and wet ingredients. When the mixture is well combined, stir through the apples.
- Grease a 20cm cake tin with removable base and line the base with a circle of baking paper. Spoon in the cake mixture, smooth over the top with a spoon, then sprinkle over the streusel topping. Scatter with the remaining 1 tbsp demerara sugar and hazelnuts. Cook in the oven for 50 mins-1 hr or until a skewer inserted into the cake comes out clean. Leave to cool in the tin for 10 mins, then turn out onto a baking rack, remove paper and cool.

Nutrition Information

- Calories: 464 calories
- Saturated Fat: 12 grams saturated fat
- Fiber: 2 grams fiber
- Sodium: 0.6 milligram of sodium
- Sugar: 42 grams sugar
- Protein: 6 grams protein
- Total Carbohydrate: 64 grams carbohydrates
- Total Fat: 22 grams fat

119. Cheat's Salted Caramels

Serving: Serves as many as you like | Prep: 5mins | Cook: | Ready in:

Ingredients

- chocolate-covered caramel(we used Rolos)
- edible goldlustre (we bought ours from Waitrose)
- sea saltflakes

Direction

- Unwrap the chocolate-covered caramels and use a small paintbrush to dust the outsides with gold lustre. Add a few flakes of sea salt to the top of each one, then arrange on a serving plate (stacking in a tower makes them look extra special). Chill for at least 1 hr before serving.

Nutrition Information

- Calories: 25 calories
- Total Carbohydrate: 4 grams carbohydrates
- Sugar: 3 grams sugar
- Sodium: 0.5 milligram of sodium
- Total Fat: 1 grams fat
- Saturated Fat: 1 grams saturated fat

120. Chocca Mocca Caramel Cake

Serving: 10-12 slices | Prep: | Cook: | Ready in:

Ingredients

- 2 tsp instant coffee granules/powder
- 2 tbsp cocoa powder
- 2 tbsp hot water
- 175g softened butter
- 175g golden caster sugar
- 2 eggs
- 2 tbsp golden syrup
- 200g self-raising flour
- 4 tbsp milk
- 2 x 50g/2 x 2oz chocolate caramel bars
- For the icing
- 100g chocolate caramel bars
- 50g butter
- 2 tbsp milk
- 100g icing sugar, sifted

Direction

- Preheat the oven to 180C/Gas 4/fan oven 160C. Butter a 20cm/8in round cake tin and line the base with baking parchment.
- Measure the coffee and cocoa into a cup, add the hot water and mix to a smooth paste. Put the butter, sugar, eggs, syrup, flour, milk and cocoa paste in a large mixing bowl and beat with a wooden spoon or electric beaters for 2-3 minutes until smooth. Break the caramel bars into sections and stir into the mixture.
- Turn the mixture into the prepared tin and smooth the top. Bake for 35-40 minutes, until the top springs back when you press it lightly. Cool in the tin for 5 minutes, then turn out, peel off the lining paper and leave to cool.
- To make the icing, break up the caramel bars and put in a small pan with the butter and milk. Gently heat until smooth, stirring all the time, then remove from the heat and stir in the icing sugar (don't worry if it doesn't dissolve immediately, just keep stirring). Leave to cool until it thickens enough to leave a trail when

you lift the spoon. Put the cake on a serving plate, spread the icing over the top, letting it fall softly down the sides, then leave to set.

121. Chocolate, Hazelnut & Salted Caramel Tart

Serving: 12 | Prep: 40mins | Cook: 50mins | Ready in:

Ingredients

- For the hazelnut pastry
- 50g blanched hazelnut
- 200g plain flour
- 1 tbsp icing sugar
- 140g cold butter, diced
- 1 egg yolk
- flour, for dusting
- For the salted caramel
- 75g caster sugar
- 25g butter
- 100ml double cream
- 1 tbsp golden syrup
- large pinch sea salt flakes
- 50g blanched hazelnut, toasted and roughly chopped
- For the chocolate fudge filling
- 100g dark chocolate (70%)
- 75g butter
- 2 large eggs, plus 1 yolk
- 50g caster sugar
- 1 tbsp cocoa

Direction

- To make the pastry, whizz the hazelnuts in a food processor until finely ground. Add the flour, icing sugar and butter, and pulse until the mixture resembles breadcrumbs. Add the egg yolk and 1-2 tbsp cold water, and pulse until the dough comes together. Tip the dough out and flatten into a disc, then wrap in cling film and chill for 30 mins.
- Heat oven to 180C/160C fan/gas 4. On a floured surface, roll out the pastry to line a

23cm loose-bottomed, deep tart tin. Trim the edges and prick the base with a fork, then line with baking parchment and fill with baking beans. Bake for 20 mins, then carefully remove the baking beans and parchment and bake for a further 5-10 mins until light golden. Allow to cool.

- Meanwhile, make the salted caramel. Tip the sugar into a small pan, add 1-2 tbsp water and heat gently to dissolve the sugar. Increase the heat and cook until the sugar turns to an ambercoloured caramel. Reduce the heat and add the butter, cream and golden syrup, and stir until the sauce is smooth and thickened. Remove from the heat and add the salt. Allow to cool for a few mins, then spread onto the tart base. Scatter with chopped hazelnuts and set aside.

- For the chocolate filling, melt the chocolate and butter in a heatproof bowl set over a pan of simmering water. Stir until smooth, then remove from the heat and allow to cool slightly. In a separate bowl, whisk the eggs, egg yolk and caster sugar for about 6 mins until thick and pale. Fold in the melted chocolate and cocoa, then pour into the tart case. Transfer to a baking sheet and cook for 20-25 mins or until set and the top has formed a crust. Allow to cool to room temperature before serving in slices.

Nutrition Information

- Calories: 424 calories
- Total Carbohydrate: 31 grams carbohydrates
- Protein: 5 grams protein
- Sugar: 19 grams sugar
- Fiber: 2 grams fiber
- Sodium: 0.6 milligram of sodium
- Total Fat: 31 grams fat
- Saturated Fat: 16 grams saturated fat

122. Chocolate, Salted Caramel & Banana Mess

Serving: 2 | Prep: 15mins | Cook: 10mins | Ready in:

Ingredients

- ½ vanilla pod, scraped of seeds
- 150ml double cream
- 2 ready-made meringue nests, crumbled into chunks
- 2 bananas, sliced
- For the salted caramel sauce
- 2 tbsp caster sugar
- 3 tbsp double cream
- 1 tbsp butter
- pinch of sea salt flakes
- For the chocolate sauce
- 2 tbsp full-fat milk
- 1 tbsp double cream
- 50g dark chocolate, broken into small pieces

Direction

- To make the salted caramel, put the sugar and 2 tbsp water in a small heavy-bottomed saucepan. Place on a low heat and swirl gently until the sugar has melted. Turn up the heat and let the sugar bubble and caramelise to a nutty brown. Take off the heat and pour in the cream, butter and salt flakes – do this carefully, as it may spit. Gently stir together until smooth and glossy.

- For the chocolate sauce, bring the milk and cream to the boil in a small saucepan. Put the chocolate bits into a bowl. Pour over two-thirds of the milk and cream mixture, stirring until melted and smooth. Adjust the consistency with the remaining hot milk mixture.

- Put the vanilla seeds into the cream and whip until just holding soft peaks. Fold the meringues and banana slices into the cream, leaving a few slices for garnish. Put in serving dishes and drizzle with the two sauces. Top with the remaining banana slices. Serve immediately.

Nutrition Information

- Calories: 938 calories
- Total Fat: 71 grams fat
- Fiber: 2 grams fiber
- Total Carbohydrate: 70 grams carbohydrates
- Protein: 5 grams protein
- Sodium: 0.5 milligram of sodium
- Sugar: 69 grams sugar
- Saturated Fat: 44 grams saturated fat

---

123. Cinder Toffee

Serving: Make a good trayful | Prep: 10mins | Cook: 20mins | Ready in:

Ingredients

- a little sunflower oil
- 200g golden caster sugar
- 100g clear honey
- 1 tbsp bicarbonate of soda

Direction

- Line a big tray with baking parchment and lightly grease with oil. Place the sugar and honey in a large saucepan with 4 tbsp water. Put over a very low heat and stir until the sugar dissolves. Once the sugar has dissolved, add a sugar thermometer and bring to the boil over a high heat. Bubble until it reaches 149C on the sugar thermometer.
- Remove from the heat and whisk in the bicarbonate of soda quickly, it will froth up madly – don't worry! Immediately pour into the tray, and leave to cool and set completely.
- Break into shards to nibble, or crumble over ice cream or our Salted honey fudge & chocolate tart (see 'Goes well with' box, right). Will keep in an airtight container between layers of baking parchment for 1-2 weeks.

---

124. Cranberry, Pumpkin Seed & Caramel Flapjacks

Serving: Makes 16 | Prep: 15mins | Cook: 40mins | Ready in:

Ingredients

- 250g pack salted butter
- 6 tbsp caramel, from a 397g can Carnation caramel (use remainder for topping, see below)
- 50g golden caster sugar
- 350g rolled oats
- 85g self-raising flour
- For the topping
- remaining caramel
- 50g salted butter
- 25g pumpkin seed
- 50g dried cranberries
- 25g dark chocolate chips

Direction

- Heat oven to 160C/140C fan/gas 3 and line a 22cm square cake tin with baking parchment. Melt the butter, caramel and sugar in a large saucepan, then tip in the oats and flour. Stir well, making sure every oat is covered in the buttery mixture, then tip into your cake tin and press down firmly with the back of a spoon to level the surface. Bake for 40 mins.
- Tip the remaining caramel and butter into a small saucepan, and bubble for 5 mins, stirring continuously, until the mixture turns dark golden brown and thickens a little. When the flapjacks have finished cooking, remove them from the oven and pour over the hot caramel. Leave to cool for 5 mins, then scatter with the seeds, cranberries and chocolate chips. Leave to cool completely in the tin before cutting into squares.

Nutrition Information

- Calories: 318 calories
- Sugar: 13 grams sugar
- Sodium: 0.4 milligram of sodium
- Total Carbohydrate: 30 grams carbohydrates
- Protein: 5 grams protein
- Saturated Fat: 11 grams saturated fat
- Total Fat: 19 grams fat
- Fiber: 3 grams fiber

125. Crème Brûlée Tartlets

Serving: 4 | Prep: 20mins | Cook: 1hours | Ready in:

Ingredients

- 175g plain flour
- 100g cold butter, cubed
- 2 tsp caster sugar
- zest ½ orange
- 1 egg yolk, beaten with 2 tbsp cold water
- 300ml carton double cream
- 1 vanilla pod, halved lengthways
- 3 egg yolksand 1 whole egg
- 2 tbsp caster sugar
- sunflower oil, for greasing
- 85g caster sugar

Direction

- Put the flour, a pinch of salt and the butter in a food processor and pulse until it resembles fine crumbs. Add the sugar and orange zest, and briefly pulse again. Pour in 2 tbsp of the egg mixture and pulse until the dough comes together, adding more liquid if needed.
- Roll out the pastry on a lightly floured surface and use to line four deep-fluted tartlet tins (8 x 3cm). Place the tins on a tray and chill for 30 mins. Heat oven to 190C/170C fan/gas 5. Line each pastry case with baking parchment and fill with baking beans. Bake for 10-15 mins, until the sides are set. Remove the parchment and beans and cook for 5-10 mins. Leave to cool. Can be made up to 1 day ahead at this

stage and be stored in an airtight container. Lower the oven to 150C/130C fan/gas 2.

- Pour the cream into a heavy-based saucepan, scrape in the seeds from the vanilla pod, then throw in the 2 halves of the pod. Heat until small bubbles begin to form around the sides of the pan, then leave to infuse for 5 mins. Remove the pod. In a bowl, beat together the egg yolks, whole egg and sugar. Keep stirring, then pour in the cream, mixing until combined. Strain through a sieve into a jug. Pour the custard into the tart shells, then bake for 18-22 mins until almost set (they should be quite wobbly in the centre but will firm up on cooling). Leave to cool completely, then chill for 30 mins.
- Meanwhile, make the caramel topping. Grease a lipped metal baking tray with a little oil. Tip the caster sugar into a frying pan with 3 tbsp water and heat gently until the sugar starts to melt. Don't be tempted to stir the sugar, as this can encourage the caramel to crystalise. However, you can tilt the pan to move it around. Once the sugar is almost melted, turn up the heat and bubble the caramel to a deep golden-brown colour. Quickly tip onto the greased tray and leave to cool completely. Once cool, turn the tray upside down and tap to release the caramel. Break into pieces, then whizz in a food processor until you have fine crystals.
- Heat the grill. Scatter a thick layer of caramel crystals over the surface of each tart, and pop a collar of foil around the top edge of the pastry. Place under the grill, not too near the heat source, and let the caramel melt – watch carefully as they will burn easily. Leave to cool, then chill for 30 mins or until ready to serve.

Nutrition Information

- Calories: 947 calories
- Total Carbohydrate: 71 grams carbohydrates
- Sugar: 41 grams sugar
- Fiber: 2 grams fiber

- Sodium: 0.6 milligram of sodium
- Total Fat: 69 grams fat
- Saturated Fat: 40 grams saturated fat
- Protein: 10 grams protein

---

126.   Galaxy Cake

Serving: 20 | Prep: 2hours | Cook: 45mins | Ready in:

Ingredients

- 250g unsalted butter
- 200g dark chocolate (70% cocoa solids)
- 350g light soft brown sugar
- 200g self-raising flour
- 1 tsp bicarbonate of soda
- ½ tsp salt
- 4 large eggs
- 300ml tub sour cream
- 100ml strong hot coffee (double shot of espresso)
- For the filling
- 250g fun size bag of mini Mars Bars
- 397g can Nestlé Carnation Caramel
- 1 tsp flaky sea salt
- For the icing
- 400g unsalted butter, softened at room temperature
- 800g icing sugar
- 2 tsp vanilla bean paste
- 4 tbsp whole milk
- For the decoration
- black, blue, purple and green food colouring gel
- navy and silver lustre dust
- edible metallic pearlescent white paint
- silver pearl balls
- thin paintbrush
- cake scraper

Direction

- Heat the oven to 180c/160 fan/gas mark 4. Grease and bottom line two deep 20cm spring form cake tins. Using the microwave on high, melt the butter with the chocolate in 30 second bursts until glossy and smooth. Alternatively melt in a bowl over a pan of simmering water. Leave to cool slightly.
- Combine the sugar and flour in a large bowl, getting rid of any lumps with your fingertips, then stir in the bicarb and salt. In a separate jug beat the eggs with the sour cream then pour into the dry ingredients and whisk until well combined. Scrape in the cooled chocolate mixture and beat until you have a smooth chocolatey batter. Stir in the hot coffee then divide the mixture between the tins and bake for 40-45mins until a skewer inserted in the centre comes out clean. Leave to cool in the tins for 10 mins then transfer to a wire rack to cool completely.
- While the cakes are cooling make the buttercream. Using a food mixer or an electric whisk beat the butter with the icing sugar, vanilla and a pinch of salt for 10 mins until very light and fluffy, then whisk in the milk. Set aside.
- Slice each of the cooled cakes into two. Break the Mars bars into small pieces and stir the sea salt through the caramel. Sandwich the cakes together using a 1/3 of the caramel and Mars between each layer, leaving the top layer free for icing.
- Crumb coat the cake completely in a layer of white buttercream then pop in the fridge to set. Meanwhile divide the remaining butter cream between 4 bowls, and colour each with the black, blue, green and purple food colouring.
- Using a palette knife dot the cake at random with a little of each coloured buttercream then using the cake scraper go around the sides to blend the colours together and smooth the cake. Keep layering different colours of buttercream until you have your desired galaxy appearance.
- Dot areas with the navy and silver lustre dust so that you create a moon beam effect around the cake. Using the paintbrush and white pearlescent paint, draw clusters of stars

and dot in silver balls, being as random or as coordinated as you and your galaxy like.

Nutrition Information

- Calories: 719 calories
- Saturated Fat: 23 grams saturated fat
- Fiber: 2 grams fiber
- Protein: 5 grams protein
- Sodium: 0.8 milligram of sodium
- Total Fat: 38 grams fat
- Total Carbohydrate: 87 grams carbohydrates
- Sugar: 78 grams sugar

127. Ginger & Caramel Apple Puddings

Serving: 6 | Prep: 30mins | Cook: 20mins | Ready in:

Ingredients

- For the caramel apples
- 50g butter, plus extra for the ramekins
- 1 large cooking apple, peeled, cored and finely chopped
- 75g light brown muscovado sugar
- For the puddings
- 140g butter, softened
- 100g light brown muscovado sugar
- 1 egg
- 125ml buttermilk
- 2 balls preserved stem ginger, finely chopped, plus 1 tbsp syrup from jar
- 100g plain flour, plus extra for dusting
- 1 ½ tbsp ground ginger
- ½ tsp baking powder
- ½ tsp bicarbonate of soda
- icing sugar, for dusting
- cream or custard, to serve

Direction

- Heat oven to 180C/160C fan/gas 4. Lightly butter and flour 6 x 8cm deep ramekins,

tapping out excess flour. Heat the butter in a pan until foaming, add the apple and cook for 1 min on a medium heat. Toss in the sugar and cook until dissolved. Divide between the ramekins.
- For the puddings, beat the butter and sugar together with an electric whisk until fully combined. In a separate bowl, mix together the egg, buttermilk, chopped ginger and ginger syrup, then stir this into the butter mixture. Fold in the flour, ground ginger, baking powder, bicarbonate of soda and a pinch of salt. Divide between the ramekins so they are filled to 1cm below the top. Place them on a baking tray and bake for 20 mins, until golden and risen.
- Serve warm, dusted with icing sugar. Accompany with cream or custard.

Nutrition Information

- Calories: 470 calories
- Fiber: 1 grams fiber
- Protein: 4 grams protein
- Total Fat: 28 grams fat
- Saturated Fat: 17 grams saturated fat
- Sodium: 1.07 milligram of sodium
- Total Carbohydrate: 53 grams carbohydrates
- Sugar: 39 grams sugar

128. Ginger Cake With Caramel Frosting

Serving: Cuts into 12 slices | Prep: 25mins | Cook: 1hours | Ready in:

Ingredients

- 200g butter, plus extra for the tin
- 200g dark muscovado sugar
- 100g black treacle
- 100g golden syrup
- 2 large eggs, beaten
- 300ml milk

- 350g plain flour
- 2 tsp ground ginger
- 2 tsp bicarbonate of soda
- few chunks crystallised ginger, chopped
- For the frosting
- 85g butter
- 175ml double or whipping cream
- 175g caster sugar (we used white - use golden for a darker icing)

Direction

- Heat oven to 160C/140C fan/gas 3. Butter and line a 23cm round cake tin. Put the butter, sugar, treacle and syrup in a large pan and gently heat, stirring until the butter has melted and the mixture is smooth. Remove from the heat and cool for 10 mins.
- Stir in the eggs and milk, then sift in the flour, ginger and bicarbonate of soda. Mix well, then pour into the prepared tin. Bake for 50 mins-1 hr until the cake is firm to the touch and springs back when pressed in the centre. Cool in the tin for 15 mins, then turn out, peel off the paper and cool on a wire rack.
- Put the frosting ingredients in a small pan over a medium heat and stir until the butter has melted and the mixture is smooth. Increase the heat and boil hard for 3-4 mins, stirring occasionally; at this stage the frosting should look like runny custard. Pour into a bowl and leave to cool for 30 mins. Beat with an electric whisk until thick and spreadable. Spread over the cooled cake and decorate with crystallised ginger.

Nutrition Information

- Calories: 527 calories
- Sodium: 1 milligram of sodium
- Total Fat: 27 grams fat
- Saturated Fat: 17 grams saturated fat
- Fiber: 1 grams fiber
- Sugar: 45 grams sugar
- Protein: 5 grams protein
- Total Carbohydrate: 65 grams carbohydrates

129.   Iced Vanilla & Caramel Profiteroles

Serving: Serves 6 (5 profiteroles each) | Prep: | Cook: 20mins | Ready in:

Ingredients

- 50g butter
- 60g plain flour
- 1 tbsp caster sugar
- 2 eggs, beaten
- For the caramel sauce
- 200g caster sugar
- 2 tbsp double cream
- splash cognac
- To serve
- 300g good-quality vanilla ice cream, bought or homemade (see below)
- Homemade vanilla ice cream (optional)
- 250ml milk
- 250ml double cream
- 50g sugar
- 6 egg yolks
- seeds of 2 vanilla pod

Direction

- Put 150ml water, the butter and a pinch of salt into a medium pan and gently heat until the butter melts. Turn up the heat and bring to the boil. As soon as it's boiling, tip in the flour in one go. Beat quickly to combine. TIP: It's important to tip the flour in as soon as the water boils, because losing too much liquid by evaporation will affect your pastry.
- The starch in the flour needs to be cooked out now. Beat well, over the heat, until the mix turns smooth and glossy and starts to come away from the edge of the pan. Tip the mix into a bowl and allow to cool a little.
- Give the mixture a quick beat, then start adding the eggs a little at a time, using a whisk, wooden spoon or electric beaters. You may not need to add all the egg – stop once the

pastry is smooth and elastic and drops easily off a spoon.

- Heat oven to 220C/fan 200C/gas 7. Drop a medium nozzle into a large piping bag and scoop the pastry into it. Line two baking sheets with non-stick paper and pipe 15 x 10p-size balls of pastry onto each one. Use a wetted finger to smooth the tops. Bake for 15-20 mins until dark golden and very firm. Transfer to a rack, turn each one upside down, then leave to cool. Will keep in an airtight container for up to 2 days. TIP: The just-piped pastry buns have pointy tops, which can quickly burn. Tap them down gently with a wet finger before you put them in to bake.

- For the sauce, heat the sugar in a large, non-stick frying pan. Melt it gently, swirling every now and again until dissolved. Turn up the heat a little, then bubble until you have a dark golden caramel, about 5 minutes in total. Keep the pan on the heat and carefully stir in the cream to make a silky sauce. Add the Cognac and stir again. Pour into a serving jug. Can be made up to 2 days ahead – warm in the microwave for a few secs and stir to loosen.

- If making your own ice cream, place the milk and double cream in a pan. Take 1 tbsp of the sugar and add to the pan, too. Whisk the remaining sugar with the egg yolks and the seeds of the vanilla pods. Heat the milk until just boiling, then pour it onto the egg mix, whisking constantly. Tip back into the pan and heat gently, stirring with a wooden spoon until the custard thickens and coats the back of a spoon. Pour through a sieve and allow to cool. Now churn the mix in an ice-cream machine, or freeze it in a shallow container, beating thoroughly at least three times, until it is frozen and smooth. Will keep frozen for up to 1 month. Makes about 500 ml, 5 mins prep, 20 mins cooking and freezing.

- Allow the ice cream to soften slightly in the fridge for 30 mins. Scoop into a piping bag then, holding the bag with a tea towel, poke the nozzle into the bottom of one of the buns. Pipe in the ice cream until completely filled (see tips). Work as quickly as you can – you need to get the profiteroles back in the freezer before the ice cream starts to melt. Will keep well-wrapped in the freezer for up to 1 week. NOTE: Wrapping a tea towel around the piping bag insulates the ice cream from the warmth of your hands. If piping in the ice cream seems too fiddly, simply cut the buns open with a serrated knife and fill with teaspoon-size scoops of ice cream.

Nutrition Information

- Calories: 509 calories
- Saturated Fat: 16 grams saturated fat
- Total Carbohydrate: 48 grams carbohydrates
- Sugar: 40 grams sugar
- Protein: 8 grams protein
- Sodium: 0.27 milligram of sodium
- Total Fat: 31 grams fat

---

130. Nutty Caramel & Choc Sundaes

Serving: Makes 6 | Prep: 15mins | Cook: 5mins | Ready in:

Ingredients

- 100g dark chocolate, broken into chunks
- 200ml milk
- 300g/11oz caramel (we used Carnation)
- 85g crunchy peanut butter
- 4 crunchy biscuits, crumbled into chunks (we used Fox's butter crinkle crunch biscuits)
- 50g salted roasted peanut, chopped
- 6 big scoops vanilla ice cream
- 6 big scoops chocolate ice cream

Direction

- Put the chocolate and 100ml milk in a small pan, and put the caramel, peanut butter and 100ml milk in another pan. Gently melt both, stirring until saucy. Set aside to cool.

- Give the sauces a good stir to loosen, then layer the 2 sauces, biscuit bits, peanuts and ice cream in 6 sundae glasses or bowls, and eat straight away.

Nutrition Information

- Calories: 608 calories
- Fiber: 3 grams fiber
- Total Carbohydrate: 62 grams carbohydrates
- Protein: 15 grams protein
- Total Fat: 34 grams fat
- Sugar: 55 grams sugar
- Saturated Fat: 15 grams saturated fat
- Sodium: 0.8 milligram of sodium

131. Orange Crème Caramel Cheesecakes

Serving: 6 | Prep: | Cook: 40mins | Ready in:

Ingredients

- 284ml pot double cream
- peel from 1 orange
- 225g caster sugar
- 4 tbsp orange liqueur
- 200g tub cream cheese
- 4 eggs
- For the biscuit base
- 250g digestive biscuit
- 85g butter, melted
- For the caramel squiggles
- 100g caster sugar
- sunflower oil

Direction

- Heat oven to 150C/fan 130C/gas 2. In a small pan, bring the cream to the boil with the orange peel, then set aside to infuse. Tip 140g/5oz sugar into another saucepan with just enough water to make it sludgy. Bring to the boil, then turn the heat down to a simmer

and boil to make a darkish caramel. Add 2 tbsp of the orange liqueur (watch out as it will splutter). Leave it to settle slightly, then pour the caramel over the base of 6 x 250ml ramekins and set aside.

- Beat the cream cheese and the remaining 85g/3oz sugar together in a large bowl, then beat in the eggs and the remaining orange liqueur. Strain in the infused cream, then beat everything together to make a custard. Skim off any froth and set aside.
- Boil the kettle. Place the ramekins in a deep roasting tin. Divide the custard between them – it will only come to halfway – then bring the tin to the oven and fill with hot water from the kettle so it comes halfway up the outside of the ramekin dishes. Bake the cheesecakes for 40 mins or until just set, then remove from the oven and the tin. Leave to cool, then chill at least overnight. These can be made up to 2 days ahead and left to chill.
- Up to 2 days before serving, make the bases. Crumble the biscuits into a food processor, then blitz to fine crumbs. Add the melted butter and pulse until everything is mixed. Line a flat baking tray with greaseproof paper, tip the base mix onto it, then top with another sheet of greaseproof paper. Gently roll the mix out until large enough to cut 6 bases the same size as the ramekins out of it. Chill.
- To make the caramel squiggles, heat the sugar with a little water in a saucepan and boil to make caramel, then set aside to cool slightly. Line a tray with baking parchment and grease with a little oil. Drizzle the caramel up and down so that all the strands of caramel stick together to create stars, then leave to set.
- To serve, use a cutter the same diameter as the ramekin to cut out 6 bases from the biscuit mix. Lift the bases onto 6 plates. Unmould the cheesecakes, saving the caramel sauce in the ramekin. Top the bases with the crème caramels, drizzle the sauce over and around the plates, garnish with a star and serve.

Nutrition Information

- Calories: 994 calories
- Protein: 10 grams protein
- Sodium: 1.28 milligram of sodium
- Sugar: 66 grams sugar
- Fiber: 1 grams fiber
- Saturated Fat: 36 grams saturated fat
- Total Fat: 67 grams fat
- Total Carbohydrate: 89 grams carbohydrates

132. Pumpkin Pancakes With Salted Pecan Butterscotch

Serving: 4 | Prep: 20mins | Cook: 25mins | Ready in:

Ingredients

- 250g pumpkin or squash, peeled, deseeded and chopped into large chunks
- 2 eggs
- 3 tbsp light brown soft sugar
- 25g butter, melted, plus a little for cooking
- 125ml buttermilk (or use the same quantity of milk, with a squeeze of lemon juice)
- 200g plain flour
- 2½ tsp baking powder
- 1 tsp ground cinnamon
- drizzle of flavourless oil, such as sunflower or groundnut, for frying
- ice cream, to serve, or yogurt or crème fraîche
- For the salted pecan butterscotch
- 50g pecans, roughly chopped
- 50g butter
- 50g light brown soft sugar
- 1 tsp sea salt flakes
- 100ml double cream

Direction

- Put the pumpkin or squash in a large heatproof bowl, add 1 tbsp water, cover with cling film and microwave on High for 5-8 mins or until really soft – different types will take a varying amount of time. Drain the pumpkin well and cool completely. If you want to eat the pancakes for breakfast, this step is best done the night before.
- Once cool, put the pumpkin in a food processer with the remaining pancake ingredients and add a good pinch of salt. Blend until everything is well combined to a smooth, thick batter (alternatively, mash the pumpkin well, then whisk in the remaining ingredients). Transfer to a jug or piping bag and set aside while you make the butterscotch sauce.
- Toast the pecans in a saucepan for 1-2 mins until a shade darker. Tip out and set aside. Add the butter, sugar, salt and cream to the pan. Bring to a simmer, then bubble gently for a few mins until you have a shiny sauce. Stir in the pecans and set aside to cool a little.
- Heat a knob of butter and a drizzle of oil in a large frying pan. Heat oven to 140C/120C fan/gas 1, to keep the pancakes warm while you cook them in batches – have a baking tray to hand. When the butter is foaming, swirl it around the pan, then pour tennis-ball-sized amounts of batter into the pan (see tip below) – they will spread a little as they cook, so leave some space between each pancake and don't overcrowd the pan. Cook over a low-medium heat. Don't touch the pancakes until you see a few bubbles appear on the surface – have a look underneath and, if the pancakes are golden, flip them over and cook for another 2 mins on the other side. Transfer the cooked pancakes to the baking tray and keep warm in the oven while you continue cooking.
- Once cooked, pile the pancakes onto plates, top with ice cream, yogurt or crème fraîche, and pour over the salted pecan butterscotch sauce.

Nutrition Information

- Calories: 717 calories
- Total Carbohydrate: 68 grams carbohydrates
- Sugar: 31 grams sugar
- Protein: 12 grams protein
- Sodium: 2.6 milligram of sodium

- Saturated Fat: 21 grams saturated fat
- Total Fat: 43 grams fat
- Fiber: 4 grams fiber

---

133. Salted Caramel & Peanut Butter Billionaire's Slice

Serving: Cuts into 15 big slices or 20 smaller ones | Prep: 45mins | Cook: 55mins | Ready in:

Ingredients

- For the base
- 225g butter, chopped into cubes, plus a little for greasing
- 140g unsalted peanut, toasted and cooled
- 225g plain flour
- 50g cornflour
- 85g golden caster sugar
- For the peanut butter layer
- 140g butter
- 225g smooth peanut butter
- 140g icing sugar
- For the salted caramel layer
- 2 X 397g cans Carnation caramel
- 1½ tsp flaky sea salt or ½ tsp fine sea salt
- For the chocolate-toffee topping
- 3 x 100g bars dark chocolate, broken into small pieces
- 140g soft dairy toffee
- 3 tbsp milk
- ½ tsp flaky sea salt

Direction

- Heat oven to 180C/160C fan/gas 4. Grease and line a 20 x 30cm rectangular cake tin with baking parchment – the best way to do this is with 2 long strips of parchment. Put the ingredients for the base in a food processor and blitz until it starts to clump together – don't worry if the peanuts are still a little chunky, they will add a lovely texture. Tip onto your work surface and knead briefly to bring together as a dough. Press the dough into the base of your tin in an even layer. Bake for 25 mins until golden, then set aside to cool.
- To make the peanut butter layer, melt the butter and peanut butter in a small pan and mix until smooth. Sieve the icing sugar into a bowl, then pour in the hot butter mixture and stir to combine. While the mixture is still warm, pour over the base and smooth out with a spatula. Chill for 2 hrs until set.
- To make the caramel layer, put the caramel and salt in a pan, bring up to the boil and simmer vigorously for 2-3 mins, whisking continuously, until the colour darkens a shade or two and the caramel thickens slightly. Leave the caramel to cool for 20 mins (see tips, below). Once cooled, pour it over the peanut butter layer and return to the fridge for a further 2 hrs.
- Melt the chocolate in a heatproof bowl set over a pan of barely simmering water. Meanwhile, put the toffees and the milk in a small saucepan and gently heat. They will clump together and struggle to melt at first, but keep heating and eventually they will turn into a runny toffee sauce.
- Remove the tin from the fridge and pour the chocolate over the salted caramel layer, tipping the tin to spread the chocolate over the surface. Use a spoon to quickly drizzle the caramel over the chocolate in a thin loopy pattern (or see tip, below). If the toffee starts to get too thick, add a splash more milk or cream and pop it back on the heat until runny. Sprinkle over the sea salt flakes and put the tin back in the fridge to chill for 2 hrs before slicing.

Nutrition Information

- Calories: 502 calories
- Fiber: 1 grams fiber
- Total Fat: 31 grams fat
- Sugar: 36 grams sugar
- Sodium: 0.7 milligram of sodium
- Protein: 8 grams protein
- Saturated Fat: 16 grams saturated fat

- Total Carbohydrate: 48 grams carbohydrates

---

134. Salted Caramel & Peanut Butter S'mores

Serving: Makes 8 | Prep: 5mins | Cook: 3mins | Ready in:

Ingredients

- 16 waffle biscuits
- 8 peanut butter cups
- 8 tsp caramel (we used Carnation)
- sea salt flakes, for sprinkling

Direction

- Preheat the grill to high and line a baking sheet with parchment. Put 8 waffle biscuits on the tray with a peanut butter cup on each and grill until it starts melting.
- Put a tsp of caramel on the other 8 waffles and sprinkle a few salt flakes over each.
- Sandwich the waffle biscuits together and enjoy with a cappuccino.

Nutrition Information

- Calories: 256 calories
- Sugar: 22 grams sugar
- Protein: 3 grams protein
- Total Fat: 12 grams fat
- Fiber: 1 grams fiber
- Sodium: 1 milligram of sodium
- Saturated Fat: 6 grams saturated fat
- Total Carbohydrate: 34 grams carbohydrates

---

135. Salted Caramel & Popcorn Crumble Choux Buns

Serving: Makes 10 | Prep: 40mins | Cook: 1hours20mins | Ready in:

Ingredients

- 125g toffee popcorn (to fill the buns)
- icing sugar, to serve
- edible gold leaf, to decorate (optional)
- For the crumble topping (craquelin)
- 50g plain flour
- 50g golden caster sugar
- 40g unsalted butter, cold and chopped into small pieces
- For the salted caramel
- 150g granulated sugar
- 125ml double cream
- 10g unsalted butter
- large pinch of flaked sea salt
- For the popcorn cream
- 600ml double cream, plus a little extra to top up
- 125g toffee popcorn
- large pinch of flaked sea salt
- For the choux pastry
- 60g unsalted butter, chopped into small cubes
- ¼ tsp golden caster sugar
- 85g plain flour
- 2-3 large eggs

Direction

- For the crumble topping (or craquelin), mix the flour and sugar together in a medium bowl. Add the butter and rub until you have a breadcrumb texture. Using your hands, press this mixture together to form a uniform dough. Place this between 2 sheets of baking parchment and roll out until it is a few millimetres thick. Pop in the freezer on a baking tray until needed.
- For the salted caramel, put the sugar in a medium-sized saucepan and set over a medium heat. Allow the sugar to melt and caramelise, stirring occasionally. Once the sugar is a dark copper caramel colour, add half the double cream. When the bubbling has subsided, add the remaining cream, the butter and salt, and stir to combine. If you have any remaining lumps, put back on the heat and stir until melted and smooth. Remove from the

heat, pour into a small bowl, cover with cling film and chill until needed.

- For the popcorn cream, put all the ingredients in a medium saucepan over a medium-high heat and bring to the boil. Remove from the heat, cover the pan and allow to infuse for 1 hour. Strain the cream through a sieve into a measuring jug, pressing down on the softened popcorn to get as much cream out as possible. Top the cream up so you still have 600ml. Press a piece of cling film onto the surface of the cream and chill until needed. Can be prepared the day before up to this point.
- For the choux pastry, heat oven to 180C/160C fan/gas 4 and line 2 baking trays with baking parchment. Using a 5cm cookie cutter as a guide, draw 5 circles onto each piece of baking parchment and turn them over. Put 140ml water, the butter, ¼ tsp salt and the sugar in a medium saucepan and, over a medium-high heat, bring the mixture to a full rolling boil. Once boiling, and the butter has melted, remove from the heat, tip in the flour and immediately mix together with a wooden spoon until a smooth paste forms. Return to the heat and beat for 1-2 mins to dry out a little. Tip the paste into a large bowl and beat for a few mins to cool down slightly.
- Add in the eggs, one at a time, beating until fully combined before adding another – add the last egg a little at a time as you may not need it all. Stop when the smooth choux drops off your spoon in a V-shape. Put the dough in a piping bag fitted with a large round nozzle, then pipe rounds of dough onto the prepared baking trays, using the circles as templates. Remove the crumble topping from the freezer and peel off the top layer of parchment. Using a 5cm cookie cutter, cut out 10 discs of the crumble topping and place one on top of each round of dough. Bake for 40 mins, or until the choux is well risen and the crumble is golden. Turn the oven off but leave the choux in until fully cooled.
- To assemble the buns, use a large serrated knife to carefully slice in half. Place a few pieces of popcorn in the base of each bun and

spoon some caramel in too (if you have prepared the caramel ahead of time, it will have firmed up, so place over a bowl of simmering water to loosen it). For the filling, remove the cream from the fridge and whip to soft peaks, then put in a piping bag fitted with a large star tip and pipe a swirl onto the base of each bun. To finish, place the top of the choux buns back on top of the cream and dust lightly with icing sugar. I finished mine with a piece of edible gold leaf.

Nutrition Information

- Calories: 681 calories
- Total Fat: 52 grams fat
- Saturated Fat: 31 grams saturated fat
- Fiber: 2 grams fiber
- Sugar: 35 grams sugar
- Total Carbohydrate: 51 grams carbohydrates
- Protein: 4 grams protein
- Sodium: 1 milligram of sodium

---

136. Salted Caramel & Popcorn Eclairs

Serving: makes 20 eclairs | Prep: 1hours45mins | Cook: 50mins | Ready in:

Ingredients

- 1 quantity eclairs and crème pâtissière recipe - see link in method
- 1 x 397g tin Nestlé Carnation Caramel
- 600g fondant icing sugar
- sea salt flakes
- 600ml double cream
- 2 tsp vanilla bean paste
- 100g chopped toffee popcorn

Direction

- Make the eclairs and crème pâtissière using our classic recipe.

- Mix 150g Carnation Caramel with the fondant icing sugar. Mix into a thick but drizzly icing, adding a splash of water if it's too thick. Cover with cling film.
- Transfer another 200g Carnation Caramel to a piping bag and pipe a line along the bottom half of the split eclairs, then sprinkle over a few sea salt flakes.
- Pour the double cream into a bowl with the remaining caramel and vanilla bean paste. Beat with an electric hand whisk to thicken the cream to stiff peaks. Fold through the crème pâtissière, then transfer to a piping bag. Pipe generous blobs of cream over the base, then sprinkle over 50g chopped toffee popcorn.
- Spread the glaze carefully over the tops of the eclairs, then position on top of the cream. After every four or five eclairs, decorate the tops, while the icing is still wet, with 50g chopped toffee popcorn and a pinch of sea salt flakes. For more help, see our how to make choux pastry and eclairs video.

Nutrition Information

- Calories: 469 calories
- Total Carbohydrate: 51 grams carbohydrates
- Sodium: 0.5 milligram of sodium
- Fiber: 1 grams fiber
- Total Fat: 27 grams fat
- Saturated Fat: 16 grams saturated fat
- Sugar: 40 grams sugar
- Protein: 5 grams protein

137. Salted Caramel Banana Tatins With Crème Fraîche Ice Cream

Serving: Serves 2 with leftover ice cream | Prep: 30mins | Cook: 25mins | Ready in:

Ingredients

- For the ice cream

- 1 vanilla pod
- 200ml double cream
- 100ml milk
- 3 egg yolks
- 85g golden caster sugar
- 300ml full-fat crème fraîche
- For the banana tatin
- 250g puff pastry
- plain flour, for dusting
- 1 banana, peeled
- 50g soft light brown sugar
- 50g butter
- 2 tbsp double cream

Direction

- To make the ice cream, split the vanilla pod in half lengthways and scrape out the seeds. Put the pod and seeds in a saucepan with the cream and milk, and bring slowly to the boil. Meanwhile, in a bowl, whisk the egg yolks and sugar together until pale. Pour the hot cream mixture over the egg and sugar, whisking continuously. Pour back into the pan, set over a gentle heat and stir with a wooden spoon. Heat gently until the custard mixture thickens enough to coat the back of the spoon, then remove from the heat.
- Pour the crème fraîche into a bowl and whisk to loosen. Slowly pour in the hot custard mixture, whisking as you go. Pour the mixture into an ice-cream machine and churn until softly frozen. Transfer to a container, then freeze for 2 hrs to firm.
- To make the Tatins, roll out the pastry on a floured surface to the thickness of a £1 coin. Using the banana as a guide, cut out 2 pastry lids big enough to fit over the banana, leaving a 1cm border around the edge. Place the pastry on a baking tray and put in the fridge.
- Set an ovenproof, heavy-bottomed frying pan over a medium heat. Add the sugar, butter and cream, and cook for 5 mins until the sugar has melted and the caramel is bubbling. Add ½ tsp sea salt flakes. Slice the banana in half lengthways and place the 2 halves, cut-side down, into the caramel.

- Heat oven to 220C/200C fan/gas 7. Place a pastry lid on top of each banana half, tucking each in tightly around the edges. This can be done 1 hr ahead. Transfer the pan to the oven and cook for 20 mins until the pastry is risen and golden. Quickly and carefully turn out the Tatins, sprinkle with a few flakes of sea salt and serve with scoops of crème fraîche ice cream.

Nutrition Information

- Calories: 1385 calories
- Saturated Fat: 63 grams saturated fat
- Protein: 12 grams protein
- Sodium: 2.8 milligram of sodium
- Total Fat: 107 grams fat
- Total Carbohydrate: 94 grams carbohydrates
- Sugar: 52 grams sugar
- Fiber: 1 grams fiber

---

138.   Salted Caramel Biscuit Bars

Serving: makes 18 | Prep: 45mins | Cook: 15mins | Ready in:

Ingredients

- For the biscuit base
- 80g porridge oats
- 20g ground almonds
- 50ml maple syrup
- 3 tbsp coconut oil, melted
- For the caramel filling
- 125g medjool dates, pitted
- 1 ½ tbsp smooth peanut butter or almond butter
- 2 tbsp coconut oil, melted
- ½ tbsp almond milk
- generous pinch of salt
- For the topping
- 150g dairy-free dark chocolate

Direction

- Heat oven to 180C/160C fan/gas 4 and line a large baking tray with baking parchment.
- For the base, blitz the oats in a food processor until flour-like. Add the remaining ingredients and whizz until the mixture starts to clump together. Scrape into a bowl, then roll and cut into 18 equal-sized rectangular bars, about 9 x 2cm. Place on the prepared tray and use a small palette knife to neaten the tops and sides of each biscuit. Bake for about 10 mins until lightly golden at the edges, then leave to cool.
- Meanwhile, put all the caramel ingredients in the food processor (no need to rinse it first) and blitz until it forms smooth, shiny clumps. Using a spatula, push the mixture together, then roll into 18 even-sized balls using your hands.
- Once the biscuits are cool, squash the caramel onto them. Use your fingers to press it into shape and smooth out any bumps, especially around the edges (as they will show underneath the chocolate coating).
- Melt the chocolate in a heatproof bowl set over a pan of simmering water – make sure the water doesn't touch the bowl (otherwise, it might seize and go grainy). Carefully dip one of the caramel-coated biscuits in the chocolate, turning it gently with a small palette knife (use this to lift it out as well). Use a spoon to drizzle over more chocolate to coat it fully. Let the excess chocolate drip into the bowl, then carefully put the biscuit back on the lined tray.
- Repeat with the remaining biscuits, then chill in the fridge for at least 30 mins or until the chocolate has set. Put the biscuits in an airtight container and store in the fridge. Will keep for five days.

Nutrition Information

- Calories: 137 calories
- Sodium: 0.1 milligram of sodium
- Total Fat: 8 grams fat
- Sugar: 8 grams sugar
- Fiber: 2 grams fiber

- Protein: 2 grams protein
- Total Carbohydrate: 13 grams carbohydrates
- Saturated Fat: 5 grams saturated fat

---

139. Salted Caramel Cheesecake

Serving: cuts into 12 slices | Prep: 30mins | Cook: 35mins | Ready in:

Ingredients

- For the base
- 50g butter, melted, plus extra for the tin
- 200g chocolate digestives
- For the filling and topping
- 750g (3 tubs) cream cheese
- 300g caramel sauce (dulce de leche) from a tin or jar
- 1 tsp vanilla extract
- 150g golden caster sugar
- 2 tbsp plain flour
- 4 medium eggs

Direction

- Heat oven to 180C/160C fan/gas 4. Butter a 23cm springform cake tin and line the base with baking parchment. Tip the biscuits into a food processor, blitz to crumbs and pour in the melted butter. (You could also tip the biscuits into a bag, bash with a rolling pin into crumbs and mix in the butter.) Press the biscuit mixture into the base of the tin – the easiest way to do this is by flattening it with your hand under a sheet of cling film. Place the tin on a tray and bake for 10 mins, then remove from the oven to cool.
- Meanwhile, scrape the cream cheese into a bowl with 3 tbsp of the caramel sauce, the vanilla, sugar and flour, and beat until smooth. Beat in the eggs, one at a time, until you have a thick, smooth custard consistency. Tip over the base, scraping the bowl clean, and bake in the oven for 10 mins. Reduce the

temperature to 140C/120C fan/gas 1 and continue to bake for 25-30 mins until there is a slight wobble in the centre. Turn off the heat and leave the door just slightly ajar – a tea towel holding the door open is ideal. This should leave you with a completely smooth top, but if there are a couple of small cracks, don't worry. Leave the cheesecake in the oven until completely cool (overnight is fine), then chill until needed. Will keep in the fridge for two days.
- On the day, loosen the sides of the cheesecake from the tin with a knife and remove the base (although I usually serve it straight from the tin base). Add a large pinch of flaky sea salt to the rest of the caramel sauce, then spoon it over the cake and swirl with the back of the spoon. The cheesecake will sit happily on a stand at room temperature for a couple of hours. Just before serving, sprinkle with extra sea salt, if you like.

Nutrition Information

- Calories: 435 calories
- Total Fat: 26 grams fat
- Sugar: 31 grams sugar
- Fiber: 1 grams fiber
- Saturated Fat: 16 grams saturated fat
- Total Carbohydrate: 41 grams carbohydrates
- Protein: 9 grams protein
- Sodium: 0.7 milligram of sodium

---

140. Salted Caramel Chocolate Torte

Serving: 8 | Prep: 1hours15mins | Cook: 10mins | Ready in:

Ingredients

- 175g digestive biscuits
- 85g butter, melted
- 397g can caramel (we used Carnation caramel)

- 1 tsp sea salt, plus extra to serve
- 300g plain chocolate (70% solids), broken into chunks
- 600ml tub double cream
- 25g icing sugar
- 2 tsp vanilla extract
- salted caramel chocolates, to decorate (find them in Waitrose, Sainsbury's or Marks & Spencer)
- single cream, to serve (optional)

Direction

- Line the base of a deep, round 20cm loose-bottomed cake tin with a circle of baking parchment. Line the sides with one long strip that comes just above the sides of the tin – staple or paper clip where the strip overlaps to hold it in place.
- Crush the biscuits in a plastic bag or bowl with the end of a rolling pin. Stir into the melted butter, then evenly press into the bottom of the tin. Chill for 10 mins.
- Reserve 2 tbsp of the caramel. Stir the sea salt into the remainder and spoon into the centre of the biscuit base. Gently spread so the base is evenly covered but a visible 1-2cm border of biscuit remains around the edge. Chill for 20 mins while you make the chocolate layer.
- Gently melt the chocolate in a large heatproof bowl over a pan of barely simmering water. Stir 1 tbsp of the cream into the reserved caramel, then cover and chill until ready to decorate. Once the chocolate has melted, turn off the heat but leave the bowl where it is, and gradually stir in the remaining cream until you have a smooth, shiny, thick chocolate sauce. Sift in the icing sugar and stir in with the vanilla extract. Lift off the heat and let the mixture cool for 10 mins.
- Ladle or pour the chocolate mixture around the edge of the torte first, so it fills the biscuit border, sealing the caramel in the centre. Then ladle or pour in the rest and gently shake to smooth the surface. Chill for at least 5 hrs or up to 24 hours until firm.

- Remove the torte from the tin, then carefully peel off the strip of paper and transfer to a serving plate. Dot the chocolates on top. Spoon the reserved caramel-cream mixture into a small food or freezer bag. Snip off the tiniest tip of the corner to make a very small opening, then squiggle lines of caramel over the top. Chill until ready to serve. Scatter with a pinch or two of sea salt before serving, then thinly slice. Eat with a drizzle of single cream, if you like.

Nutrition Information

- Calories: 925 calories
- Saturated Fat: 39 grams saturated fat
- Total Carbohydrate: 74 grams carbohydrates
- Sugar: 61 grams sugar
- Total Fat: 69 grams fat
- Sodium: 1.27 milligram of sodium
- Fiber: 2 grams fiber
- Protein: 8 grams protein

---

141.   Salted Caramel Parsnips

Serving: 6 | Prep: 5mins | Cook: 40mins | Ready in:

Ingredients

- 1kg parsnip, peeled
- 3 tbsp rapeseed oil
- 50g golden caster sugar
- large knob of butter
- 1 tsp sea salt

Direction

- Heat oven to 220C/200C fan/gas 7. Halve the parsnips, then cut the thicker end in two lengthways. Boil for 5 mins, then drain well and leave to steam-dry for a few mins. Meanwhile, pour the oil into a shallow roasting tin or a lipped baking tray and heat in the oven for 3 mins.

- Remove the tin from the oven and carefully add the parsnips to the hot oil. Turn them to coat, and make sure they aren't overcrowded (otherwise they won't crisp up). Roast for 30-35 mins or until golden and crisp, turning them halfway through the cooking time.
- About 10 mins before the parsnips are ready, tip the sugar and 2 tbsp water into a small frying pan. Heat very gently until the sugar has dissolved. Turn up the heat and bring the liquid to the boil. Measure 3½ tbsp cold water into a jug. Keep swirling the pan around until the sugar reaches a rich, dark-reddish caramel colour, then remove from the heat. Stand well back and add the water (it will splutter!). Return to the heat, add the butter and the salt, and stir to remove any lumps. The caramel should be runny, so add a splash more water if needed. Pile the parsnips into a serving dish, then drizzle over the salted caramel.

Nutrition Information

- Calories: 205 calories
- Total Fat: 9 grams fat
- Fiber: 8 grams fiber
- Saturated Fat: 2 grams saturated fat
- Sugar: 18 grams sugar
- Protein: 3 grams protein
- Sodium: 1.4 milligram of sodium
- Total Carbohydrate: 28 grams carbohydrates

---

142. Salted Caramel Pecan Sour

Serving: 6 | Prep: 15mins | Cook: 5mins | Ready in:

Ingredients

- 100g pecans, finely chopped
- 160g golden caster sugar
- ½ tsp sea salt flakes
- Reyka vodka
- 3 egg whites

- 120ml fresh clementine juice (about 2-3 clementines)
- 18 drops chocolate bitters (we used Fee brothers Aztec chocolate bitters)
- ice
- 6 dehydrated orange slices, to serve
- good grating of nutmeg, to serve

Direction

- Toast the pecans in a dry saucepan for 1-2 mins, then take off the heat. Quickly add the sugar and 80ml water, stir rapidly to dissolve the sugar, add the salt, then leave the mixture to cool completely. Pour through a sieve to remove the pecans.
- Pour the pecan salted caramel syrup, vodka, egg whites, clementine juice and bitters into a cocktail shaker. Shake hard for 30 secs to add volume to the egg white. Add some ice and shake again for a further 15 secs, then strain into rocks or coupe glasses. Garnish each with a dehydrated orange slice and grate fresh nutmeg over, to taste. Serve immediately.

Nutrition Information

- Calories: 358 calories
- Total Carbohydrate: 29 grams carbohydrates
- Total Fat: 12 grams fat
- Sodium: 0.5 milligram of sodium
- Sugar: 29 grams sugar
- Fiber: 2 grams fiber
- Protein: 3 grams protein
- Saturated Fat: 1 grams saturated fat

---

143. Salted Caramels

Serving: Makes 55 | Prep: 5mins | Cook: 20mins | Ready in:

Ingredients

- 70g unsalted butter, plus extra for the tin
- 200ml double cream

- ½ tsp vanilla extract
- 150g golden granulated sugar
- 150g golden syrup
- 1 heaped tsp flaky sea salt
- flavourless oil, for the knife
- You will need
- sugar thermometer or digital probe

Direction

- Butter and line the base and sides of a 20 x 30cm tin with baking parchment.
- Pour the cream into a saucepan along with the butter and vanilla, then bring to a simmer. Swirl the pan to melt the butter, then remove from the heat.
- In a separate pan, melt the sugar and golden syrup together, stirring occasionally. Once the sugar granules have dissolved, bring to the boil and cook until the temperature reaches 155C on a sugar thermometer. Remove from the heat and swiftly whisk through the cream mixture. Return to the heat and cook until the mixture reaches 127C, constantly whisking so it doesn't catch.
- Pour the caramel into the tin, tilting so it reaches the corners. Leave to set for 15 mins, then sprinkle with the salt. Leave to cool completely at room temperature (preferably overnight). Cut into squares using a very sharp, slightly oiled knife, then wrap each one in a square of baking parchment.

Nutrition Information

- Calories: 47 calories
- Total Fat: 3 grams fat
- Saturated Fat: 2 grams saturated fat
- Total Carbohydrate: 5 grams carbohydrates
- Sugar: 5 grams sugar
- Protein: 0.1 grams protein
- Sodium: 0.15 milligram of sodium

144.   Shallot Tatin

Serving: 4 | Prep: 25mins | Cook: 35mins | Ready in:

Ingredients

- 450g shallot
- 3 tbsp demerara sugar
- 50g butter
- 1 tsp fresh thyme leaf
- 1 tbsp balsamic vinegar or a few grindings of cracked black pepper
- plain flour, for dusting
- 500g pack puff pastry

Direction

- Heat oven to 200C/180C fan/gas 6. Pour boiling water over the shallots and leave them until the water cools. (This makes it easier to slip the skins off.) Peel and halve the shallots, then set aside. Put the sugar in a 23cm ovenproof frying pan and heat until it dissolves and you have a sticky caramel. Add the butter, thyme and a splash of balsamic vinegar or cracked black pepper – take care as it will spit.
- Remove the pan from the heat and put all the shallots into the pan, cut-side down. On a lightly floured surface, roll out the pastry and cut out a round 2cm larger than the pan. Drape the pastry over the shallots and tuck in the edges, so that it 'hugs' the shallots. Place the pan in the oven and cook for 25-30 mins until the pastry is puffed up and golden. Leave to rest for 1 min, then invert the tart onto a plate. Serve with a punchy salad of rocket and goat's cheese.

Nutrition Information

- Calories: 649 calories
- Fiber: 2 grams fiber
- Sodium: 1.2 milligram of sodium
- Total Carbohydrate: 63 grams carbohydrates
- Protein: 9 grams protein
- Total Fat: 40 grams fat

- Saturated Fat: 21 grams saturated fat
- Sugar: 21 grams sugar

145. Utterly Nutterly Caramel Layer Cake

Serving: 8 | Prep: 30mins | Cook: 30mins | Ready in:

Ingredients

- 250g pack salted butter, softened, plus extra for greasing
- 175g mixed nut, we used Brazil nuts, hazelnuts, pecans and almonds, roughly chopped
- 250g soft light brown sugar
- 3 tbsp golden syrup
- 4 large eggs
- 140g self-raising flour
- 75g ground almond
- ½ tsp baking powder
- 1 tsp almond extract
- 3 tbsp milk
- For the filling
- 200ml double cream
- 5 tbsp caramel, from a can (we used Carnation)

Direction

- Heat oven to 180C/160C fan/gas 4. Line 2 x 20cm loose-bottomed Victoria sandwich cake tins with baking parchment, then grease one of the tins over the top of the parchment (this will help to prevent the caramel-nut topping from sticking when you turn it out). Tip the nuts into a frying pan and toast over a medium heat until golden. Add 50g of the butter, 50g sugar, the golden syrup and a good pinch of salt. Stir until the butter has melted, then bubble for 2 mins until the buttery sauce is golden brown – don't let it bubble for too long or the topping will set hard once cooled. Tip into the cake tin with the greased parchment and smooth over. Leave to cool while you make the cake.
- Tip the remaining butter and sugar into a large bowl and beat with an electric whisk until pale and fluffy. Add the eggs, one at a time, mixing well between each addition. Add the flour, almonds, baking powder, 1/2 tsp salt, almond extract and milk, and mix again until just combined. Divide the cake mixture between the tins and smooth over the surface. Bake for 25 mins, or until a skewer comes out clean. Leave to cool in the tins for 10 mins, then flip out onto a wire rack and remove the parchment. Allow to cool completely.
- Whisk the cream and 2 tbsp of the caramel until softly whipped and just holding its shape. To assemble the cake, place the plain cake on a plate or stand. Top with the whipped cream, swirling it out towards the edges. Drizzle over the remaining caramel (give it a good mix first to loosen it), letting it dribble down the sides. Top with the remaining sponge, nutty-side up. Serve within 1 day, or store in fridge for 3 days, removing it from the fridge 10 mins before serving.

Nutrition Information

- Calories: 531 calories
- Protein: 9 grams protein
- Sugar: 27 grams sugar
- Fiber: 1 grams fiber
- Sodium: 0.9 milligram of sodium
- Saturated Fat: 19 grams saturated fat
- Total Fat: 39 grams fat
- Total Carbohydrate: 36 grams carbohydrates

146. Walnut Caramel Tart

Serving: Cuts into 8-10 slices | Prep: 40mins | Cook: 25mins | Ready in:

Ingredients

- 175g plain flour, plus extra for dusting
- 85g butter, cut into small cubes
- 50g caster sugar
- 1 egg yolk
- For the filling
- 200g caster sugar
- 100g butter, cut into small pieces
- 200ml whipping or double cream
- 200g shelled walnut half

Direction

- Heat oven to 190C/170C fan/gas 5. Put the flour in a food processor with the butter and sugar, and mix until it forms fine breadcrumbs. Add the egg yolk and 1-2 tbsp cold water, and pulse to make a firm dough.
- Have ready a 24cm tart tin. Briefly knead the pastry on a lightly floured surface, then roll out to a round about 5cm larger than your tin. Lift onto the tin with the help of your rolling pin, then press into the corners using your finger. Do not trim the pastry. Fill the pastry case with a round of baking parchment and baking beans. Chill for 10 mins. Blindbake for 10 mins, remove the paper and beans, then bake for 5 mins more.
- To make the filling, put the sugar in a large pan with 3 tbsp cold water. Heat gently, stirring to dissolve the sugar. When the sugar is completely dissolved, increase heat and bubble until the syrup has turned a rich caramel colour. Remove from the heat and stir in the butter until it has dissolved, then stir in the cream. Return to the heat and boil hard, stirring until the sauce is thick enough to leave a gap on the base of the pan when you draw your spoon across it. Stir in the walnuts.
- Fill the pastry case with the nut mixture, levelling it with a fork. Return to the oven for 8-10 mins until the filling is bubbling. Cool for 10 mins before removing carefully from the tin. Serve warm or cold.

Nutrition Information

- Calories: 539 calories

- Total Fat: 40 grams fat
- Total Carbohydrate: 38 grams carbohydrates
- Saturated Fat: 18 grams saturated fat
- Protein: 5 grams protein
- Sugar: 26 grams sugar
- Fiber: 2 grams fiber
- Sodium: 0.3 milligram of sodium

Chapter 5: Cookie Recipes

***

| 147. | Anzac Biscuits |

Serving: Makes 20 | Prep: | Cook: | Ready in:

Ingredients

- 85g porridge oat
- 85g desiccated coconut
- 100g plain flour
- 100g caster sugar
- 100g butter, plus extra butter for greasing
- 1 tbsp golden syrup
- 1 tsp bicarbonate of soda

Direction

- Heat oven to 180C/fan 160C/gas 4. Put the oats, coconut, flour and sugar in a bowl. Melt the butter in a small pan and stir in the golden syrup. Add the bicarbonate of soda to 2 tbsp boiling water, then stir into the golden syrup and butter mixture.
- Make a well in the middle of the dry ingredients and pour in the butter and golden syrup mixture. Stir gently to incorporate the dry ingredients.

- Put dessertspoonfuls of the mixture on to buttered baking sheets, about 2.5cm/1in apart to allow room for spreading. Bake in batches for 8-10 mins until golden. Transfer to a wire rack to cool.

Nutrition Information

- Calories: 118 calories
- Fiber: 1 grams fiber
- Sodium: 0.28 milligram of sodium
- Protein: 1 grams protein
- Total Carbohydrate: 13 grams carbohydrates
- Total Fat: 7 grams fat
- Sugar: 6 grams sugar
- Saturated Fat: 5 grams saturated fat

your hand and bake them in the oven for around 10-12 mins until they are golden brown and slightly firm on top. Leave the cookies on a cooling rack for around 15 mins before serving.

Nutrition Information

- Calories: 125 calories
- Protein: 1 grams protein
- Total Fat: 8 grams fat
- Sodium: 0.2 milligram of sodium
- Fiber: 0.4 grams fiber
- Saturated Fat: 5 grams saturated fat
- Sugar: 4 grams sugar
- Total Carbohydrate: 13 grams carbohydrates

---

148.   Basic Cookies

Serving: Makes 25 | Prep: 20mins | Cook: 12mins | Ready in:

Ingredients

- 225g butter, softened
- 110g caster sugar
- 275g plain flour
- 1 tsp cinnamon or other spices (optional)
- 75g white or milk chocolate chips (optional)

Direction

- Heat the oven to 190C/170C fan/gas 5. Cream the butter in a large bowl with a wooden spoon or in a stand mixer until it is soft. Add the sugar and keep beating until the mixture is light and fluffy. Sift in the flour and add the optional ingredients, if you're using them. Bring the mixture together with your hands in a figure-of-eight motion until it forms a dough. You can freeze the dough at this point.
- Roll the dough into walnut-sized balls and place them slightly apart from each other on a baking sheet (you don't need to butter or line it). Flatten the balls a little with the palm of

---

149.   Blueberry & Pecan Oaties

Serving: 12 cookies | Prep: 20mins | Cook: 15mins | Ready in:

Ingredients

- 175g plain flour, plus extra for dusting
- ½ tsp baking powder
- 85g porridge oat
- 175g golden caster sugar
- 1 tsp ground cinnamon
- 140g butter, chopped
- 70g pack dried blueberry(or use raisins or dried cranberries)
- 50g pecan, roughly broken
- 1 egg, beaten

Direction

- Tip the flour, baking powder, oats, sugar and cinnamon into a bowl, then mix well with your hands. Add the butter, then rub it into the mixture until it has disappeared.
- Stir in the blueberries and pecans, add the egg, then mix well with a cutlery knife or wooden spoon until it all comes together in a big ball.

Lightly flour the work surface, then roll the dough into a fat sausage about 6cm across. Wrap in cling film, then chill in the fridge until solid.

- To bake, heat oven to 180C/fan 160C/ gas 4. Unwrap the cookie log, thickly slice into discs, then arrange on baking sheets. Bake for 15 mins (or a few mins more if from frozen) until golden, leave on the trays to harden, then cool completely on a wire rack before tucking in.

Nutrition Information

- Calories: 274 calories
- Total Fat: 14 grams fat
- Saturated Fat: 7 grams saturated fat
- Total Carbohydrate: 36 grams carbohydrates
- Sugar: 20 grams sugar
- Protein: 4 grams protein
- Sodium: 0.27 milligram of sodium

---

150.   Blueberry & Pretzel Cookies

Serving: Makes 20 | Prep: 20mins | Cook: 18mins | Ready in:

Ingredients

- 175g butter, softened
- 200g light soft brown sugar
- 100g golden caster sugar
- 1 tbsp vanilla extract
- 1 large egg
- 250g plain flour
- ½ tsp bicarbonate of soda
- 200g blueberry
- 50g small salted pretzel, broken into chunky pieces
- 100g white chocolate chunks

Direction

- Heat oven to 190C/170C fan/gas 5. Line 2 baking trays with baking parchment. Tip the butter, sugars and vanilla into a bowl. Beat with a hand-held electric whisk until pale and fluffy. Add the egg and beat again. Tip the flour, bicarb and a pinch of salt into the bowl, and use a spatula to mix together. Add the blueberries, pretzel pieces and chocolate chunks, and mix again until everything is combined.
- Scoop golf-ball-sized mounds of cookie dough onto the baking trays, making sure you leave plenty of space between each one. (You should fit 4-6 cookies on each tray, so you'll have to bake in batches to make the total 20 cookies.) Can be frozen at this point – simply defrost in the fridge before baking. Bake for 18 mins, swapping the trays around halfway through.
- Remove the trays from the oven and leave to cool for 10 mins before transferring to a wire rack, then bake the second batch. Continue until all the cookies are baked. Will keep in a cookie jar for up to 1 week.

Nutrition Information

- Calories: 211 calories
- Protein: 2 grams protein
- Sodium: 0.3 milligram of sodium
- Saturated Fat: 6 grams saturated fat
- Fiber: 1 grams fiber
- Total Fat: 9 grams fat
- Total Carbohydrate: 29 grams carbohydrates
- Sugar: 19 grams sugar

---

151.   Bumper Oat Cookies

Serving: Makes 18 | Prep: | Cook: | Ready in:

Ingredients

- 175g butter
- 175g demerara sugar
- 100g golden syrup

114

- 85g plain flour
- ½ tsp bicarbonate of soda
- 250g porridge oats
- 1 tsp ground cinnamon
- 100g each of ready-to-eat dried apricots, chopped and stem ginger, chopped
- 75-80g pack dried sour cherries
- 2 tbsp boiling water
- 1 medium egg, beaten

Direction

- Heat the oven to 180C/fan160C/gas 4. Line several baking sheets with baking parchment or non-stick sheets. Warm the butter, sugar and golden syrup in a large saucepan over a medium heat until the butter has melted. Stir in the flour, bicarbonate of soda, oats, cinnamon, dried fruits and ginger, then the water and finally the egg. Leave to cool until easy to handle.
- With dampened hands, shape the mixture into 18 large balls, then flatten them onto the baking sheets – allowing plenty of space for spreading – and bake for 15-20 mins until golden. (This will give a soft, chewy cookie. For a crisper one, reduce the heat to 160C/fan140C/gas 3 and bake for a further 5-10 mins.)
- Allow the cookies to cool on the trays briefly, then lift onto to a cooling rack. Will keep in an airtight container, separated with baking parchment, for up to 1 week.

Nutrition Information

- Calories: 236 calories
- Saturated Fat: 5 grams saturated fat
- Total Fat: 10 grams fat
- Fiber: 2 grams fiber
- Total Carbohydrate: 37 grams carbohydrates
- Sugar: 13 grams sugar
- Protein: 3 grams protein
- Sodium: 0.3 milligram of sodium

---

152.   Butterscotch Cookies

Serving: Makes 10 | Prep: 10mins | Cook: 20mins | Ready in:

Ingredients

- 100g unsalted butter, softened, plus extra for the baking sheet
- 100g light soft brown sugar
- 2 tbsp golden syrup
- 175g self-raising flour
- 25g puffed rice cereal, such as Rice Krispies
- dark chocolate chips, for decoration

Direction

- Heat oven to 160C/140C fan/gas 3. In a large bowl, beat together the butter, sugar and golden syrup until smooth.
- Sift in the flour and mix together, then fold through the puffed rice cereal. Roll into walnut-sized balls and place, well spaced, on a lightly buttered baking sheet. Decorate each ball with a few chocolate chips.
- Bake for 15-20 mins until golden. Leave on the baking sheet for 1 min before removing to a wire rack to cool.

Nutrition Information

- Calories: 188 calories
- Sodium: 0.2 milligram of sodium
- Total Carbohydrate: 27 grams carbohydrates
- Sugar: 13 grams sugar
- Saturated Fat: 5 grams saturated fat
- Total Fat: 8 grams fat
- Protein: 2 grams protein
- Fiber: 1 grams fiber

153. Cherry & Coconut Florentines

Serving: Makes 24 | Prep: 30mins | Cook: 20mins | Ready in:

Ingredients

- 140g light muscovado sugar
- 100g clear honey
- 200g salted butter
- 100g desiccated coconut
- 140g flaked almonds
- 300g glacé cherry, sliced
- 4 tbsp plain flour
- 250g dark, milk or white chocolate, or a mix

Direction

- Heat oven to 200C/180C fan/gas 6. Put the sugar, honey and butter in a large pan and gently melt together. When all the sugar has dissolved stir in the coconut, flaked almonds, sliced cherries and flour.
- Line a large baking tray with greaseproof paper (about 40 x 30cm), and roughly spread the Florentine mixture out to a thin layer – don't worry if you have small gaps, it should melt together in the oven. Bake for 10-12 mins until a rich golden colour, then set aside to cool and firm up.
- Melt the chocolate(s) all in separate heatproof bowls over gently simmering water. Line a second large tray or board with greaseproof paper and carefully flip the cooled Florentine bake onto it. Peel off the greaseproof paper. Spread the melted chocolate over, if you're using a few types just leave a gap between each.
- Leave aside until set, then stamp out shapes using cookie star cutters - if the cutter is digging into your hands (as the Florentine mix may be a little hard), rest a small plate or pan on top of it and push down on this instead.

Nutrition Information

- Calories: 247 calories
- Total Fat: 15 grams fat
- Saturated Fat: 9 grams saturated fat
- Sugar: 25 grams sugar
- Total Carbohydrate: 26 grams carbohydrates
- Protein: 2 grams protein
- Fiber: 1 grams fiber
- Sodium: 0.15 milligram of sodium

154. Chewy Chocolate Chip Cookies

Serving: Makes 12 | Prep: 10mins | Cook: 10mins | Ready in:

Ingredients

- 150g butter, softened
- 150g soft brown sugar, golden caster sugar, or ideally half of each
- 1 egg
- 1 tsp vanilla extract
- 180-200g plain flour (see tip below)
- ½ tsp baking powder
- 200g chocolate chips or chopped chocolate

Direction

- Mix the butter and sugar together using an electric whisk or hand whisk until very light and fluffy, then beat in the egg and vanilla. Fold in the flour, baking powder, chocolate and ¼ tsp salt as quickly as you can. Don't overwork the dough as this will toughen the cookies.
- For the best flavour, leave the mixture overnight: either cover the bowl and chill, or roll the mixture into balls and chill.
- Heat the oven to 180C/160C fan/gas 4 and line two baking sheets with parchment. Divide the mixture into balls, the craggier the balls, the rougher the cookies will look. If you want to give the dough more texture, tear the balls in half and squidge them lightly back together. Space out evenly on the baking sheets, leaving

enough space between each to allow for spreading.

- Bake the fresh cookies for 8-10 mins and the chilled ones for 10-12 mins, or until browned and a little crisp at the edges but still very soft in the middle – they will harden a little as they cool. Leave to cool on the tray for a few minutes before eating warm, or transfer to a wire rack to cool completely. Will keep for three days in an airtight container.

Nutrition Information

- Calories: 299 calories
- Sugar: 18 grams sugar
- Protein: 3 grams protein
- Fiber: 2 grams fiber
- Sodium: 0.4 milligram of sodium
- Total Fat: 17 grams fat
- Total Carbohydrate: 31 grams carbohydrates
- Saturated Fat: 10 grams saturated fat

---

155. Chilli Chocolate Cookies

Serving: Makes 40 cookies | Prep: 20mins | Cook: 12mins | Ready in:

Ingredients

- 225g unsalted butter, softened
- 100g caster sugar
- 175g dark muscovado sugar
- 2 tsp vanilla extract
- 2 eggs, beaten
- 300g plain flour
- 50g cocoa powder
- 1 tsp baking powder
- 1 ½ tsp cayenne pepper (less or more to taste)
- 100g bar dark chilli chocolate, roughly chopped
- 100g bar white chocolate, roughly chopped
- 100g bar dark chocolate, roughly chopped
- vanilla ice cream

Direction

- Beat the butter and sugars together, then gradually mix in the vanilla and eggs. In another bowl, combine the flour, cocoa, a pinch of salt, baking powder and cayenne pepper, then mix these into the butter and fold in all the chocolate.
- Heat oven to 180C/160C fan/gas 4. Place walnut-sized spoonfuls of the mixture on baking sheets lined with baking parchment, leaving enough space between so they don't melt together. Bake in batches, for 10-12 mins, depending on how gooey you like your cookies. Allow to cool on the baking sheets for 1 min before removing to a plate to cool completely. Serve with vanilla ice cream.

Nutrition Information

- Calories: 142 calories
- Fiber: 1 grams fiber
- Saturated Fat: 5 grams saturated fat
- Protein: 2 grams protein
- Total Fat: 8 grams fat
- Sugar: 11 grams sugar
- Sodium: 0.2 milligram of sodium
- Total Carbohydrate: 17 grams carbohydrates

---

156. Choc Chunk, Cashew & Cranberry Cookies

Serving: Makes 30 | Prep: 20mins | Cook: 12mins | Ready in:

Ingredients

- 100g pack cashew nuts, or more if you like
- 140g unsalted butter, at room temperature, plus extra for greasing
- 250g plain flour
- ½ tsp baking powder
- 200g white caster sugar

- 100g crunchy cashew nut butter, or use peanut butter
- 1 large egg, beaten
- 2 tbsp golden syrup
- 200g bar chocolate, 50% cocoa solids, chopped into 1cm chunks
- 50g dried cranberries (optional)

Direction

- Heat oven to 180C/160C fan/gas 4. Scatter the cashews over a baking tray and toast for 5-7 mins until golden. Cool, then roughly chop.
- Meanwhile, grease and line 2 baking sheets with parchment. Sift the flour, baking powder and 1/2 tsp salt into a large bowl, then stir in the sugar. Cut the butter into rough cubes, and add this and the nut butter to the bowl. Rub together until the mixture resembles damp breadcrumbs.
- Using a cutlery knife, work the egg and syrup into the bowl to make a soft dough. Tip in the chocolate, nuts and cranberries (if using), and stir to combine. Try not to overwork the dough at this point.
- Roll slightly heaped tablespoons of dough into balls and place onto each baking sheet, leaving plenty of room for the cookies to spread. Bake for 12 mins or until golden at the edges and risen in the middle. Let them cool for 5 mins, then move to a rack to cool completely. Repeat until all the dough is shaped and baked. To make ahead, freeze the raw cookies on a baking sheet, then transfer to a freezer bag or box once solid. Bake from frozen, adding 5 mins to the cooking time.

Nutrition Information

- Calories: 178 calories
- Protein: 3 grams protein
- Sodium: 0.1 milligram of sodium
- Total Carbohydrate: 21 grams carbohydrates
- Fiber: 1 grams fiber
- Total Fat: 9 grams fat
- Saturated Fat: 4 grams saturated fat
- Sugar: 13 grams sugar

157. Chocolate & Hazelnut Thumbprint Cookies

Serving: Makes 25 | Prep: 20mins | Cook: 20mins | Ready in:

Ingredients

- 180g hazelnuts, toasted
- 100g plain flour
- 90g buckwheat flour
- 60g golden caster sugar
- 180g unsalted butter
- 100g dark chocolate, roughly chopped
- 1 tsp coconut oil (or use any flavourless oil)

Direction

- Line a baking tray with baking parchment. Tip the hazelnuts into the bowl of a food processor and pulse until finely chopped. Add the flours, sugar and a pinch of flaked sea salt, and process for 20-30 secs until fully combined. Add the butter and pulse until the mixture just starts to come together. Tip the dough out onto a work surface and knead by hand until smooth.
- Roll the dough into 25 small balls, then transfer to the prepared baking tray. Using your thumb or the handle of a wooden spoon, make an indent in the centre of each piece of dough. Put the tray in the fridge and chill for 30 mins before baking. Heat oven to 180C/160C fan/gas 4.
- Bake in the oven for 15-20 mins or until light golden brown. Put the chocolate and oil in a heatproof bowl and set over a pan of simmering water, stirring occasionally, until fully melted. Use a teaspoon to top each cookie with a little melted chocolate. Put aside until the chocolate has set.

Nutrition Information

- Calories: 163 calories
- Fiber: 1 grams fiber
- Protein: 2 grams protein
- Total Fat: 12 grams fat
- Saturated Fat: 5 grams saturated fat
- Total Carbohydrate: 9 grams carbohydrates
- Sugar: 4 grams sugar

- Total Fat: 20 grams fat
- Sodium: 0.44 milligram of sodium
- Saturated Fat: 8 grams saturated fat
- Total Carbohydrate: 27 grams carbohydrates
- Sugar: 17 grams sugar
- Protein: 4 grams protein
- Fiber: 2 grams fiber

158. Chocolate Chunk Pecan Cookies

Serving: Makes 12 | Prep: | Cook: 12mins | Ready in:

Ingredients

- 200g dark chocolate, broken into squares (we like Green & Black's)
- 100g butter, chopped
- 50g light muscovado sugar
- 85g golden caster sugar
- 1 tsp vanilla extract
- 1 egg, beaten
- 100g whole pecan
- 100g plain flour
- 1 tsp bicarbonate of soda

Direction

- Heat oven to 180C/fan 160C/gas 4. Melt 85g chocolate in the microwave on High for 1 min or over a pan of simmering water.
- Beat in the butter, sugars, vanilla and egg until smooth, then stir in three-quarters of both the nuts and remaining chocolate, then the flour and bicarbonate of soda.
- Heap 12 spoonfuls, spaced apart, on 2 baking sheets (don't spread the mixture), then poke in the reserved nuts and chocolate. Bake for 12 mins until firm, then leave to cool on the sheets. Can be stored in a tin for up to 3 days.

Nutrition Information

- Calories: 294 calories

159. Clove Sugar Cookies

Serving: Makes about 28 | Prep: 30mins | Cook: 15mins | Ready in:

Ingredients

- 250g butter, softened
- 100g hazelnuts
- 1 tsp vanilla extract
- 250g icing sugar
- 1 ½ tsp ground cloves
- 350g plain flour

Direction

- Put the butter, hazelnuts, vanilla extract and 85g of the icing sugar in a food processor and whizz to a paste. Add 1 tsp of the ground cloves and the flour, and pulse together until a dough forms.
- Heat oven to 200C/180C fan/gas 6. Line a couple of baking sheets with baking parchment. Roll the dough into walnut- sized balls and arrange on the baking sheets. Use the back of a fork to lightly squash each ball, then bake for 12-15 mins until they turn a pale biscuit colour – if they get too brown, they will become dry.
- Mix the remaining icing sugar and ground cloves, then sieve thickly over the hot biscuits. Leave to cool slightly before eating just warm, or cool.

Nutrition Information

- Calories: 168 calories

- Total Carbohydrate: 19 grams carbohydrates
- Fiber: 1 grams fiber
- Protein: 2 grams protein
- Sugar: 10 grams sugar
- Sodium: 0.11 milligram of sodium
- Total Fat: 10 grams fat
- Saturated Fat: 5 grams saturated fat

160.   Cookie Dough Pizza

Serving: 15 | Prep: 15mins | Cook: 25mins | Ready in:

Ingredients

- 185g butter, softened
- 185g golden caster sugar
- 150g soft light brown sugar
- 2 medium eggs, beaten
- 2 tsp vanilla extract
- 335g self raising flour
- 1 tsp salt
- 200g chocolate chips
- 200g dark chocolate, melted
- 25g giant white chocolate buttons
- 25g mini marshmallows
- 25g strawberries, hulled and sliced

Direction

- Heat the oven to 180C/160 fan/ gas 4. Beat the butter and sugars together in a large bowl using an electric whisk or table top mixer. Pour in the beaten eggs and vanilla, beating well until combined.
- Sift in the flour and salt and fold until evenly combined. Scatter over the chocolate chips and stir until they are rippled throughout the dough.
- Roll into a big round cookie and place onto a large baking sheet covered with parchment. If the dough feels very soft at this stage pop it in the fridge for 30 mins to firm up. Bake in the preheated oven for 25 mins until golden at the edges and still a little wobbly in the middle. Leave to cool for a couple of mins before

topping. Spread the melted chocolate over the cookie, sprinkle with giant chocolate buttons, mini marshmallows and strawberries. Cut into about 15 slices and serve while it is still a little warm.

Nutrition Information

- Calories: 432 calories
- Fiber: 2 grams fiber
- Protein: 5 grams protein
- Saturated Fat: 12 grams saturated fat
- Total Fat: 21 grams fat
- Total Carbohydrate: 55 grams carbohydrates
- Sodium: 0.8 milligram of sodium
- Sugar: 36 grams sugar

161.   Double Choc Peanut Butter Cookies

Serving: 12 | Prep: 20mins | Cook: 10mins | Ready in:

Ingredients

- 100g unsalted butter, softened at room temperature
- 100g light brown sugar
- 100g caster sugar
- 1 egg, beaten
- 150g self-raising flour
- 2 tbsp cocoa powder
- ¼ tsp salt
- 200g milk chocolate, 150g chopped into chunks and 50g melted for drizzling
- 75g peanut butter (crunchy or smooth is fine)
- handful of salted peanuts, roughly chopped
- milk to serve, optional

Direction

- Heat the oven to 180c/160 fan/gas mark 4 and line two baking trays with parchment. Using a food mixer or electric whisk beat the butter and sugar together until light and fluffy. Add in the egg and whisk to combine then beat in the flour, cocoa powder, salt and chocolate chunks until fully incorporated. Using a spoon swirl the peanut butter through the cookie dough.

- Scoop the dough into 12 large cookies onto the two trays using a dessert spoon, leaving plenty of room between each cookie as they'll spread. Bake in the oven for 9-10 mins until still soft and melty in the middle. They will look underbaked but will harden once cool. Drizzle over the melted milk chocolate and top with a few chopped peanuts and a pinch of flaky sea salt. Serve with a glass of milk for dunking.

Nutrition Information

- Calories: 328 calories
- Sodium: 0.4 milligram of sodium
- Saturated Fat: 9 grams saturated fat
- Total Carbohydrate: 36 grams carbohydrates
- Sugar: 26 grams sugar
- Fiber: 2 grams fiber
- Total Fat: 19 grams fat
- Protein: 6 grams protein

162. Double Ginger Cookies

Serving: Makes 24 | Prep: 20mins | Cook: 12mins | Ready in:

Ingredients

- 350g plain flour
- 1 tbsp ground ginger
- 1 tsp bicarbonate of soda
- 175g light muscovado sugar
- 100g butter, chopped
- 8 pieces of stem ginger, chopped (not too finely), plus thin slices, to decorate (optional)
- 1 large egg
- 4 tbsp golden syrup
- 200g bar dark chocolate, chopped

Direction

- Mix the flour, ground ginger, bicarbonate of soda, 1/2 tsp salt and sugar in a bowl, then rub in the butter to make crumbs. Stir in the chopped stem ginger.
- Beat together the egg and syrup, pour into the dry ingredients and stir, then knead with your hands to make a dough. Cut the dough in half and shape each piece into a thick sausage about 6cm across, making sure that the ends are straight. Wrap in cling film and chill for 20 mins. You can now freeze all or part of the dough for 2 months.
- Heat oven to 180C/160C fan/gas 4 and line 2 baking sheets with baking parchment. Thickly slice each sausage into 12 and put the slices on the baking sheets, spacing them well apart and reshaping any, if necessary, to make rounds. Bake for 12 mins, then leave to cool for a few mins to harden before transferring to a wire rack to cool completely.
- Melt the chocolate in a bowl over a pan of gently simmering water, making sure that the water isn't touching the bottom of the bowl. Dip half of each cookie into the chocolate – you may need to spoon it over when you get to the final few. Decorate with a slice of ginger, if you like, and leave to set. Will keep for 1 week in an airtight container.

Nutrition Information

- Calories: 180 calories
- Total Fat: 7 grams fat
- Sugar: 13 grams sugar
- Fiber: 2 grams fiber
- Saturated Fat: 4 grams saturated fat
- Total Carbohydrate: 25 grams carbohydrates
- Sodium: 0.2 milligram of sodium
- Protein: 2 grams protein

163. Double Dipped Shortbread Cookies

Serving: Makes 15 | Prep: 20mins | Cook: 30mins | Ready in:

Ingredients

- 200g salted butter, softened
- 100g icing sugar
- 1 tsp vanilla extract
- 250g plain flour
- 1 tbsp milk, plus extra if needed
- 50g white chocolate, chopped
- 50g milk chocolate, chopped

Direction

- Heat the oven to 180C/160C fan/gas 4. Beat the butter with the icing sugar using an electric whisk until the mixture is light and fluffy. Beat in the vanilla and flour (the mixture will stiffen and look like crumble as the flour is added). Add the milk and keep beating until the mixture softens and sticks together (add some more milk if needed).
- Scoop the dough into a piping bag fitted with a large star nozzle and pipe swirled rings onto a baking sheet lined with baking parchment. If the mixture is too stiff to pipe easily, you can roll the dough into balls and put them on the sheet instead. The cookies will spread as they cook so don't worry if there's a small gap in the centre of the piped swirls, but ensure there is enough space between each cookie so they don't stick together as they cook. Bake for 15 mins, or until lightly golden, then transfer to a wire rack to cool.
- Put the white and milk chocolate in separate bowls and microwave each in 20-second bursts until melted. Dip the cookies into each chocolate, milk at one end and white on the other, then let any excess drip off before returning them to the rack to set. Will keep in an airtight tin for up to four days.

Nutrition Information

- Calories: 224 calories
- Total Carbohydrate: 23 grams carbohydrates
- Sugar: 10 grams sugar
- Sodium: 0.2 milligram of sodium
- Fiber: 1 grams fiber
- Protein: 2 grams protein
- Saturated Fat: 8 grams saturated fat
- Total Fat: 13 grams fat

164. Forgotten Cookies

Serving: Makes 32 | Prep: 30mins | Cook: | Ready in:

Ingredients

- 2 large egg whites
- 120g golden caster sugar
- 120g pecan, roughly chopped
- 150g dark chocolate (at least 70% cocoa solids), roughly chopped
- 1 tsp vanilla extract

Direction

- Preheat the oven to 180C/gas 4/fan 160C. Line two baking sheets with foil to cover. In a large clean bowl, whisk the egg whites with a pinch of salt until stiff and dry. Gradually whisk in the sugar a little at a time to make a thick and glossy meringue. Tip in the pecan nuts and chocolate, then the vanilla extract and gently fold into the meringue with a large metal spoon.
- Spoon heaped teaspoonfuls of the meringue mixture, spaced apart, on to the lined baking sheets. Put the sheets in the oven, then turn it off and leave the cookies for at least 3 hours, overnight or until the oven is cold.
- Carefully peel the cookies from the foil. Store in an airtight tin where they will keep for 3-4 days.

Nutrition Information

- Calories: 66 calories
- Total Carbohydrate: 7 grams carbohydrates
- Sugar: 7 grams sugar
- Protein: 1 grams protein
- Sodium: 0.06 milligram of sodium
- Total Fat: 1 grams fat

165. Freezer Biscuits

Serving: Makes 30 biscuits | Prep: | Cook: 15mins | Ready in:

Ingredients

- 200g pack butter, softened
- 200g soft brown sugar
- 2 eggs
- 1 tsp vanilla extract
- 200g self-raising flour
- 140g oats
- Your choice of flavours
- 50g chopped nuts such as pecan, hazelnuts or almonds
- 50g desiccated coconut
- 50g raisin, or mixed fruit

Direction

- When the butter is really soft, tip it into a bowl along with the sugar. Using an electric hand whisk or exercising some arm muscle, beat together until the sugar is mixed through. Beat in the eggs, one at a time, followed by the vanilla extract and a pinch of salt, if you like. Stir in the flour and oats. The mixture will be quite stiff at this point. Now decide what else you would like to add – any or all of the flavours are delicious – and stir through.
- Tear off an A4-size sheet of greaseproof paper. Pile up half the mixture in the middle of the sheet, then use a spoon to thickly spread the mixture along the centre of the paper. Pull over one edge of paper and roll up until you get a tight cylinder. If you have problems getting it smooth, then roll as you would a

rolling pin along a kitchen surface. You'll need it to be about the width of a teacup. When it is tightly wrapped, twist up the ends and then place in the freezer. Can be frozen for up to 3 months.

- To cook, heat oven to 180C/fan 160C/gas 4 and unwrap the frozen biscuit mix. Using a sharp knife, cut off a disk about ½cm wide. If you have difficulty slicing through, dip the knife into a cup of hot water. Cut off as many biscuits as you need, then pop the mix back into the freezer for another time. Place on a baking sheet, spacing them widely apart as the mixture will spread when cooking, then cook for 15 mins until the tops are golden brown. Leave to cool for at least 5 mins before eating.

Nutrition Information

- Calories: 138 calories
- Total Fat: 8 grams fat
- Protein: 2 grams protein
- Sodium: 0.21 milligram of sodium
- Total Carbohydrate: 16 grams carbohydrates
- Saturated Fat: 5 grams saturated fat
- Sugar: 8 grams sugar
- Fiber: 1 grams fiber

166. Fruity Cookies

Serving: Makes 20 | Prep: 20mins | Cook: 25mins | Ready in:

Ingredients

- 200g butter
- 175g soft brown sugar
- 2 tbsp thin-cut marmalade
- 2 tsp ground mixed spice
- 1 tsp ground cinnamon
- 1 tsp ground ginger
- 175g porridge oats
- 200g self-raising flour, plus extra for dusting
- 2 tsp baking powder

- 175g dried fruit - try chopped glacé cherries, apricots and sultanas
- 100g nuts, chopped (we used hazelnuts)

Direction

- Heat oven to 160C/140C fan/gas 3. Cream the butter and sugar until light and fluffy. Mix the marmalade with 2 tbsp boiling water. Stir into the creamed mix, then add the spices, oats, flour and baking powder. Mix in the fruit and nuts.
- Dust your hands and surface with flour and roll the dough into a long sausage shape. Cut into about 20 discs. Place on a baking tray lined with baking parchment, spaced out as they will spread. Bake for about 25 mins until golden brown.

Nutrition Information

- Calories: 236 calories
- Total Fat: 12 grams fat
- Total Carbohydrate: 30 grams carbohydrates
- Sugar: 16 grams sugar
- Protein: 4 grams protein
- Sodium: 0.42 milligram of sodium
- Saturated Fat: 6 grams saturated fat
- Fiber: 2 grams fiber

---

167. Gingerbread Cookies

Serving: Makes 20 cookies | Prep: 20mins | Cook: 12mins | Ready in:

Ingredients

- 120g unsalted butter, softened
- 1½ tbsp black treacle
- 170g soft light brown sugar
- ½ tsp fine sea salt
- 1 medium egg
- 200g plain flour
- ¼ tsp bicarbonate of soda

- ¼ tsp ground cloves
- 1½ tsp ground ginger
- ½ tsp ground cinnamon
- 60g golden caster sugar

Direction

- Beat together the butter, treacle, brown sugar and salt in a large mixing bowl. Add the egg, then beat through all of the remaining dry ingredients apart from the caster sugar. Chill the mixture in the fridge for 1 hr.
- Heat the oven to 200C/180C fan/gas 4. Line two baking sheets with baking parchment. Roll the mixture into 20 even-sized balls (weighing for accuracy, if you like). Tip the caster sugar onto a small plate, then add each ball and roll around to coat. Space each ball out on the baking sheets. Bake for 9-10 mins until golden brown. Leave to cool completely on a wire rack.

Nutrition Information

- Calories: 135 calories
- Protein: 1 grams protein
- Sodium: 0.18 milligram of sodium
- Saturated Fat: 3 grams saturated fat
- Total Carbohydrate: 20 grams carbohydrates
- Fiber: 1 grams fiber
- Total Fat: 5 grams fat
- Sugar: 12 grams sugar

---

168. Hazelnut & Chocolate Cookie Sandwiches

Serving: Makes 12 | Prep: 20mins | Cook: 12mins | Ready in:

Ingredients

- 120g unsalted butter, softened
- 100g light brown soft sugar
- 75g golden caster sugar

- ½ tsp fine sea salt
- 1 medium egg, lightly beaten
- 1 tsp vanilla extract
- 200g plain flour
- ¼ tsp bicarbonate of soda
- 100g milk chocolate, roughly chopped
- 70g skinless hazelnuts, roughly chopped and toasted
- 120g chocolate hazelnut spread

Direction

- Heat the oven to 200C/180C fan/gas 4. Line two baking sheets with baking parchment and set aside.
- Cream the butter with both sugars in a large mixing bowl using an electric whisk, then beat in the salt, egg and vanilla. Stir in the flour, bicarbonate of soda, chocolate and hazelnuts using a wooden spoon until well combined.
- Scoop the dough onto the baking sheets in 24 heaps, well spaced apart. Bake for 10-12 mins or until lightly golden at the edges. Remove from the oven and allow to cool completely on the baking sheets. Spread 1 tsp of chocolate spread on the bottoms of half the cookies, then sandwich with the other halves. Will keep in a cake tin or airtight container for up to five days.

Nutrition Information

- Calories: 336 calories
- Total Carbohydrate: 37 grams carbohydrates
- Total Fat: 18 grams fat
- Protein: 4 grams protein
- Saturated Fat: 8 grams saturated fat
- Sugar: 24 grams sugar
- Fiber: 2 grams fiber
- Sodium: 0.5 milligram of sodium

169. Macadamia & Cranberry American Cookies

Serving: Makes 55 | Prep: 20mins | Cook: 12mins |Ready in:

Ingredients

- 3 x 200g/7oz white chocolate bars, chopped
- 200g butter
- 2 eggs
- 100g light muscovado sugar
- 175g golden caster sugar
- 2 tsp vanilla extract
- 350g plain flour
- 2 tsp baking powder
- 1 tsp cinnamon
- 100g dried cranberry
- 100g macadamia nut, chopped

Direction

- Heat oven to 180C/160C fan/gas 4. Melt 170g of the chocolate, then allow to cool. Beat in the butter, eggs, sugars and vanilla, preferably with an electric hand whisk, until creamy. Stir in the flour, baking powder, cinnamon and cranberries with two-thirds of the remaining chocolate and macadamias, to make a stiff dough.
- Using a tablespoon measure or a small ice-cream scoop, drop small mounds onto a large baking dish, spacing them well apart, then poke in the reserved chocolate, nuts and berries. Bake in batches for 12 mins until pale golden, leave to harden for 1-2 mins, then cool on a wire rack.
- To freeze, open-freeze the raw cookie dough scoops on baking trays; when solid, pack them into a freezer container, interleaving the layers with baking parchment. Use within 3 months. Bake from frozen for 15-20 mins.

Nutrition Information

- Calories: 149 calories
- Saturated Fat: 4 grams saturated fat

- Total Carbohydrate: 18 grams carbohydrates
- Sugar: 13 grams sugar
- Protein: 2 grams protein
- Sodium: 0.14 milligram of sodium
- Total Fat: 8 grams fat

170. Mango Crunch Cookies

Serving: Makes about 14 large or 28 small cookies | Prep: 15mins | Cook: 15mins | Ready in:

Ingredients

- 140g butter, at room temperature
- 50g golden caster sugar
- 1 egg yolk
- 1 tsp vanilla extract
- 1 tbsp maple syrup
- 100g dried mango, roughly chopped
- 175g plain flour, plus extra for dusting
- To decorate (optional)
- 200g icing sugar, sifted
- 3 tbsp mango juice
- sprinkles

Direction

- Heat the oven to 180C/160C fan/gas 4. Place the butter and sugar in a food processor and blitz until smooth and creamy. Add the egg yolk, vanilla, maple syrup and mango. Whizz to blend in and chop the mango a little more finely. Add the flour and briefly blitz to form a soft dough. Turn out onto a floured surface and shape into a ball. Chill for 20 mins.
- Using a rolling pin, roll the cookie dough to the thickness of a £1 coin on a lightly floured surface, then cut out biscuit shapes with a 10cm cutter for large, or a 5cm cutter for smaller cookies.
- Transfer to a baking tray lined with baking parchment, and cook for 12-15 mins or until lightly golden and firm. Remove and leave to cool on a wire rack.

- If decorating, mix the icing sugar with the mango juice to make a runny icing. Drizzle or spoon the icing over the biscuits, then add the sprinkles if using, and leave to set. Will keep in a biscuit tin for up to 1 week.

Nutrition Information

- Calories: 156 calories
- Total Fat: 5 grams fat
- Fiber: 1 grams fiber
- Total Carbohydrate: 17 grams carbohydrates
- Sodium: 0.2 milligram of sodium
- Protein: 2 grams protein
- Saturated Fat: 1 grams saturated fat
- Sugar: 8 grams sugar

171. Oatmeal Raisin Cookies

Serving: Makes 25 | Prep: 15mins | Cook: 15mins | Ready in:

Ingredients

- 100g raisin
- 150ml vegetable oil
- 200g golden caster sugar
- 1 large egg, beaten
- 1 tsp ground cinnamon
- 1 tsp vanilla extract
- 140g plain flour
- ¼ tsp bicarbonate of soda
- 300g oats

Direction

- Heat oven to 180C/160C fan/gas 4 and line 2 baking trays with baking parchment. Pour 50ml/2fl oz boiling water over the raisins and leave to soak for 20 mins until plump. Drain, reserving the liquid.
- Meanwhile, in a large bowl, mix together the oil and sugar. Gradually beat in the egg, along with the reserved water from the raisins, the

cinnamon and vanilla extract. Sift the flour, bicarbonate of soda and a pinch of salt into the bowl, then add the oats. Finally, mix in the raisins.

- Drop heaped tbsps of the cookie dough onto the baking trays, well spaced apart as they will spread when cooking. Bake for 12-15 mins until golden. Leave to cool on the trays for 10 mins before tucking in, or transfer to a cooling rack to cool completely. Will keep in an airtight container for up to 3 days.

Nutrition Information

- Calories: 166 calories
- Total Fat: 7 grams fat
- Sodium: 0.2 milligram of sodium
- Total Carbohydrate: 22 grams carbohydrates
- Sugar: 11 grams sugar
- Fiber: 2 grams fiber
- Protein: 3 grams protein
- Saturated Fat: 1 grams saturated fat

172.   Oaty Hazelnut Cookies

Serving: makes 9 | Prep: 15mins | Cook: 30mins | Ready in:

Ingredients

- 50g butter, plus a little for greasing
- 2 tbsp maple syrup
- 1 dessert apple, unpeeled and coarsely grated (you need 85g)
- 1 tsp cinnamon
- 50g raisins
- 50g porridge oats
- 50g spelt flour
- 40g unblanched hazelnuts, cut into chunky slices
- 1 egg

Direction

- Heat oven to 180C/160C fan/gas 4 and lightly grease a non-stick baking tray (or line a normal baking tray with baking parchment). Tip the butter and syrup into a small non-stick pan and melt together, then add the apple and cook, stirring, over a medium heat until it softens, about 6-7 mins. Stir in the cinnamon and raisins.
- Mix the oats, spelt flour, and hazelnuts in a bowl, pour in the apple mixture, then add the egg and beat everything together really well.
- Spoon onto the baking tray, well spaced apart to make 9 mounds, then gently press into discs. Bake for 18-20 mins until golden, then cool on a wire rack. Will keep for 3 days in an airtight container or 6 weeks in the freezer.

Nutrition Information

- Calories: 146 calories
- Saturated Fat: 3 grams saturated fat
- Sugar: 8 grams sugar
- Fiber: 2 grams fiber
- Protein: 2 grams protein
- Total Carbohydrate: 15 grams carbohydrates
- Sodium: 0.1 milligram of sodium
- Total Fat: 8 grams fat

173.   Orange Pumpkin Face Cookies

Serving: Makes 12 | Prep: | Cook: | Ready in:

Ingredients

- 140g butter, softened
- 175g plain flour
- 50g icing sugar
- finely grated zest 1 medium orange
- For the filling
- 100g mascarpone
- 1 tsp icing sugar
- 25g plain chocolate (55% cocoa solids is fine), melted

- For the glaze
- 50g icing sugar
- about 1 tbsp orange juice

Direction

- Preheat the oven to fan 160C/ conventional 180C/gas 4. Put the butter in a bowl and beat with a wooden spoon until smooth. Add the flour, icing sugar and orange zest and beat together to make a softish dough. Knead into a ball and wrap in cling film. Chill for 1 hour.
- Roll the dough out on a lightly floured surface to a thickness of about 3mm. Cut 24 circles with a 7.5 cm round plain cutter. Put them on a couple of baking sheets.
- Using a small sharp knife, cut out Hallowe'en faces on 12 of the circles. Gather up the spare biscuit dough and press into pumpkin stem shapes, trimming with a sharp knife. Press to the top of each biscuit with a knife to join. Make lines on the face biscuits with the back of a roundbladed knife, to look like the markings on a pumpkin. Bake all the biscuits for about 15 minutes until pale golden. Leave to set for a while, then cool completely on a wire rack.
- Mix the glaze ingredients to make a smooth, runny icing, adding a bit more juice if needed, then set aside. For the filling, beat the mascarpone with the icing sugar, then stir in the cooled melted chocolate.
- Spread the filling over the cooled plain biscuits, then press the 'face' ones on top – do this just before you want to eat them, otherwise they go soft. Brush with the glaze, using a clean paint brush or pastry brush. Eat the same day.

Nutrition Information

- Calories: 219 calories
- Saturated Fat: 9 grams saturated fat
- Fiber: 1 grams fiber
- Protein: 2 grams protein
- Sugar: 10 grams sugar
- Sodium: 0.25 milligram of sodium
- Total Fat: 14 grams fat

- Total Carbohydrate: 22 grams carbohydrates

174.   Peanut Butter Cookies

Serving: Makes 16 | Prep: 15mins | Cook: 12mins | Ready in:

Ingredients

- 200g peanut butter (crunchy or smooth is fine)
- 175g golden caster sugar
- ¼ tsp fine table salt
- 1 large egg

Direction

- Heat oven to 180C/160C fan/gas 4 and line 2 large baking trays with baking parchment.
- Measure the peanut butter and sugar into a bowl. Add ¼ tsp fine table salt and mix well with a wooden spoon. Add the egg and mix again until the mixture forms a dough.
- Break off cherry tomato sized chunks of dough and place, well spaced apart, on the trays. Press the cookies down with the back of a fork to squash them a little. The cookies can now be frozen for 2 months, cook from frozen adding an extra min or 2 to the cooking time.
- Bake for 12 mins, until golden around the edges and paler in the centre. Cool on the trays for 10 mins, then transfer to a wire rack and cool completely. Store in a cookie jar for up to 3 days.

Nutrition Information

- Calories: 126 calories
- Total Carbohydrate: 12 grams carbohydrates
- Sodium: 0.2 milligram of sodium
- Sugar: 11 grams sugar
- Saturated Fat: 2 grams saturated fat
- Fiber: 0.5 grams fiber
- Protein: 4 grams protein
- Total Fat: 7 grams fat

175.   Rainbow Cookies

Serving: Makes 22 | Prep: 30mins | Cook: 15mins | Ready in:

Ingredients

- 175g softened butter
- 50g golden caster sugar
- 50g icing sugar
- 2 egg yolks
- 2 tsp vanilla extract
- 300g plain flour
- zest and juice 1 orange
- 140g icing sugar, sifted
- sprinkles, to decorate

Direction

- Heat oven to 200C/180C fan/gas 6. Mix the butter, sugars, egg yolks and vanilla with a wooden spoon until creamy, then mix in the flour in 2 batches. Stir in the orange zest. Roll the dough into about 22 walnut-size balls and sit on baking sheets. Bake for 15 mins until golden, then leave to cool.
- Meanwhile, mix the icing sugar with enough orange juice to make a thick, runny icing. Dip each biscuit half into the icing, then straight into the sprinkles. Dry on a wire rack.

Nutrition Information

- Calories: 168 calories
- Total Carbohydrate: 26 grams carbohydrates
- Sugar: 15 grams sugar
- Protein: 2 grams protein
- Sodium: 0.1 milligram of sodium
- Total Fat: 7 grams fat
- Saturated Fat: 4 grams saturated fat

176.   Red Nose Day Raspberry Cookies

Serving: Makes 14 | Prep: | Cook: | Ready in:

Ingredients

- 1 quantity basic biscuit dough - link in recipe
- 1 tsp cinnamon
- 6 tbsp raspberry jam
- 6 tbsp icing sugar, sifted
- icing, to decorate

Direction

- Heat oven to 180C/fan 160C/gas 4. Make up the basic biscuit dough (click here for the recipe), sifting in the cinnamon when you add the flour. Shape into 2 balls, wrap in cling film and chill for 20-30 mins.
- Roll out the dough on a lightly floured surface, then stamp out 28 biscuits with a 7-8cm wide cutter. Lay these on non-stick baking sheets. Using a 4cm cutter, cut out the 'noses' from half the biscuits. Bake for 10-12 mins until pale golden, then lift onto a cooling rack.
- Mix the raspberry jam with the sifted icing sugar. When the biscuits are cool, spoon a little of the jam onto each whole biscuit, then carefully sandwich the other biscuits on top. Serve as they are, or pipe icing, made with a little water, to draw funny faces.

Nutrition Information

- Calories: 295 calories
- Total Fat: 15 grams fat
- Total Carbohydrate: 39 grams carbohydrates
- Fiber: 1 grams fiber
- Protein: 2 grams protein
- Sugar: 22 grams sugar
- Saturated Fat: 10 grams saturated fat
- Sodium: 0.29 milligram of sodium

177. Red Velvet Cookies

Serving: Makes 16-18 | Prep: 20mins | Cook: 15mins | Ready in:

Ingredients

- 175g soft salted butter
- 200g light brown soft sugar
- 100g caster sugar
- 1 large egg
- 2 tsp vanilla extract
- ½-1 tbsp red food colouring gel, depending on strength
- 225g plain flour
- 25g cocoa powder
- ½ tsp bicarbonate of soda
- 150g white chocolate chips or chunks
- For the drizzle
- 2 tbsp soft cheese
- 6 tbsp icing sugar

Direction

- Beat the butter and sugars together with an electric whisk until pale and fluffy. Beat in the egg, vanilla and food colouring until you have a bright red batter. Sieve over the flour, cocoa and bicarb. Fold everything together to make a stiff evenly-coloured dough, then fold in the chocolate chips.
- Put the dough on a sheet of baking parchment, fold the parchment over the dough and mould into a sausage shape about 6cm wide. Chill until ready to bake. Will keep for a week in the fridge or one month in the freezer.
- Heat the oven to 190C/170C fan/gas 5. Cut the cookie dough into 1cm thick slices using a sharp knife and arrange on two large baking sheets lined with baking parchment well-spaced apart so they have room to spread in the oven. Bake in batches, keeping the unbaked cookies on the sheet in the fridge while the rest are baking.
- Bake in the middle of the oven for 13-15 mins until the cookies are crisp at the edges, but still soft in the centre. Leave to cool on the baking sheet for a few minutes, then transfer to a wire rack to cool completely. Beat the soft cheese in a small bowl to a loose consistency, then stir in the icing sugar. Use a piping bag or spoon to drizzle the icing over the cookies. Un-iced cookies keep for five days in an airtight container, or two days iced.

Nutrition Information

- Calories: 268 calories
- Saturated Fat: 7 grams saturated fat
- Sugar: 26 grams sugar
- Protein: 3 grams protein
- Sodium: 0.3 milligram of sodium
- Total Carbohydrate: 36 grams carbohydrates
- Fiber: 1 grams fiber
- Total Fat: 12 grams fat

178. Show Your Spots Cookie Sandwiches

Serving: Makes 20 | Prep: 30mins | Cook: 12mins | Ready in:

Ingredients

- 200g butter, softened
- 140g icing sugar
- 1 tsp vanilla extract
- 2 large eggs, 1 beaten for glazing
- 350g plain flour, plus extra for dusting
- 147g bag Smarties
- 4 tbsp hundreds and thousands
- 100g butter, softened
- 140g icing sugar
- ¼ tsp vanilla extract

Direction

- In a food processor, whizz the butter, icing sugar and vanilla until smooth. Add 1 egg and blend to combine, then tip in the flour and blitz once more. Scoop the dough into a ball and wrap in cling film. Chill for 30 mins.

- Heat oven to 200C/180C fan/gas 6. Dust 2 large baking trays with flour. Break the dough into large cherry-sized pieces. Roll into balls and put on the baking trays, spaced a little apart. Squash down the balls slightly with 3 fingers. Bake (in batches, if necessary) for 8 mins – the cookies will still be very pale at this stage.
- Remove the cookies from the oven. While still warm, quickly brush the tops with the beaten egg, then dip half in the hundreds & thousands, and press a few Smarties onto each of the remaining cookies – do this while the egg is still wet, so the toppings will stick once cooked. Bake for a further 4 mins. Leave to cool on wire racks.
- To make the icing, beat together the butter, icing sugar and vanilla. Once the cookies are completely cool, use the icing to sandwich together the 2 different cookies. Un-iced cookies can be made up to 4 days ahead and kept in an airtight container. You can fill with the icing up to 1 day ahead.

Nutrition Information

- Calories: 270 calories
- Sodium: 0.3 milligram of sodium
- Fiber: 1 grams fiber
- Protein: 3 grams protein
- Total Fat: 14 grams fat
- Saturated Fat: 9 grams saturated fat
- Total Carbohydrate: 32 grams carbohydrates
- Sugar: 19 grams sugar

179.   Sparkling Vanilla Christmas Cookies

Serving: Makes 20 biscuits | Prep: 10mins | Cook: 12mins | Ready in:

Ingredients

- 140g icing sugar, sieved

- 1 tsp vanilla extract
- 1 egg yolk
- 250g butter, cut into small cubes
- 375g plain flour, sieved
- To decorate
- 200g icing sugar, sieved
- edible food colouring, optional
- edible gold and silver balls
- approx 2m thin ribbon cut into 10cm lengths

Direction

- Tip the icing sugar, vanilla extract, egg yolk and butter into a mixing bowl, then stir together with a wooden spoon (or pulse in a food processor until well combined). Add the flour and mix to a firm dough. Shape the dough into two flat discs and wrap them. Chill for 20-30 mins. Heat oven to 190C/fan 170C/gas 5 and line two baking sheets with non-stick baking paper.
- Roll out the dough on a lightly floured surface to about the thickness of two £1 coins. Cut out Christmassy shapes (use a cutter if you like) and place on the baking sheets. Using the tip of a skewer, cut a small hole in the top of each cookie. Bake for 10-12 mins until lightly golden.
- Lift the biscuits onto a wire rack to cool. Meanwhile, mix the icing sugar with a few drops of cold water to make a thick, but still runny icing. Colour with edible food colouring, if you like. Spread it over the cooled biscuits, decorate with edible balls and thread with ribbon when dry.

Nutrition Information

- Calories: 233 calories
- Saturated Fat: 7 grams saturated fat
- Sodium: 0.2 milligram of sodium
- Total Carbohydrate: 34 grams carbohydrates
- Fiber: 1 grams fiber
- Protein: 2 grams protein
- Total Fat: 11 grams fat
- Sugar: 19 grams sugar

180. Sugar Dusted Vanilla Shortbread

Serving: Makes 35 biscuits | Prep: | Cook: 20mins | Ready in:

Ingredients

- 325g plain flour
- 200g chilled salted butter, plus a little more for the sheets
- 125g golden caster sugar
- 2 tsp good-quality vanilla extract
- 2large free range egg yolks
- icing sugar, for dusting

Direction

- Tip the flour into a food processor. Cut the butter into small pieces and drop them into the bowl, then whizz until the mixture looks like breadcrumbs. Add the sugar, vanilla and egg yolks and whizz to a smooth dough.
- With your hands, roll the dough on a lightly floured surface into a sausage shape about 25cm/9in long and 5cm/2½in in diameter. Wrap the roll and chill for at least 1 hour. (The roll can be frozen for up to 6 weeks. To use, remove from the freezer and allow to thaw for one hour at room temperature so that the dough is soft enough to be sliced into biscuits.)
- Preheat the oven to 180C/gas 4/fan 160C and lightly grease 2 large baking sheets. Using a sharp knife, cut the dough into slices, each a generous 5mm/¼in thick, then arrange them on the greased baking sheets, spacing the biscuits slightly apart so they have a bit of room to spread as they cook.
- Bake for 20 minutes until the biscuits are just turning pale golden around the edges, then transfer to a wire rack to cool. Dust generously with icing sugar. The biscuits will keep fresh for up to one week stored in an airtight tin.

181. Sugar Dusted Wedding Cookies

Serving: Makes about 60-70 - easily increased | Prep: 30mins | Cook: 20mins | Ready in:

Ingredients

- 250g salted butter, softened
- 140g caster sugar
- 1 egg, separated, plus 2 egg yolks
- 2 tsp vanilla extract
- 100g ground rice
- 300g plain flour
- 140g preserving sugar (or demerara sugar)

Direction

- In a large bowl, mix the butter, caster sugar, three yolks and vanilla with a wooden spoon until creamy. Stir in the ground rice and flour – you may need to get your hands in at the end to get all of the dry ingredients incorporated. Roughly divide the mixture into 3.
- Lay out 3 large sheets of greaseproof paper, and on each one, roll out a third of the dough into a long, thin sausage – about 1in thick. Use the paper to help you to roll it out as smoothly and evenly as possible. Lightly beat the egg white, then brush all over the dough. Scatter over the preserving sugar and roll so the dough is completely coated. Wrap up in the paper and carefully transfer to the fridge to chill for 30-40 mins until firm. At this stage you can freeze for up to 2 months, wrapped well in cling film.
- Heat oven to 200C/180C fan/gas 6. Using a sharp knife, slice each roll into roughly 20-30 small biscuits. Arrange over baking parchment-lined baking trays – they will spread a little so leave gaps. Bake for 8-12 mins until pale golden. Cool on the trays until firm. Can also be frozen at this stage for up to a month.

182. Toffee Apple Cookies

Serving: Makes 24 cookies | Prep: 15mins | Cook: 12mins | Ready in:

Ingredients

- 175g unsalted butter, at room temperature
- 140g golden caster sugar
- 2 egg yolks
- 50g ground almond
- 85g chewy toffees, roughly chopped
- 85g/3oz ready-to-eat dried apple chunks, roughly chopped
- 225g self-raising flour
- 2 tbsp milk

Direction

- Preheat the oven to fan 170C/conventional 190C/gas 5. Using an electric whisk, beat together the butter and sugar until pale and creamy.
- Stir in the egg yolks, ground almonds, toffees, dried apple and flour. Mix well together then roll into walnut-sized balls.
- Place well apart on two non-stick or lined baking sheets and flatten slightly with your hand. Brush with milk and bake for 8-12 minutes until golden. Leave to firm up for 5 minutes, then transfer to a wire rack and leave to cool completely.

Nutrition Information

- Calories: 148 calories
- Total Fat: 8 grams fat
- Sodium: 0.12 milligram of sodium
- Saturated Fat: 5 grams saturated fat
- Sugar: 7 grams sugar
- Fiber: 1 grams fiber
- Protein: 2 grams protein
- Total Carbohydrate: 17 grams carbohydrates

Chapter 6: Tray Bake Recipes

***

183. Apricot Crumb Squares

Serving: 16 | Prep: 25mins | Cook: 50mins | Ready in:

Ingredients

- 175g plain flour
- 140g light muscovado sugar
- 140g butter, softened
- 1 tsp ground cinnamon
- 175g butter, softened
- 200g golden caster sugar
- 3 large eggs
- 175g plain flour
- 1 tsp baking powder
- 2-3 tbsp milk
- 8 fresh apricots, quartered (or canned in natural juice)
- icing sugar for dusting

Direction

- Preheat oven to fan 160C/ conventional 180C/gas 4 and butter a shallow 22cm square cake tin. Put all the topping ingredients in a food processor with 1/2 tsp salt and blend to make a sticky crumble.
- Using an electric hand whisk or wooden spoon, blend the cake ingredients, except milk and apricots, gradually adding enough milk to make a creamy mixture that drops from the spoon. Spread in the tin and scatter with apricots. Top with the crumble and press down.
- Bake for 45-50 minutes until golden and a skewer comes out clean. Cool in tin, cut into 16 squares and dust with icing sugar. (Keeps up to 5 days in a plastic container in the fridge.)

Nutrition Information

- Calories: 332 calories
- Saturated Fat: 11 grams saturated fat
- Total Carbohydrate: 42 grams carbohydrates
- Sodium: 0.52 milligram of sodium
- Sugar: 22 grams sugar
- Fiber: 1 grams fiber
- Protein: 4 grams protein
- Total Fat: 18 grams fat

184. Banoffee Traybake

Serving: 12 | Prep: 20mins | Cook: 30mins |Ready in:

Ingredients

- 200g butter, softened, plus extra for the tin
- 2 large ripe bananas (250g peeled weight)
- 250g light brown soft sugar
- 4 large eggs
- 1½ tsp vanilla extract
- 250g self-raising flour
- 100g natural yogurt
- 100g dark chocolate, chopped into chunks
- 100g thick caramel or dulce de leche (we used a can of Carnation caramel)
- 12 dried banana chips, to serve (optional)

Direction

- Heat oven to 180C/160C fan/gas 4. Butter and line a 20 x 30cm baking tin with two strips of criss-crossed baking parchment. In a jug, mash the bananas with a fork, then add the butter and sugar and mix with an electric whisk until smooth and creamy.
- Add the eggs one at a time, beating well after each addition, then add the vanilla and a pinch of salt. Use a spatula to fold through the flour, yogurt and chocolate chunks. Scrape the mixture into the tin and smooth over the surface. Bake for 30 mins until risen and

golden and a skewer inserted into the centre of the cake comes out clean. Cool for 10 mins in the tin, then transfer to a wire rack.
- Cut the traybake into 12 squares, then top each one with a spoonful of caramel and a banana chip, if you like. Will keep in a tin for up to five days, or in the freezer – without the toppings – for up to a month.

Nutrition Information

- Calories: 406 calories
- Sodium: 0.7 milligram of sodium
- Total Fat: 20 grams fat
- Total Carbohydrate: 48 grams carbohydrates
- Saturated Fat: 12 grams saturated fat
- Fiber: 2 grams fiber
- Sugar: 31 grams sugar
- Protein: 7 grams protein

185. Blackberry & Apple Mallow Traybake

Serving: Makes 16 squares | Prep: 30mins | Cook: 1hours |Ready in:

Ingredients

- For the cake
- 140g unsalted butter, softened, plus a little for greasing
- 140g golden caster sugar
- 1 egg and 2 yolks, beaten together
- ½ tsp vanilla extract
- 100g self-raising flour
- 100g ground almond
- 1 tsp baking powder
- 1 tsp freshly grated nutmeg (or ½ ground)
- 1 large Bramley apple, about 200g, peeled and sliced (to give about 140g)
- 125g blackberry (avoid 'dessert' blackberries, as they lack bite)
- For the mallow and to finish
- 25g blackberry

- 100g white caster sugar, plus 1 tsp for the ripple
- 2 egg whites
- 1 tsp lemon juice
- 1-2 tbsp toasted flaked almond
- a little icing sugar, to dust (optional)

Direction

- First make the blackberry sauce to ripple through the mallow. Put the berries and 1 tsp sugar in a small bowl and cover with cling film. Microwave for 30 secs on High. Alternatively, add 1 tsp water then soften in a pan over a low heat. Mash well until saucy, then leave to cool.
- Heat oven to 160C/140C fan/gas 3. Grease and line the base and sides of a 23cm square traybake tin, leaving some overhang. Using electric beaters or a hand whisk, beat the butter and sugar in a large bowl until very pale and creamy, then beat in the egg and yolks, followed by the vanilla. Mix the flour, almonds, baking powder, nutmeg and a pinch of salt, then fold into the fluffy mix to make a very thick batter.
- Fold in the apple, then spoon into the tin and smooth over the top. Scatter with the blackberries, poke them in just a little, then bake for 45 mins until golden and a skewer inserted into the middle comes out clean. After removing, leave the oven on.
- For the mallow topping, you'll need a large piping bag with a 1cm nozzle, or a food bag with a corner snipped off. Whisk the egg whites, lemon juice and a pinch of salt to stiff peaks. Add the sugar 1 tbsp at a time, whisking well after each spoonful, to make a shiny, stiff meringue. Ripple with the cooled blackberry mix, then spoon into the bag. Pipe 16 evenly spaced, walnut-sized meringues on top of the cake (you'll have some left over), scatter with the toasted almonds, then bake for 10-12 mins until the meringues are just set. Cool in the tin for 30 mins, then remove to a rack to cool completely. Add a dusting of icing sugar, if you like, then cut into squares.

Nutrition Information

- Calories: 207 calories
- Sugar: 17 grams sugar
- Total Carbohydrate: 21 grams carbohydrates
- Fiber: 1 grams fiber
- Saturated Fat: 5 grams saturated fat
- Protein: 3 grams protein
- Total Fat: 12 grams fat
- Sodium: 0.2 milligram of sodium

---

186. Blackberry & Coconut Squares

Serving: Cuts into 12 squares | Prep: 15mins | Cook: 1hours15mins |Ready in:

Ingredients

- 250g self-raising flour
- 25g oats
- 280g soft brown sugar
- 200g cold butter, cut into pieces
- 75g desiccated coconut
- 2 medium eggs, beaten
- 350g frozen or fresh blackberry

Direction

- Heat oven to 180C/160C fan/gas 4. Tip the flour, oats and sugar into a large bowl. Rub the butter into the flour mixture using your fingertips until only small pea-size pieces remain. Stir through the coconut, then fill a teacup with the mixture and set this aside.
- Stir the eggs into the bowl of mixture, then spread over the bottom of a lined baking tin (31 x 17cm), or a 21cm square tin. Smooth the surface with the back of a spoon, then scatter over the blackberries. Scatter over the reserved teacup mixture and bake for 1 hr-1 hr 15 mins until golden and cooked through (if you poke a skewer in, it should come out with moist

crumbs but no wet mixture). Leave to cool, then remove from the tin and cut into squares. Serve with some extra berries, if you like. Great for teatime or to pop into a lunchbox.

Nutrition Information

- Calories: 347 calories
- Sugar: 26 grams sugar
- Total Carbohydrate: 43 grams carbohydrates
- Fiber: 3 grams fiber
- Protein: 4 grams protein
- Total Fat: 19 grams fat
- Sodium: 0.5 milligram of sodium
- Saturated Fat: 12 grams saturated fat

187. Blueberry Lemon Cake With Coconut Crumble Topping

Serving: 16 | Prep: | Cook: 45mins |Ready in:

Ingredients

- 300g butter, softened
- 425g caster sugar
- zest 1 lemon
- 6 eggs, beaten
- 250g self-raising flour
- 300g blueberry
- 200g desiccated coconut
- 200g lemon curd

Direction

- Heat oven to 180C/fan 160/gas 4 and grease and line a 20 x 30 cm cake tin with baking parchment. Beat together 250g of the butter with 250g sugar and the lemon zest until light and fluffy. In a separate bowl, break up 4 eggs with a fork, then gradually beat into the butter and sugar mixture, adding a spoonful of flour if it begins to curdle. When the eggs are incorporated, fold in the flour and a third of the blueberries, then spoon into the tin. Flatten

the surface with a spatula, sprinkle over another third of the blueberries, and bake for 20 mins until the surface is set.

- To make the topping, melt the rest of the butter, then stir in the coconut and remaining sugar and eggs until combined. Warm the lemon curd gently for a few mins in a small pan until it is runny and pourable.
- After the initial baking, scatter the remaining blueberries over the top of the cake, drizzle over the lemon curd, and crumble over the coconut mixture. Bake for a further 20-25 mins until the coconut is golden. Leave the cake in the tin to cool. Cut into 16 squares and store in a tin, interlined with greaseproof paper.

Nutrition Information

- Calories: 446 calories
- Total Carbohydrate: 50 grams carbohydrates
- Sugar: 34 grams sugar
- Saturated Fat: 17 grams saturated fat
- Protein: 5 grams protein
- Fiber: 43 grams fiber
- Sodium: 0.55 milligram of sodium
- Total Fat: 27 grams fat

188. Butternut Bakewell Bars

Serving: Serves 20 | Prep: 45mins | Cook: 1hours50mins |Ready in:

Ingredients

- Seville orange marmalade, for spreading
- 1 small butternut squash
- 200g pecans
- 100g softened butter
- 150g light brown sugar
- 2 large eggs
- 1 tsp cinnamon
- 150g light spelt flour
- ½ tsp baking powder
- 1 orange, zested

- 250g light spelt flour
- 150g cold butter, cut into cubes
- 1 egg yolk
- 50g icing sugar
- good pinch cinnamon
- a few pecans, toasted and roughly chopped

Direction

- Heat oven to 180C/160C fan/gas 4. Halve the butternut lengthways, scrape out and discard the pith and seeds, then put in a roasting tin, cut-side down. Roast in the oven for 1 hr 10 mins until completely soft. When it has 20 mins left, cook the pecans on a baking tray in the oven, then leave to cool. Scrape the flesh out of the butternut and purée in a food processor. Set both aside to cool. The purée and pecans can be prepared up to three days ahead.
- For the pastry, blitz together the flour, butter and a pinch of salt in a food processor until it resembles coarse breadcrumbs. Add the egg and pulse until the pastry comes together. Wrap in cling film and chill for 2 hrs.
- Heat oven to 200C/180C fan/gas 6. Butter and line a 20 x 30cm loose-bottomed baking tin. Roll out the pastry, then lift into the tin. Don't worry if it falls apart a little, patch it up with your fingers and press down into the corners. Chill for 20 mins, then prick the base all over with a fork and bake for 10-12 mins until lightly coloured. Reduce oven to 180C/160C fan/gas 4.
- Grind the pecans in a food processor, then tip into a large bowl with all the sponge filling ingredients and a pinch of salt. Beat with an electric whisk until well combined. Warm the marmalade, then spread over the pastry. Smooth the cake batter on top and bake for 20-25 mins. Leave to cool.
- Mix the icing sugar with the cinnamon and enough water to make a thick drizzling consistency. Drizzle over the cake and scatter over the pecans. Once the icing is set, cut into 20 bars.

Nutrition Information

- Calories: 299 calories
- Fiber: 2 grams fiber
- Saturated Fat: 7 grams saturated fat
- Total Carbohydrate: 27 grams carbohydrates
- Sugar: 13 grams sugar
- Protein: 5 grams protein
- Sodium: 0.3 milligram of sodium
- Total Fat: 19 grams fat

---

189.   Coconut & Jam Macaroon Traybake

Serving: Makes 16-20 | Prep: 15mins | Cook: 30mins | Ready in:

Ingredients

- 250g caster sugar
- 4 egg whites, beaten
- 1 tsp vanilla extract
- 300g desiccated coconut
- 25g plain flour
- 200g raspberry jam
- 100g dark chocolate, chopped

Direction

- Line a 20 x 30cm baking tin with baking parchment. Heat the oven to 180C/160C fan/gas 4.
- Mix the sugar, egg whites, vanilla and a pinch of salt together in a bowl. Add the coconut and flour and stir until thoroughly combined – the mixture will be quite thick and sticky. Tip into the tin and gently spread out with a spatula. Dot the jam over the top using a teaspoon, nestling it into the batter. Bake for 25-30 mins, until set and golden around the edges. Leave to cool completely in the tin.
- Melt the chocolate in the microwave, or in a bowl set over a pan of simmering water. Remove the cake from the tin, drizzle with chocolate and leave to set before cutting into

squares. Will keep in an airtight container for up to a week.

Nutrition Information

- Calories: 210 calories
- Fiber: 3 grams fiber
- Total Carbohydrate: 23 grams carbohydrates
- Protein: 2 grams protein
- Total Fat: 11 grams fat
- Sugar: 21 grams sugar
- Sodium: 0.1 milligram of sodium
- Saturated Fat: 9 grams saturated fat

---

190. Coconut Carrot Slices

Serving: 15 | Prep: 10mins | Cook: 40mins | Ready in:

Ingredients

- 250g pack unsalted butter
- 300g light muscovado sugar
- 1 tsp vanilla extract
- 3 large eggs
- 200g self-raising flour
- 50g desiccated coconut
- 200g grated carrot
- 2 tsp mixed spice
- For the topping
- 85g desiccated coconut
- 25g light muscovado sugar
- 25g butter, melted

Direction

- Butter and line a traybake or small roasting tin, about 20 x 30cm. Heat oven to 180C/160C fan/gas 4. Gently melt the butter in a large saucepan, cool for 5 mins, add the sugar, vanilla and eggs, then beat until smooth with a wooden spoon. Stir in the flour, coconut and ¼ tsp salt. Stir the carrot and mixed spice into the mix. Bake for 30 mins.

- Meanwhile, evenly mix 85g more coconut with 25g light muscovado sugar and 25g melted butter. Smooth this over the cake, then bake for 10 mins more until golden and a skewer inserted comes out clean. Cool, then cut into squares.

Nutrition Information

- Calories: 347 calories
- Total Carbohydrate: 35 grams carbohydrates
- Total Fat: 22 grams fat
- Sodium: 0.22 milligram of sodium
- Sugar: 25 grams sugar
- Fiber: 2 grams fiber
- Protein: 4 grams protein
- Saturated Fat: 15 grams saturated fat

---

191. Dorset Apple Traybake

Serving: Cuts into 16 pieces | Prep: 20mins | Cook: 50mins | Ready in:

Ingredients

- 225g butter, softened, plus extra for the tin
- 450g cooking apples (such as Bramley)
- ½ lemon, juiced
- 280g golden caster sugar
- 4 eggs
- 2 tsp vanilla extract
- 350g self-raising flour
- 2 tsp baking powder
- demerara sugar, to sprinkle

Direction

- Heat the oven to 180C/160C fan/gas 4. Butter and line a rectangular baking tin (approx 27 x 20cm) with baking parchment. Peel, core and thinly slice the apples, then squeeze over the lemon juice. Set aside.
- Put the butter, caster sugar, eggs, vanilla, flour and baking powder into a large bowl and mix

well until smooth. Spread half the mixture into the prepared tin. Arrange half the apples over the top of the mixture, then repeat the layers. Sprinkle over the demerara sugar.

- Bake for 45-50 mins until golden and springy to the touch. Leave to cool for 10 mins, then turn out of the tin and remove the paper. Cut into bars or squares.

Nutrition Information

- Calories: 285 calories
- Total Fat: 13 grams fat
- Saturated Fat: 8 grams saturated fat
- Protein: 4 grams protein
- Sodium: 0.7 milligram of sodium
- Total Carbohydrate: 39 grams carbohydrates
- Sugar: 23 grams sugar
- Fiber: 1 grams fiber

| 192. | Double Choc & Coconut Traybake |

Serving: Makes 12 squares | Prep: 30mins | Cook: 40mins | Ready in:

Ingredients

- 200g unsalted butter, softened
- 100g golden caster sugar
- 100g light brown soft sugar
- 3 large eggs
- 60g desiccated coconut
- 200g self-raising flour
- 100g Greek yogurt
- ½ tsp coconut flavouring (optional, see tip below)
- For the topping
- 200g milk or dark chocolate, chopped into small pieces
- 200ml double cream
- 40g white chocolate, melted
- handful of coconut flakes, toasted, or desiccated coconut or sprinkles

Direction

- Line a 22 x 28cm rectangular cake tin with baking parchment. Heat the oven to 180C/160C fan/gas 4.
- First, prepare the topping. Put the milk or dark chocolate pieces in a large heatproof bowl. Heat the double cream in a medium pan until just steaming, then slowly pour over the chocolate, whisking until the chocolate has melted and the mix is smooth. Leave to cool slightly, then chill for 1 hr 30 mins until soft, but still spoonable.
- Beat the butter, sugars and ¼ tsp salt together in a stand mixer or using an electric whisk for 5 mins, or until light and fluffy. Add the eggs one at a time, beating well after each addition. Add the desiccated coconut, flour, yogurt and coconut flavouring, if using, and briefly beat until just combined. Spoon the mix into the tin, smooth the surface using the back of a spoon, then bake for 30 mins until golden and firm to the touch. Leave in the tin to cool completely.
- When fully cool, spread over the chocolate topping, then drizzle with the white chocolate and scatter over the toasted coconut flakes. Chill for around 15 mins until the topping is set. Cut into 12 squares, then serve.

Nutrition Information

- Calories: 513 calories
- Total Carbohydrate: 41 grams carbohydrates
- Fiber: 2 grams fiber
- Total Fat: 35 grams fat
- Protein: 6 grams protein
- Sodium: 0.4 milligram of sodium
- Saturated Fat: 23 grams saturated fat
- Sugar: 28 grams sugar

| 193. | Fruity Flag Traybake |

Serving: Cuts into 15 squares | Prep: 45mins | Cook: 30mins | Ready in:

Ingredients

- 100g butter or baking spread (Stork for cakes), softened, plus extra for the tin
- 175g self-raising flour
- 50g ground almond
- 2 tsp baking powder
- 4 large eggs
- 225g caster sugar
- 125ml full-fat Greek yogurt
- zest 2 lemons
- For the butter icing
- 175g butter, softened
- 350g icing sugar, sieved
- To decorate
- 300g raspberry
- 175g blueberry

Direction

- Heat oven to 180C/160C fan/gas 4. Butter and line a 30 x 20cm traybake tin with baking parchment. Measure all the sponge ingredients into a mixing bowl and mix together using an electric hand whisk until smooth. Spoon into the tin and level the surface.
- Bake for 25-30 mins until lightly golden and the top of the cake springs back when pressed with your finger, and the sides of the sponge are shrinking away from the sides of the tin. Carefully lift the sponge out of the tin, then transfer to a wire rack to cool. Remove the baking parchment.
- To make the icing, tip the butter into a bowl and whisk using an electric hand whisk until light and fluffy. Add half the icing sugar and whisk again until incorporated. Add the remaining sugar and whisk again until smooth. Spread the icing over the top of the cold cake.
- To decorate, place a double row of raspberries across the centre and down the length of the cake to make a cross. Next, place a single row diagonally from each corner to the middle. Now fill in the empty spaces with blueberries. Cut into squares to serve.

Nutrition Information

- Calories: 390 calories
- Saturated Fat: 11 grams saturated fat
- Total Carbohydrate: 49 grams carbohydrates
- Protein: 4 grams protein
- Sugar: 41 grams sugar
- Fiber: 1 grams fiber
- Total Fat: 20 grams fat
- Sodium: 0.6 milligram of sodium

---

194.   Fruity Traybake

Serving: Cuts into 15 pieces | Prep: 20mins | Cook: 40mins | Ready in:

Ingredients

- 175ml vegetable oil, plus extra for greasing
- 175g dark muscovado sugar
- 3 large eggs
- 1 small ripe banana, mashed
- 140g grated eating apple
- 100g grated carrot
- 1 small mango, peeled and cut into small dice
- zest 1 lemon
- 250g self-raising flour
- 1 tsp bicarbonate of soda
- 1 tsp mixed spice
- For the icing
- 225g icing sugar, sieved
- For the icing
- 75g passion fruit or lemon curd
- 75g cream cheese

Direction

- Heat oven to 180C/160C fan/gas 4. Grease and line a 22cm square tin with baking parchment. Whisk the oil and sugar in a large mixing bowl until light and fluffy. Beat in the eggs, one at a time, followed by the banana. Stir through the apples, carrots, mango and lemon zest. Combine the flour, bicarb and mixed spice in another bowl, then fold into the fruit mixture.

- Pour the mixture into the tin and bake for 40 mins, until a skewer inserted comes out clean. Cool for 10 mins before turning out onto a wire rack.

- To make the icing, beat together the icing sugar, passion fruit or lemon curd and the cream cheese. Spread over the top of the cake and cut into square pieces to serve.

Nutrition Information

- Calories: 339 calories
- Sodium: 0.4 milligram of sodium
- Fiber: 2 grams fiber
- Protein: 3 grams protein
- Total Fat: 16 grams fat
- Saturated Fat: 4 grams saturated fat
- Total Carbohydrate: 45 grams carbohydrates
- Sugar: 33 grams sugar

---

195.   Gingery Plum Cake

Serving: Cuts into 16 squares | Prep: 25mins | Cook: 1hours | Ready in:

Ingredients

- butter, for greasing
- 2 tbsp demerara sugar
- 500g plum
- For the cake
- 175g butter
- 175g dark muscovado sugar
- 140g golden syrup
- 2 eggs, beaten
- 200ml milk
- 300g self-raising flour
- ½ tsp bicarbonate of soda
- 1 tbsp ground ginger
- 1 tsp mixed spice

Direction

- Heat oven to 180C/160C fan/gas 4. Grease and line the base of a 23cm square cake tin with baking parchment. Butter the paper generously and sprinkle with the demerara sugar. Halve the plums and arrange in the base of the tin in 1 layer, cut-sides down.

- For the cake, melt the butter, muscovado sugar and syrup in a large pan over a low heat, stirring until smooth. Cool for 10 mins, then stir in the eggs and milk. Sift in the flour, bicarbonate of soda and spices, then mix to a smooth batter.

- Pour the batter into the tin, over the plums, and bake for 45-55 mins until firm to the touch. Cool in the tin for 10 mins, then turn out onto a wire rack and leave to cool. Will keep in the fridge, wrapped in baking parchment and foil, for up to 5 days.

Nutrition Information

- Calories: 252 calories
- Sugar: 24 grams sugar
- Saturated Fat: 6 grams saturated fat
- Sodium: 0.5 milligram of sodium
- Fiber: 1 grams fiber
- Total Fat: 11 grams fat
- Total Carbohydrate: 36 grams carbohydrates
- Protein: 3 grams protein

---

196.   Lemon & Raspberry Doughnut Pudding

Serving: Serves 8-10 | Prep: 15mins | Cook: 10mins | Ready in:

Ingredients

- butter, for the baking dish
- 8 raspberry jam doughnut
- 150g raspberries
- 500ml shop-bought fresh custard
- 250ml whole milk
- 150g lemon curd

Direction

- Heat the oven to 200C/180C fan/gas 6 and butter a 20 x 20cm baking dish. Quarter the raspberry jam doughnuts and arrange in overlapping layers in the prepared dish. Scatter over 100g raspberries.
- Heat the custard with the milk until steaming, then whisk through the lemon curd. Pour the lemon custard over the doughnuts, then leave to soak for 30 mins, ensuring some of the doughnuts stick out so they'll crisp up when baked.
- Scatter over another 50g raspberries and bake for 35-40 mins, or until golden brown and just set.

Nutrition Information

- Calories: 314 calories
- Sodium: 0.7 milligram of sodium
- Sugar: 27 grams sugar
- Fiber: 2 grams fiber
- Protein: 6 grams protein
- Total Carbohydrate: 46 grams carbohydrates
- Total Fat: 12 grams fat
- Saturated Fat: 5 grams saturated fat

---

197.   Lemon Drizzle Flapjacks

Serving: Makes 12 | Prep: 15mins | Cook: 25mins | Ready in:

Ingredients

- 250g butter
- 250g soft brown sugar
- 175g golden syrup
- 425g porridge oats
- 150g lemon curd
- 50g icing sugar
- ½ lemon, juiced

Direction

- Heat oven to 180C/160C fan/gas 4 and line a 20 x 20 cm tin with baking parchment. Melt the butter, sugar and golden syrup in a pan until bubbling. Tip in the oats and stir until everything is well coated. Press ¾ into the tin, spread over the lemon curd then sprinkle over the remaining flapjack mix. Bake for 30 mins then leave to cool.
- Mix the icing sugar with the lemon juice then drizzle across the cooled flapjack and cut into 12 pieces.

Nutrition Information

- Calories: 473 calories
- Total Carbohydrate: 66 grams carbohydrates
- Fiber: 3 grams fiber
- Protein: 4 grams protein
- Sodium: 0.5 milligram of sodium
- Total Fat: 21 grams fat
- Sugar: 42 grams sugar
- Saturated Fat: 11 grams saturated fat

---

198.   Lighter Spiced Carrot Cake

Serving: Cuts into 15 squares | Prep: 30mins | Cook: 30mins | Ready in:

Ingredients

- 125ml rapeseed oil, plus a little extra for greasing
- 300g wholemeal flour
- 2 tsp baking powder
- 1 tsp bicarbonate of soda
- 1 tbsp mixed spice
- 100g dark soft brown sugar
- 140g carrot, grated
- 140g sweet potato, peeled and grated
- 200g sultana
- 2 large eggs
- 4 tbsp agave syrup
- juice 2 oranges

- For the icing
- 200g quark
- 50g fromage frais
- 3 tbsp icing sugar, sifted
- zest 1 orange

Direction

- Heat oven to 180C/160C fan/gas 4. Grease and line a 20 x 30cm traybake tin with baking parchment. Mix together the flour, baking powder, bicarb, spice and sugar in a big mixing bowl. Stir in the grated carrots, sweet potatoes and sultanas. In a jug, whisk together the eggs, rapeseed oil, agave syrup and juice from 1 orange. Tip the wet ingredients into the bowl and stir to combine, then scrape into the tin. Bake for 25-30 mins until a skewer poked in comes out clean. Prick all over with a skewer and drizzle over the remaining orange juice. Cool in the tin.
- Once cool, make the icing. Stir the quark with a spoon to make it a bit smoother, then fold in the fromage frais, icing sugar and orange zest. Spread all over the cake and slice into squares to eat.

Nutrition Information

- Calories: 269 calories
- Fiber: 3 grams fiber
- Total Carbohydrate: 38 grams carbohydrates
- Total Fat: 10 grams fat
- Saturated Fat: 1 grams saturated fat
- Sugar: 25 grams sugar
- Protein: 6 grams protein
- Sodium: 0.4 milligram of sodium

---

199. Morello Cherry & Almond Traybake

Serving: Cuts into 24 | Prep: 40mins | Cook: 35mins | Ready in:

Ingredients

- 300g butter, softened, plus extra for greasing
- 300g golden caster sugar
- 375g self-raising flour, plus extra for dusting
- zest 1 lemon (save the juice for the icing)
- 85g ground rice or ground almonds
- 4 eggs, lightly beaten
- 25g marzipan, chilled until firm, then grated
- 2 tsp almond extract
- 1 tsp baking powder
- 3 tbsp whole milk
- 200g morello glacé cherries, washed, dried and quartered
- For the icing and decoration
- 500g fondant icing sugar
- juice 1 lemon (from the lemon above)
- 50g marzipan
- red and green food colouring gels (we used Dr Oetker)

Direction

- Heat oven to 180C/160C fan/gas 4. Grease and line a large square traybake tin, about 28 x 28cm, with baking parchment. Put all the cake ingredients (apart from the cherries) in a large mixing bowl or tabletop mixer and beat together until thoroughly combined. Toss the cherries in a little flour, then fold them into the cake mixture using a spatula. Spoon the mixture into the prepared tin and bake for 30-35 mins until the cake is golden brown, springy to the touch, and a skewer inserted into the centre comes out clean. Leave to cool completely in the tin.
- To make the icing, sift the icing sugar into a bowl, then add the lemon juice and enough water to make a thick yet fairly fluid icing. Transfer 3 tbsp of the icing to a small bowl and set aside. Spoon the remaining icing over the cooled cake – it should be liquid enough to level itself out; if not, use a knife to smooth it. Knead the marzipan to soften it, then incorporate enough red food colouring to turn it bright red. Roll into 48 cherry balls.

- When the icing is almost set, place 2 balls directly next to each other on the icing, in rows of 4, with enough space between each to cut 24 equal pieces. Colour the reserved icing with green food colouring, then transfer to a piping bag fitted with a very fine nozzle, or simply snip off the end, and pipe cherry stalks next to the marzipan balls. When all the icing is completely set, take the cake out of the tin and cut into 24 pieces.

Nutrition Information

- Calories: 334 calories
- Protein: 4 grams protein
- Total Carbohydrate: 48 grams carbohydrates
- Sodium: 0.4 milligram of sodium
- Total Fat: 14 grams fat
- Saturated Fat: 7 grams saturated fat
- Sugar: 36 grams sugar
- Fiber: 1 grams fiber

200.   Nutty Florentine Bars

Serving: Cuts into 18-21 bars | Prep: 15mins | Cook: 50mins | Ready in:

Ingredients

- 225g salted butter, at room temperature
- 175g golden caster sugar
- ¼ tsp almond extract
- 200g plain flour, plus 1 tbsp extra
- 100g ground rice
- 75ml double cream
- 50g toasted flaked almonds
- 25g whole blanched almonds
- 25g walnuts, roughly chopped
- 25g pecans
- 25g blanched hazelnuts, halved
- 50g glacé cherries, sliced
- 25g dried cherries
- 50g dark chocolate, melted

Direction

- Start with the base. Line a 20cm square tin with some baking parchment. Put 200g of the butter and 100g of the sugar in a food processor and whizz until smooth. Add the almond extract, flour and ground rice, and pulse until the mixture comes together. Press the mixture into the base of your tin, flattening the surface as much as possible. Chill for at least 30 mins, or for up to 2 days.
- Heat oven to 180C/160C fan/gas 4. Peel off the cling film, prick the base a few times with the prongs of a fork. Bake for 25 mins.
- Meanwhile, put the remaining 25g butter, 75g sugar and 1 tbsp flour in a small pan. Heat gently, stirring, until the butter and sugar have melted. Stir in the cream until smooth, then the nuts, glacé and dried cherries.
- When the base has baked, dot the hot nut mixture all over the top and gently spread with the back of a spoon. Return to oven and bake for another 10-20 mins until the top is golden – check every 5 mins. Cool to room temperature, then melt the dark chocolate in a microwave or in a bowl over, but not touching, a pan of hot water. Drizzle the chocolate all over the top, and leave to set solid before removing and cutting into thin bars.

Nutrition Information

- Calories: 257 calories
- Total Fat: 16 grams fat
- Saturated Fat: 8 grams saturated fat
- Total Carbohydrate: 24 grams carbohydrates
- Fiber: 1 grams fiber
- Protein: 3 grams protein
- Sugar: 12 grams sugar
- Sodium: 0.2 milligram of sodium

201. Orange & Passion Fruit Traybake

Serving: Serves 12-16 | Prep: 20mins | Cook: 25mins | Ready in:

Ingredients

- 150g margarine or butter, plus extra for the tin
- 150g caster sugar
- 3 eggs
- 150g self-raising flour
- 1 orange, zested and juiced
- For the mascarpone topping
- 250g tub mascarpone
- 1 tbsp icing sugar
- 4 tbsp fresh orange juice
- 1 tsp vanilla extract
- 2 passion fruit

Direction

- Heat oven to 180C/160C fan/gas 4. Butter and line a 20 x 24cm cake tin with baking parchment. Cream the margarine or butter with the caster sugar using an electric whisk until light and fluffy, then beat in the eggs one at a time. Sieve in the flour and fold it in. Add the orange zest and juice, fold that in as well, then pour into the prepared tin, smoothing over the top. Bake for 25 mins until golden. A skewer should come out clean when inserted in the middle.
- Remove the cake from the oven, leave for 5 mins, then remove from the tin, peel away the parchment and leave to cool on a wire rack.
- Meanwhile, make the topping by mixing the mascarpone, icing sugar, orange juice and vanilla until smooth. Cut open the passion fruit, scoop out the seeds, then add half to the mix, reserving the rest.
- Use a palette knife to spread the topping over the cooled cake, then drizzle over the remaining passion fruit seeds.

Nutrition Information

- Calories: 231 calories
- Sugar: 12 grams sugar
- Total Fat: 16 grams fat
- Saturated Fat: 6 grams saturated fat
- Protein: 3 grams protein
- Sodium: 0.2 milligram of sodium
- Fiber: 1 grams fiber
- Total Carbohydrate: 19 grams carbohydrates

202. Peach Melba Squares

Serving: 12 | Prep: 10mins | Cook: 1hours | Ready in:

Ingredients

- 250g pack unsalted butter
- 300g golden caster sugar
- 1 tsp vanilla extract
- 3 large eggs
- 200g self-raising flour
- 50g ground almonds
- 2 just-ripe peaches, stoned, halved, then each half cut into 3
- 100g raspberries
- handful flaked almonds
- 1 tbsp icing sugar, to finish

Direction

- Butter and line a traybake or small roasting tin, about 20 x 30cm. Heat oven to 180C/160C fan/gas 4. Gently melt the butter in a large saucepan, cool for 5 mins, add the sugar, vanilla and eggs, then beat until smooth with a wooden spoon. Stir in the flour, almonds and ¼ tsp salt.
- Tip the mix into the tin, then lay the peach slices evenly on top – that way each square of cake will have a bite of fruit. Scatter the raspberries and almonds over, then bake for 1 hr-1 hr 10 mins, covering with foil after 40 mins. Test with a skewer: the middle should have just a tiny hint of squidginess, which will

firm up once the cake cools. Cool in the tin for 20 mins, then lift out onto a cooling rack. Once cold, dredge with icing sugar, then cut into squares.

Nutrition Information

- Calories: 385 calories
- Total Fat: 23 grams fat
- Sugar: 31 grams sugar
- Protein: 5 grams protein
- Sodium: 0.22 milligram of sodium
- Saturated Fat: 12 grams saturated fat
- Fiber: 2 grams fiber
- Total Carbohydrate: 43 grams carbohydrates

203. Plum & Almond Crumble Slice

Serving: Cuts into 16 slices | Prep: 15mins | Cook: 1hours5mins | Ready in:

Ingredients

- 250g pack butter (this must be very cold)
- 225g caster sugar
- 300g ground almond
- 140g plain flour, plus 25g/1oz
- 2 eggs
- 1 tsp cinnamon
- 1 tsp baking powder
- approx 6 plums, stoned and cut into sixths
- 50g flaked almond

Direction

- Heat oven to 180C/fan 160C/gas 4. Butter and line a 20 x 30cm baking tin with baking paper. Put the butter, sugar and ground almonds into a food processor, then pulse until the mixture resembles very rough breadcrumbs. Spoon out half the mix into a bowl and set aside.
- Add 140g flour into the mix in the processor and whizz until it just forms a dough. Tip into

the tin and press down with the back of a spoon. Bake for 15-20 mins until golden. Leave to cool for 10 mins.

- To make the filling, put the remaining butter and the sugar and almond mix back into the processor, saving a few tbsp for the topping. Add the eggs, the 25g flour, cinnamon and baking powder and whizz to a soft batter. Spread over the base.
- Top with the plum pieces and a little extra caster sugar and cinnamon. Bake for 20 mins, then sprinkle with the remaining crumble mix and flaked almonds. Cook for another 20 mins or until golden. Leave to cool in the tin before slicing.

Nutrition Information

- Calories: 360 calories
- Sugar: 18 grams sugar
- Fiber: 2 grams fiber
- Saturated Fat: 9 grams saturated fat
- Total Fat: 26 grams fat
- Total Carbohydrate: 26 grams carbohydrates
- Protein: 7 grams protein
- Sodium: 0.37 milligram of sodium

204. Plum, Raspberry Jam & Cardamom Crumble Squares

Serving: 16 | Prep: 30mins | Cook: 55mins | Ready in:

Ingredients

- 4 cardamom pods, seeds crushed
- 1 tbsp lemon juice (reserve the lemon, see below)
- 250g low-sugar, high-fruit raspberry jam
- 10 slightly unripe plums, halved and stoned (you may need more, depending on size)
- For the pastry
- 125g cold butter, cut into chunks, plus extra for the tin
- 150g ground almonds

- 150g plain flour
- 115g caster sugar
- ½ lemon, zested
- ½ tsp vanilla extract
- For the crumble
- 50g plain flour
- 35g ground almonds
- 45g cold butter, cut into small chunks
- 50g light brown soft sugar
- ½ lemon, zested
- 25g flaked almonds
- icing sugar, for dusting (optional)

Direction

- Butter and line a 30 x 20cm baking tin with baking parchment, leaving an overhang so you can lift out the traybake later, then butter the parchment. Heat the oven to 180C/160C fan/gas 4.
- To make the pastry, put all the ingredients, except the vanilla, into a food processor and blitz until the mixture resembles breadcrumbs. Add a couple of teaspoons of very cold water and the vanilla, then blitz again. The mixture should come together into a ball. If it doesn't, add a little more cold water and blitz again. Press into the tin using your fingers and the back of a large spoon, then bake in the oven for 15-18 mins until pale golden. Leave to cool for 15 mins.
- Stir the cardamom seeds and the lemon juice into the jam until smooth. Spread the jam over the pastry base, leaving a 2cm border all the way round. Cut each plum half into 1cm slices. Lay these in rows, overlapping, on top of the jam.
- To make the crumble, put the flour, ground almonds, butter, sugar and lemon zest into a food processor (you don't need to wash it out first), and blitz until the mixture looks like breadcrumbs. Tip this over the plums and scatter the flaked almonds on top. Bake for about 35-40 mins until the top is golden and the plums are tender. Leave to cool completely in the tin.

- Carefully lift the traybake out of the tin onto your work surface using the baking parchment. Leave for a few hours so the fruit can settle. Cut into squares or rectangles, then sift some icing sugar over the top, if you like.

Nutrition Information

- Calories: 294 calories
- Total Carbohydrate: 31 grams carbohydrates
- Saturated Fat: 6 grams saturated fat
- Sodium: 0.2 milligram of sodium
- Sugar: 21 grams sugar
- Fiber: 1 grams fiber
- Protein: 5 grams protein
- Total Fat: 16 grams fat

205.	Raspberry & Almond Traybake

Serving: Cuts into 16-24 slices | Prep: | Cook: |Ready in:

Ingredients

- 250g self-raising flour
- 50g ground almonds
- 200g butter, diced
- 280g golden granulated sugar
- 50g desiccated coconut
- 2 medium eggs
- 350-450g/12oz-1lb fresh or frozen raspberries

Direction

- Heat the oven to 180C/fan160C/gas 4. Butter an oblong cake tin (about 31 x 17 x 3cm). Tip the flour, ground almonds, butter and sugar into a food processor and whizz just until the butter is evenly distributed – or rub together by hand. Remove 85g/3oz of the mix, stir in the coconut and put to one side. Add the eggs to the remaining mixture in the food processor and whizz quickly – or mix with a wooden spoon. It doesn't need to be very smooth.

- Spread this mixture over the base of the tin, then scatter half the raspberries over the top. Sprinkle with the coconut mixture and bake for 45 mins. Dot the remaining fruit over the surface and cook for a further 15 mins, until firm to the touch. Cool in the tin and cut into slices, squares, whichever shape you want. They will keep for up to 2 days in the fridge.

Nutrition Information

- Calories: 179 calories
- Total Fat: 10 grams fat
- Total Carbohydrate: 21 grams carbohydrates
- Sugar: 12 grams sugar
- Protein: 3 grams protein
- Fiber: 1 grams fiber
- Saturated Fat: 6 grams saturated fat
- Sodium: 0.3 milligram of sodium

206. Raspberry & Apple Crumble Squares

Serving: Cuts into 16 | Prep: 15mins | Cook: 50mins | Ready in:

Ingredients

- 1 Bramley apple, peeled and diced
- 100g butter, softened
- 175g golden caster sugar
- 1 egg
- 280g self-raising flour
- 125ml milk
- 200g raspberries
- For the crumble topping
- 50g butter, diced
- 85g self-raising flour
- 100g golden caster sugar
- zest 1 lemon

Direction

- Heat oven to 180C/160C fan/gas 4 and line a 20 x 30cm cake tin with baking parchment. Put the apple in a small pan with 2 tbsp water. Cook for a few mins or until the apple starts to soften.
- Meanwhile, make the crumble topping. Rub the butter into the flour, sugar and lemon zest until it resembles big breadcrumbs, then set aside.
- Beat the butter and sugar in a large bowl until fluffy, then gradually add the egg. Tip in the flour and milk, and continue to beat until everything is combined. Incorporate the apples then spoon the mixture into the tin, smooth the surface, then dot with the raspberries. Sprinkle over the crumble topping and bake for 45 mins or until a skewer inserted comes out clean, and the topping is golden.

Nutrition Information

- Calories: 230 calories
- Protein: 3 grams protein
- Saturated Fat: 5 grams saturated fat
- Total Carbohydrate: 37 grams carbohydrates
- Sugar: 21 grams sugar
- Sodium: 0.35 milligram of sodium
- Total Fat: 9 grams fat
- Fiber: 1 grams fiber

207. Raspberry & Blueberry Lime Drizzle Cake

Serving: Cuts into 12 pieces | Prep: 25mins | Cook: 1hours | Ready in:

Ingredients

- For the cake
- 225g softened butter, plus extra for greasing
- 225g golden caster sugar
- 4medium eggs
- 2 limes, grated zest and juice

- 250g self-raising flour, sifted with a pinch of salt, plus extra flour
- 25g ground almond
- 100g each blueberry and raspberries
- For the syrup
- 8 tbsp lime juice (about 4 limes)
- 1 lime, grated zest
- 140g golden caster sugar

Direction

- Line the base and sides of a 20cm/8in square cake tin (not loose-based) with greaseproof paper and butter the paper. Set oven to 180C/Gas 4/fan oven 160C.
- Cream the butter and sugar together until light. Gradually beat in the eggs, adding a little flour towards the end to prevent curdling. Beat in the lime zest, then fold in the flour and almonds. Fold in enough lime juice – about 3 tablespoons – to give you a good dropping consistency (the mixture should drop easily from the spoon when tapped).
- Fold in three quarters of the blueberries and raspberries and turn into the prepared tin. Smooth the surface, then scatter the remaining fruit on top – it will sink as the cake rises.
- Bake for about 1 hour (cover with foil if beginning to brown too much), or until firm to a gentle prod in the centre. A skewer pushed into the centre should be clean when removed.
- Meanwhile make the syrup: put the lime juice, zest and sugar in a small saucepan. Put over a gentle heat and stir, without allowing to bubble. The sugar should dissolve a little. As soon as the cake comes out of the oven, prick all over with a skewer then spoon the syrup over it. To store, cool before wrapping in paper and/or foil.
- Carefully remove the cake from the tin, discard the lining paper and cut into 12 pieces to serve.

Nutrition Information

- Calories: 370 calories
- Total Carbohydrate: 49 grams carbohydrates
- Sodium: 0.61 milligram of sodium
- Total Fat: 19 grams fat
- Protein: 5 grams protein
- Saturated Fat: 10 grams saturated fat
- Sugar: 32 grams sugar
- Fiber: 1 grams fiber

208. Raspberry & White Chocolate Financier Traybake

Serving: Serves 8 (or 4-6 with leftovers) | Prep: 20mins | Cook: 30mins | Ready in:

Ingredients

- 200g butter, plus extra for the tin
- 200g golden caster sugar
- 100g plain flour
- 100g ground almonds
- small pinch of ground cinnamon
- 6 large egg whites (freeze the egg yolks for another recipe)
- 150g raspberries
- 100g white chocolate chips or chunks
- icing sugar, for dusting
- 227g tub clotted cream, to serve

Direction

- Melt the butter in a small pan until sizzling. Watch it carefully – the butter will foam, and, when the foam subsides, it will turn from yellow to a nutty brown. Remove from the heat, tip into a bowl to stop it cooking and leave to cool.
- Heat the oven to 180C/160C fan/gas 4. Butter a 20 x 25cm baking tin at least 4cm deep and line with baking parchment. Mix the sugar, flour, almonds and cinnamon together. Beat the egg whites in a separate large bowl using an electric whisk to soft peaks. Fold the beaten egg whites into the flour mix using a large metal spoon. Slowly pour in the brown butter, folding it in until everything is combined and

the batter is light. Scrape into the prepared tin. Scatter over the raspberries and chocolate.

- Bake for 20-25 mins until firm. Leave to cool in the tin, then dust with some icing sugar and cut into squares or bars. Will keep, well wrapped, for up to three days at room temperature. Serve with clotted cream.

Nutrition Information

- Calories: 494 calories
- Protein: 8 grams protein
- Saturated Fat: 16 grams saturated fat
- Sugar: 33 grams sugar
- Total Fat: 32 grams fat
- Sodium: 0.6 milligram of sodium
- Total Carbohydrate: 43 grams carbohydrates
- Fiber: 1 grams fiber

---

209. Raspberry & White Chocolate Traybake

Serving: Cuts into 16 pieces | Prep: 10mins | Cook: 30mins | Ready in:

Ingredients

- 375g pack ready-rolled shortcrust pastry
- 500g mascarpone
- 100g golden caster sugar
- 100g ground almonds
- 2 large eggs
- 250g fresh raspberries
- 100g white chocolate, roughly chopped

Direction

- Heat oven to 160c/fan 140c/gas 4. roll out the pastry a little more on a floured surface and use to line a 30 x 20cm tin, or a Swiss roll tin. Line with greaseproof paper, fill with baking beans and cook for 10 mins. Take out the beans and paper, then return to the oven for a further 5 mins.

- Whisk together the mascarpone, sugar, almonds and eggs until well blended. Fold in the raspberries and chocolate, then pour into the tin. Bake for 20-25 mins until just set and lightly golden. Turn off the oven, open the door and leave the tray bake to cool gradually. For the best results, chill for at least 1 hr before slicing.

Nutrition Information

- Calories: 314 calories
- Fiber: 2 grams fiber
- Total Fat: 25 grams fat
- Total Carbohydrate: 19 grams carbohydrates
- Sodium: 0.18 milligram of sodium
- Sugar: 13 grams sugar
- Protein: 5 grams protein
- Saturated Fat: 12 grams saturated fat

---

210. Raspberry Bakewell Slice

Serving: 10 | Prep: 45mins | Cook: 35mins | Ready in:

Ingredients

- 375g pack sweet shortcrust pastry
- 5 tbsp thick seedless raspberry jam
- 100g frozen raspberries, just thawed
- 25g flaked almonds
- 4 tbsp apricot jam
- For the sponge
- 200g butter, very soft, plus a little extra for the tin
- 200g golden caster sugar
- 100g ground almonds
- 100g self-raising flour
- 1 tsp baking powder
- ½ tsp almond extract
- 4 eggs, beaten

Direction

- Heat oven to 200C/180C fan/gas 6. Line the base and sides of a buttered traybake tin, about 18-20cm x 30cm, with baking parchment. Roll out the pastry to line. Lift into the tin and evenly press right into the corners. Prick with a fork and chill for 20 mins.
- Bake the pastry for 8-10 mins until it's cooked but not too coloured. Cool for a few mins and turn down the oven to 180C/160C fan/gas 4. Dot the raspberry jam over the pastry (there's no need to spread) and scatter over the raspberries.
- For the sponge, put all the ingredients into a large bowl and beat with an electric whisk until soft and very well mixed. Spoon this over the raspberry layer, then smooth evenly. Scatter over the flaked almonds and bake for 35-40 mins until golden and firm. Cool completely in the tin. Will freeze for up to 3 months – overwrap the tin with baking parchment and foil beforehand.
- To serve, thaw for 4 hrs at room temperature, then reheat in a low oven. Melt the apricot jam with 1 tbsp water and brush over the top of the sponge just before serving.

Nutrition Information

- Calories: 595 calories
- Total Carbohydrate: 57 grams carbohydrates
- Saturated Fat: 16 grams saturated fat
- Protein: 9 grams protein
- Fiber: 2 grams fiber
- Sodium: 0.76 milligram of sodium
- Sugar: 36 grams sugar
- Total Fat: 38 grams fat

211. Rhubarb, Marzipan & Citrus Cake

Serving: 15 | Prep: 20mins | Cook: 50mins |Ready in:

Ingredients

- 300g softened butter, plus a little for the tin
- 400g thin-stemmed rhubarb, cut into thick pieces
- 350g golden caster sugar
- ½ orange, zested
- 1/2 lemon, zested
- 3 large eggs
- 200g self-raising flour
- 50g fine polenta
- 50g ground almonds
- 1 tsp baking powder
- 100g marzipan, chopped into small chunks

Direction

- Heat oven to 180C/160C fan/gas 4. Butter and line a 20 x 30cm traybake tin with baking parchment. Toss the rhubarb in 50g sugar and set aside to macerate for 20 mins.
- Tip the butter, remaining sugar and zests into a large bowl. Beat with an electric whisk until light and fluffy. Add the eggs, one at a time, mixing well between each addition. Add the flour, polenta, almonds, baking powder and a good pinch of salt, and mix until just combined. Fold through half the rhubarb (reserving the rest for the top), plus any juices, and the marzipan.
- Scrape the mixture into the tin. Smooth the surface up to the edges and top with the remaining rhubarb. Bake for 45-50 mins until risen and golden, and a skewer inserted in the centre of the cake comes out clean. If there is any wet mixture, return it to the oven for 5 mins, then check again. Cool in the tin for 10 mins, then serve warm with crème fraîche, or cool completely to serve as a cake. Will keep in an airtight container for three days.

Nutrition Information

- Calories: 371 calories
- Fiber: 1 grams fiber
- Saturated Fat: 11 grams saturated fat
- Total Carbohydrate: 41 grams carbohydrates
- Protein: 5 grams protein
- Total Fat: 21 grams fat

- Sodium: 0.6 milligram of sodium
- Sugar: 28 grams sugar

212. Sour Cream Rhubarb Squares

Serving: Makes 15 squares | Prep: 1hours20mins | Cook: | Ready in:

Ingredients

- 100g butter, room temperature
- 100g golden caster sugar
- 100g mixed nuts, such as walnuts, brazil nuts, almonds and hazelnuts, roughly chopped (you can buy these as a mixed pack)
- 1 tsp ground cinnamon
- 250g dark muscovado sugar
- 1 large egg
- 225g plain flour
- 1 tsp bicarbonate of soda
- 2 x cartons soured cream
- 300g rhubarb, cut into 1cm pieces

Direction

- Preheat the oven to 180C/gas 4/fan 160C. If baking to cut into squares, line a 33 x 23 x 5cm baking tin with non-stick baking parchment. If serving as a pudding simply grease a similar-sized ovenproof dish with a little butter.
- Melt about 15g/1/2oz of the butter and stir into the caster sugar, nuts and cinnamon in a bowl. Set aside.
- Cream together the rest of the butter with the muscovado sugar and egg. When smooth and creamy, stir in the flour, bicarbonate of soda, 1/2 tsp salt and the soured cream. Lastly, stir in the rhubarb.
- Pour the rhubarb mixture into the prepared tin and sprinkle with the sugar and nut topping. Bake for 30-35 minutes or until a skewer inserted in the centre comes out clean. Serve immediately as a pudding, or leave to cool and

cut into squares. Keeps for 4-5 days in an airtight tin.

Nutrition Information

- Calories: 277 calories
- Saturated Fat: 7 grams saturated fat
- Sugar: 24 grams sugar
- Total Carbohydrate: 37 grams carbohydrates
- Fiber: 1 grams fiber
- Sodium: 0.63 milligram of sodium
- Protein: 4 grams protein
- Total Fat: 13 grams fat

213. Swirly Lemon Drizzle Fingers

Serving: Makes 18 fingers | Prep: 15mins | Cook: 40mins | Ready in:

Ingredients

- 200g butter, well softened, plus extra
- 200g golden caster sugar
- 4 large eggs
- 100g fine polenta or fine cornmeal
- 140g self-raising flour
- zest 3 lemons
- For the swirl and drizzle
- 4 tbsp lemon curd
- 5 tbsp golden or white caster sugar
- zest and juice 1 lemon

Direction

- Heat oven to 180C/fan 160C/gas 4 and make sure there's a shelf ready in the middle of the oven. Butter a rectangular baking tray or small roasting tin, about 20cm x 30cm. Cut out a sheet of baking paper a bit larger than the tin, then push it in and smooth it out with your hands so it sticks to the butter. Snip into the corners with a pair of scissors to get the paper to lie neatly.

- Put all the cake ingredients and a pinch of salt into a large bowl, then use electric beaters to beat until creamy and smooth. Scoop into the tin, then level the top. Spoon the lemon curd over the batter in thick stripes. Use the handle of the spoon to swirl the curd into the cake – not too much or you won't see the swirls once it's cooked. Bake for about 35 mins or until golden and risen. It should have shrunk away from the sides of the tin ever so slightly and feel springy. Don't open the oven before 30 mins cooking is up.
- Leave the cake in the tin for 10 mins or until just cool enough to handle. Carefully lift out of the tin and put it onto a cooling rack, sat over a tray or something similar to catch drips of drizzle. To make the drizzle, mix 4 tbsp sugar and the lemon juice together and spoon over the cake. Toss the lemon zest with the final 1 tbsp sugar and scatter over the top. Let the cake cool completely, then lift onto a board, peel away the sides of the baking paper and cut the cake into fingers. Will keep in an airtight tin for 3 days.

Nutrition Information

- Calories: 214 calories
- Total Fat: 11 grams fat
- Saturated Fat: 6 grams saturated fat
- Total Carbohydrate: 27 grams carbohydrates
- Sugar: 17 grams sugar
- Protein: 3 grams protein
- Sodium: 0.3 milligram of sodium

214.   The Ultimate Makeover: Carrot Cake

Serving: Cuts into 16 squares | Prep: 30mins | Cook: 1hours |Ready in:

Ingredients

- For the cake
- 1 medium orange
- 140g raisin
- 125ml rapeseed oil
- 115g plain wholemeal flour
- 1 tsp baking powder, plus a pinch
- 1 tsp bicarbonate of soda
- 1 rounded tsp ground cinnamon
- 140g dark muscovado sugar
- 280g finely grated carrot (about 375-400g carrots before peeling)
- 2 eggs
- 115g self-raising flour
- For the frosting
- 100g light soft cheese, straight from the fridge
- 100g quark
- 3 tbsp sifted icing sugar
- ½ tsp finely grated orange zest
- 1½ tsp lemon juice

Direction

- Heat oven to 160C/fan 140C/gas 3. For the cake, finely grate the zest from the orange and squeeze 3 tbsp of juice. Pour the juice over the raisins in a bowl, stir in zest, then leave to soak while you make the cake. Lightly oil and line the base of a deep 20cm square cake tin. Mix the flours with 1 tsp baking powder, bicarbonate of soda and cinnamon.
- Separate one of the eggs. Put the white in a small bowl and the yolk in a large one. Break the remaining whole egg in with the yolk, then tip in the sugar. Whisk together for 1-2 mins until thick and foamy. Slowly pour in the oil and continue to whisk on a low speed until well mixed. Tip in the flour mix, half at a time, and gently stir it into the egg mixture with a rubber spatula or big spoon. The mix will be quite stiff. Put the extra pinch of baking powder in with the egg white and whisk to soft peaks.
- Fold the carrot, raisins (and any liquid) into the flour mixture. Gently fold in the whisked egg white, then pour into the tin. Jiggle the tin to level the mixture. Bake for 1 hr until risen and firm or until a skewer inserted in the centre comes out clean. Leave to cool in the tin

5 mins, turn out onto a wire rack, peel off the paper, then leave until cold.

- To make the frosting, stir the soft cheese, Quark, icing sugar and orange zest together - don't overbeat. Stir in the lemon juice. Swirl the frosting over the cake and cut into 16 square. This cake is even better if left well wrapped for a day or two before icing and eating. Will keep up to 5 days uniced in an airtight tin, or in the fridge if iced.

Nutrition Information

- Calories: 217 calories
- Saturated Fat: 1 grams saturated fat
- Sugar: 21 grams sugar
- Protein: 4 grams protein
- Total Carbohydrate: 31 grams carbohydrates
- Total Fat: 9 grams fat
- Fiber: 2 grams fiber
- Sodium: 0.52 milligram of sodium

215. Triple Ginger & Spice Cake

Serving: Cuts into 16 squares | Prep: 20mins | Cook: 15mins | Ready in:

Ingredients

- 250g pack butter
- 250g dark brown muscovado sugar
- 250g black treacle
- 300ml milk
- 2 eggs
- 100g glacé ginger from a jar, finely chopped
- 375g plain flour
- 2 tsp bicarbonate of soda
- 1 tsp allspice
- 2 tsp ground ginger
- For the icing
- 3 tbsp ginger syrup from the jar
- 5 tbsp icing sugar

Direction

- Butter and line a 23cm square baking tin (or use a shallow roasting tin, approx 30 x 20cm). Heat oven to 160C/fan 140C/gas 3. Put the butter, sugar and treacle into a saucepan and heat gently for about 5 mins until the butter and sugar have melted. Stir in the milk. The mix should be just warm to the touch; if not, leave to cool a little longer, then beat in the eggs.
- Mix the chopped ginger and dry ingredients together in a large bowl and make a well in the centre. Pour the melted mix into the well, then gradually draw the dry ingredients into the wet with a wooden spoon, until you have a thick, smooth batter.
- Pour the batter into the prepared tin, then bake for 1 hr until risen and firm to the touch. Resist taking a peek beforehand; the cake will sink if the oven temperature drops too quickly before it's cooked through. Poke a skewer into the centre to check that it's cooked - it should come out clean. If not, give it 10 mins more and check again. Leave the cake to cool in the tin. Once completely cool, turn out of the tin ready for icing, or wrap well in cling film and keep in a cool, dry place for up to a week.
- To make the icing, sift the icing sugar into a bowl and add the gingery syrup. Beat well until you have a smooth, runny icing. Once the cake has cooled, drizzle with icing and cut into squares. If you're planning to let the cake mature for a while, make the icing on the day you want to cut it.

Nutrition Information

- Calories: 360 calories
- Total Fat: 14 grams fat
- Saturated Fat: 9 grams saturated fat
- Total Carbohydrate: 57 grams carbohydrates
- Sugar: 39 grams sugar
- Protein: 46 grams protein
- Sodium: 0.81 milligram of sodium

216. Upside Down Peach Sponge

Serving: Cuts into 15 squares | Prep: 25mins | Cook: 1hours | Ready in:

Ingredients

- For the traybake sponge base
- 250g softened butter, plus extra for greasing
- 280g self-raising flour
- 250g golden caster sugar
- ½ tsp baking powder
- 4 eggs
- 150ml pot natural yogurt
- 1 tsp vanilla paste or extract
- For the topping
- 2 tbsp caster sugar mixed with 1 tbsp flour
- small punnet raspberries
- 2-3 x 400g/14oz cans peach halves, drained

Direction

- First make the topping. Heat oven to 180C/160C fan/gas 4. Grease a 20 x 30cm baking or roasting tin and line with baking parchment. Sprinkle with the sugar-flour mix. Push a raspberry or cherry into the cavity of each peach half, then place the peaches, cut-side down, in the tin.
- To make the sponge batter, beat the butter, flour, sugar, baking powder, eggs, yogurt and vanilla in a large bowl with an electric whisk until lump-free. Spoon the mix into the tin, over and around the peaches, then bake for 50 mins-1 hr until golden and risen and a skewer poked in comes out clean.
- Cool briefly, then carefully run a cutlery knife around the edges to release any stuck bits. Turn the cake out onto a board and cut into squares. Delicious eaten warm with ice cream.

Nutrition Information

- Calories: 326 calories

- Fiber: 1 grams fiber
- Total Carbohydrate: 43 grams carbohydrates
- Sodium: 0.5 milligram of sodium
- Sugar: 29 grams sugar
- Protein: 5 grams protein
- Total Fat: 16 grams fat
- Saturated Fat: 10 grams saturated fat

Chapter 7: Easy Baking Recipes

***

217. Apple & Walnut Cake With Treacle Icing

Serving: Serves 10 | Prep: 20mins | Cook: 45mins | Ready in:

Ingredients

- 300g plain flour
- 1 tsp ground cinnamon
- ½ tsp bicarbonate of soda
- 140g dark brown soft sugar
- 50g golden caster sugar
- 250ml rapeseed or sunflower oil
- 4 eggs
- 3 unpeeled apples, coarsely grated
- 100g walnuts, roughly chopped
- For the icing
- 100g butter, softened
- 50g dark soft brown sugar
- 1 tbsp black treacle
- 200g tub full fat soft cheese

Direction

- Heat oven to 150C/130C fan/gas 2. Line two 20cm cake tins. Put the flour, cinnamon and bicarbonate of soda in a big bowl, then stir in the sugars, making sure there are no lumps of sugar. Add the oil, eggs and apples, and beat everything together. Fold in the walnuts then divide the mixture between the tins and bake for 45 mins or until a skewer comes out clean. Allow to cool for a few mins in the tin then remove and cool completely on a wire rack.

- For the icing, beat all the ingredients together then chill until the mixture is thick but spreadable. Spread half the icing on top of one cake, sandwich with the other and spread the remaining icing on top

Nutrition Information

- Calories: 535 calories
- Total Fat: 14 grams fat
- Protein: 15 grams protein
- Total Carbohydrate: 89 grams carbohydrates
- Sugar: 51 grams sugar
- Saturated Fat: 8 grams saturated fat
- Fiber: 2 grams fiber
- Sodium: 0.46 milligram of sodium

218.	Bakewell Tarts

Serving: 12 | Prep: 30mins | Cook: 40mins | Ready in:

Ingredients

- 2 x 320g sheets of all butter shortcrust pastry
- For the frangipane
- 120g butter, softened
- 120g golden caster sugar
- 1 egg
- 1 tbsp plain flour
- 110g ground almonds
- 90g cherry jam
- For the icing
- 200g icing sugar
- 12 glacé cherries

Direction

- Heat the oven to 180C/160C fan/gas 4. Lightly butter a 12 hole muffin tin. Unroll the sheet of pastry and use a 10cm circular pastry cutter to cut 12 circles out of the pastry sheet. Press the cut circles into the holes of the tin, making sure they come right up and slightly over the top – pushing out any creases. Chill the pastry in the fridge for 20mins. Scrunch up 10cm x 10cm squares of baking paper and then un-scrunch and use to line each of the pastry tarts, then fill with baking beans, rice or dried pulses. Bake for 10 mins, then remove the paper and beans and bake for 10 mins longer, until golden brown. Set aside to cool a little.
- Make the filling by beating together the butter and sugar until light and fluffy, then whisk in the egg, followed by the flour (the flour will prevent the mixture from splitting). Fold in the ground almonds. Spoon a level tsp of cherry jam into each of the pastry shells, followed by a tablespoon of the frangipane mixture. Bake for 20 mins, until the frangipane is golden and springy. Set aside to cool completely. Neaten the edges of the pastry with a small knife or scissors if you like.
- Mix the icing sugar with 2 tbsp water. Spread the icing over each of the tarts, top each with a glacé cherry, leave to set for 20 mins, then serve with tea.

Nutrition Information

- Calories: 534 calories
- Fiber: 2 grams fiber
- Total Fat: 30 grams fat
- Total Carbohydrate: 57 grams carbohydrates
- Protein: 6 grams protein
- Sodium: 0.5 milligram of sodium
- Saturated Fat: 12 grams saturated fat
- Sugar: 32 grams sugar

219.   Blueberry & Orange Traybake Pancake

Serving: 6 | Prep: 5mins | Cook: 30mins |Ready in:

Ingredients

- 1 tbsp melted unsalted butter, plus extra for the tin
- 200g self-raising flour
- 1 tsp baking powder
- 1 egg
- 250ml milk
- 2 tbsp golden caster sugar
- 1 large orange, zested and juiced
- 150g blueberries
- icing sugar, for dusting
- extra blueberries, blueberry compote or ice cream, to serve (optional)

Direction

- Heat oven to 180C/160C fan/gas 4. Brush a 25 x 20 x 2cm baking tray with butter. Tip the flour and baking powder into a bowl and mix in the egg, milk, butter and caster sugar. Stir in the orange zest and 50ml juice.
- Scrape the mixture into the tin and level the surface. Dot the blueberries over the top and bake for 20 mins or until the middle of the pancake feels cooked through when pressed lightly. Dust with icing sugar and serve with more blueberries, blueberry compote or ice cream, if you like.

Nutrition Information

- Calories: 230 calories
- Protein: 6 grams protein
- Sodium: 0.6 milligram of sodium
- Fiber: 2 grams fiber
- Total Carbohydrate: 38 grams carbohydrates
- Total Fat: 6 grams fat
- Saturated Fat: 3 grams saturated fat
- Sugar: 12 grams sugar

220.   Blueberry Bakewell Muffins

Serving: Makes 12 | Prep: 20mins | Cook: 20mins |Ready in:

Ingredients

- 100g unsalted butter, softened, plus 1 tbsp, melted, for greasing
- 140g golden caster sugar
- 2 large eggs
- 140g natural yogurt
- 1 tsp vanilla extract
- 1 tsp almond extract
- 2 tbsp milk
- 250g plain flour
- 2 tsp baking powder
- 1 tsp bicarbonate of soda
- 125g pack blueberries (or use frozen)
- For the topping
- 3 tbsp demerara sugar
- ¼ tsp ground cinnamon
- 3 tbsp flaked almonds, roughly chopped
- 2 tbsp ground almonds
- 3 tbsp plain flour
- 1 tbsp cold butter diced
- 12 tsp wild blueberry conserve (I used Felix wild blueberry jam, available from ocado.com)

Direction

- Heat oven to 200C/180C fan/gas 6 and line a 12-hole muffin tin with paper cases. Put all the topping ingredients, apart from the jam, in a bowl and rub together.
- Beat the butter and caster sugar together until pale and fluffy. Add the eggs and beat in for 1 min, then mix in the yogurt, extracts and milk. Combine the flour, baking powder and bicarb in a bowl with 1/4 tsp fine salt, then tip this into the wet ingredients and stir in. Finally, fold in the blueberries and divide the mixture between the muffin cases. Top each muffin

with 1 tsp blueberry jam, then scatter over the crumble mixture.

- Bake for 5 mins, then reduce oven to 180C/160C fan/gas 4 and bake for 15-18 mins more until risen and golden, and a cocktail stick inserted in comes out with just jam on it – no wet cake mixture.
- Cool in the tin for 10 mins, then carefully lift out onto a wire rack to finish cooling. Will keep for 3-4 days in an airtight container – after a day or two, pop them in the microwave for 10-15 secs on High to freshen up.

Nutrition Information

- Calories: 312 calories
- Protein: 6 grams protein
- Fiber: 1 grams fiber
- Sodium: 0.6 milligram of sodium
- Saturated Fat: 6 grams saturated fat
- Total Carbohydrate: 40 grams carbohydrates
- Sugar: 24 grams sugar
- Total Fat: 14 grams fat

---

221. Butterfly Cakes

Serving: Makes 10 | Prep: 15mins | Cook: 15mins | Ready in:

Ingredients

- 110g butter, softened
- 110g caster sugar
- 2 eggs
- 1 tsp vanilla extract
- 110g self-raising flour
- ½ tsp baking powder
- 1 tbsp milk, plus 2 tbsp if needed, to loosen the buttercream
- strawberry jam (optional)
- sprinkles (optional)
- For the buttercream
- 300g icing sugar
- 150g butter, softened

- 2 tsp vanilla paste

Direction

- Heat the oven to 180C/160C fan/gas 4. Line a cupcake tin with 10 cases. To make the sponge, tip the butter, sugar, eggs, vanilla, flour, baking powder and milk into a large mixing bowl and beat with either a hand whisk or electric mixer until smooth, pale and combined. Divide the batter between the cases and bake for 15 mins until golden brown and a skewer inserted in the middle of a cake comes out clean. Leave on a wire rack to cool.
- While the cakes are cooling, make the buttercream by beating together the icing sugar, butter and vanilla until pale and fluffy. Mix in the extra milk if the icing feels too stiff.
- Once the cakes are cool, use a sharp knife to slice off the tops, then cut the tops in half. Pipe or spread the buttercream on top of the cakes, then gently push two semi-circular halves into the buttercream on each cake, doing this at an angle to look like butterfly wings. You can serve the cupcakes at this stage, or decorate them with a little blob of jam in the centre and a scattering of sprinkles, if you like.

Nutrition Information

- Calories: 419 calories
- Saturated Fat: 14 grams saturated fat
- Total Carbohydrate: 50 grams carbohydrates
- Sugar: 42 grams sugar
- Protein: 3 grams protein
- Sodium: 0.7 milligram of sodium
- Total Fat: 23 grams fat

---

222. Cherry Bakewell Cake

Serving: 8 | Prep: 15mins | Cook: 30mins | Ready in:

Ingredients

- For the cake
- 200g butter, well softened, plus extra for greasing
- 200g golden caster sugar
- 100g ground almond
- 100g self-raising flour
- 1 tsp baking powder
- ½ tsp almond extract or essence
- 4 large eggs
- For the filling and top
- ½ a 340g jar morello cherry conserve
- 175g icing sugar
- 5-6 tsp water or lemon juice
- 1 tbsp ready-toasted flaked almonds

Direction

- Heat oven to 180C/160C fan/gas 4 and make sure there's a shelf ready in the middle. Butter and line the bases of two 20cm round sandwich tins with baking paper.
- Using electric beaters, beat together all the cake ingredients with a pinch of salt until smooth, then spoon into the tins and level the tops. Bake for 30 mins or until golden and springy. Don't open the oven before 25 mins cooking time has passed.
- When they're ready, cool the sponges for a few mins, then tip out of the tins and cool completely on a wire rack. Make sure the top of one of the cakes is facing up as you'll want a smooth surface for the icing later on.
- When cool, put one sponge on a serving plate, then spread with jam. Sandwich the second sponge on top. Sieve the icing sugar into a large bowl. Add the water or lemon juice, then stir until smooth and thick. Spread evenly over the top and let it dribble over the sides. Scatter with the nuts and leave to set for a few mins before cutting.

Nutrition Information

- Calories: 600 calories
- Protein: 8 grams protein
- Saturated Fat: 15 grams saturated fat

- Fiber: 1 grams fiber
- Total Carbohydrate: 75 grams carbohydrates
- Sugar: 65 grams sugar
- Sodium: 0.83 milligram of sodium
- Total Fat: 32 grams fat

223. Chocolate Concrete With Caramel Sauce

Serving: 12 | Prep: 15mins | Cook: 30mins | Ready in:

Ingredients

- 175g plain flour
- 50g ground almonds
- 60g cocoa
- 115g golden caster sugar
- 145g butter, softened, plus extra for the tin
- demerara sugar, for sprinkling over
- 4 tbsp caramel
- 50ml single cream

Direction

- Heat oven to 180C/160C fan/gas 4. Put the flour, almonds, cocoa, caster sugar and a large pinch of salt into a food processor and whizz briefly. Add the butter and whizz until the mixture resembles damp sand.
- Generously butter the base and sides of a small (15 x 25cm) baking tin. Tip the mixture into the tin and press it down. Bake for 30 mins. Remove from the oven, sprinkle over some demerara sugar and cut into squares using a sharp knife while still it's soft.
- Meanwhile, heat the caramel and cream together in a pan. Serve the concrete warm with the caramel sauce. You can cool any leftovers and eat them cold – they will harden like shortbread.

Nutrition Information

- Calories: 257 calories

- Total Carbohydrate: 25 grams carbohydrates
- Fiber: 1 grams fiber
- Saturated Fat: 8 grams saturated fat
- Sugar: 13 grams sugar
- Total Fat: 15 grams fat
- Protein: 4 grams protein
- Sodium: 0.2 milligram of sodium

224.   Chocolate Peppermint Mini Rolls

Serving: 12 | Prep: 45mins | Cook: 20mins | Ready in:

Ingredients

- butter for the tin
- 3 eggs
- 100g golden caster sugar, plus extra for dusting
- 80g plain flour
- 2 tbsp cocoa powder
- ½ tsp baking powder
- ¼ tsp vanilla extract
- 300g dark chocolate
- For the filling
- 125g butter, softened
- 125g icing sugar
- 1 tsp milk
- few drops peppermint extract

Direction

- Heat oven to 200C/180C fan/gas 6. Line a 24 x 32cm Swiss roll tin with a piece of baking parchment and grease well. Whisk the eggs and sugar together with an electric hand whisk for 2-3 mins or until thickened and very pale.
- Fold the flour, cocoa powder, baking powder and vanilla extract into the egg mixture with a large metal spoon until there are no pockets of flour visible.
- Gently scrape the mixture into your prepared Swiss roll tin with a spatula then smooth it out so it fills the tin evenly. Bake in the oven for 15

mins or until puffed up and springy when you touch it.
- Remove from the oven, allow to cool for 1-2 mins or until cool enough to handle. Run a rolling pin over it very gently to slightly flatten it, then carefully roll up the sponge along the longest edge while it's still warm (keeping the baking parchment attached). Take it halfway in, stopping when you get to the middle, then turn it around and start rolling from the other side to meet your first roll – just as you would making a scroll or palmier biscuits. Leave to cool completely in its rolled-up shape. Clean the electric beaters.
- While the sponge cools make the buttercream. Put the butter in a bowl with half the icing sugar, milk and peppermint extract. Beat well with a wooden spoon until smooth then stir in the rest of the icing sugar and switch to using the electric beaters and whisk up until pale. Taste a bit and add more peppermint extract if you like. Set aside somewhere cool until needed.
- Once the sponge is cold, slice it through the middle where the two rolls meet and uncurl them. Carefully spread or pipe the buttercream on top of each length of sponge in an even layer. Smooth it out with a palette knife or the back of a spoon then roll it up again as tightly as you can. Trim off the ends and cut each roll into 6 equal-sized sections. Chill them in the fridge on the tray while you prepare the topping.
- Melt the chocolate, either in a bowl set over a pan of simmering water or in the microwave (checking and stirring it every 30 secs until melted).
- Take the mini rolls out of the fridge then spoon the melted chocolate over them to cover them completely. Sit them on baking parchment until the chocolate has set firmly then serve. Keep in an airtight container in a cool place for up to 1 day.

Nutrition Information

- Calories: 348 calories
- Total Carbohydrate: 33 grams carbohydrates
- Protein: 5 grams protein
- Saturated Fat: 12 grams saturated fat
- Fiber: 3 grams fiber
- Sodium: 0.3 milligram of sodium
- Total Fat: 21 grams fat
- Sugar: 25 grams sugar

225. Chocolate Traybake

Serving: 10 | Prep: 15mins | Cook: 30mins | Ready in:

Ingredients

- For the chocolate sponge
- 185ml vegetable oil, plus extra for the tin
- 250g plain flour
- 80g cocoa powder
- 2 ½ tsp baking powder
- 1 tsp bicarbonate of soda
- 325g light brown soft sugar
- 250ml buttermilk
- 125ml strong coffee or espresso, (can be warm, but not hot)
- 2 tsp vanilla extract
- 2 large eggs
- For the icing
- 150g salted butter, softened
- 200g icing sugar
- 4 tbsp cocoa powder
- 2 tbsp milk
- sprinkles, sweets, chocolate shavings or nuts, to decorate

Direction

- Heat oven to 180C/160C fan/gas 4. Oil and line the base and sides of a 33cm x 23cm roasting tin or cake tin with a lip of at least 2½ cm. Combine the flour, cocoa powder, baking powder, bicarb, sugar and a good pinch of salt in a large bowl. Rub any lumps of sugar between your fingers, shaking the bowl a few times to bring them to the surface.

- Whisk the oil, buttermilk, coffee, vanilla and eggs in a jug, then pour the wet ingredients into the dry. Use a spatula to stir well, removing any pockets of flour. Pour the mixture into the lined tin and bake for 25-30 mins until a skewer inserted into the centre comes out clean. If any wet cake mixture clings to the skewer, return the cake to the oven for 5 mins, then check again. Once cooked, remove from the oven and leave to cool in the tin for at least 20 mins.
- Meanwhile, make the icing. Melt the butter in a saucepan, then remove from the heat and stir in the icing sugar, cocoa powder and milk. The icing will be very runny but will thicken a little as it cools. (If the icing has set too much before the cake has cooled, reheat it slightly to make it easier to pour.)
- Pour the icing over the cake and leave to set. Decorate with the sweets, sprinkles, chocolate shavings or nuts, then cut into squares and dig in.

Nutrition Information

- Calories: 330 calories
- Saturated Fat: 6 grams saturated fat
- Total Fat: 18 grams fat
- Fiber: 2 grams fiber
- Sodium: 0.5 milligram of sodium
- Total Carbohydrate: 37 grams carbohydrates
- Sugar: 26 grams sugar
- Protein: 4 grams protein

226. Chorizo & Manchego Scones

Serving: 6 | Prep: 20mins | Cook: 14mins | Ready in:

Ingredients

- 225g self-raising flour, plus extra for dusting
- ¼ tsp salt
- 50g butter, very cold, diced

- 60g chorizo
- 110g manchego
- pinch of smoked paprika
- 150ml buttermilk (or milk)

Direction

- Heat oven to 220C/200C fan/gas 7. Put the flour, salt and butter in a food processor and pulse until you can't feel any lumps of butter (or rub in any remaining lumps with your fingers).
- Cut 60g chorizo and 60g manchego into small cubes and add them to the pulsed dry flour mixture with a pinch of smoked paprika.
- Stir the buttermilk into the mixture and use a knife to quickly combine everything together to form a dough – stop when it has just combined and don't overmix it.
- Tip the dough onto a floured surface and lightly bring it together with your hands a couple of times. Press out gently until about 4cm thick, then stamp out 6-7cm rough squares. Re-shape any trimmings until all the dough is used. Grate another 50g manchego over the scones before baking. Spread out on a lightly floured baking sheet and bake for 10-12 mins or until well risen and golden.

Nutrition Information

- Calories: 332 calories
- Protein: 12 grams protein
- Sugar: 2 grams sugar
- Fiber: 2 grams fiber
- Sodium: 1.38 milligram of sodium
- Total Fat: 18 grams fat
- Saturated Fat: 11 grams saturated fat
- Total Carbohydrate: 30 grams carbohydrates

227. Cinnamon Apple Pecan Pudding

Serving: 6 | Prep: 10mins | Cook: 45mins | Ready in:

Ingredients

- 85g softened butter
- 85g xylitol (we used Total Sweet)
- 125g self-raising flour
- 25g oats
- 1 tsp ground cinnamon
- 1 heaped tsp baking powder
- 2 large eggs
- 3 tbsp milk
- 1 Bramley apple (about 280g), peeled, cored, a quarter grated, the rest diced
- 25g pecans, roughly chopped or broken
- Greek yogurt or cream, to serve

Direction

- Heat oven to 180C/160C fan/gas 4 and lightly grease a 1-litre (20 x 16cm) pie or oven dish. Tip the butter and xylitol into a bowl with the flour, oats, cinnamon and baking powder. Break in the eggs, add the milk, then beat with an electric hand whisk until evenly mixed and smooth. Stir in all the apple, then scrape into the dish, level the top and scatter with the pecans.
- Bake for 35-45 mins until risen and golden and a skewer inserted into the centre comes out clean. Serve with Greek yogurt or cream.

Nutrition Information

- Calories: 328 calories
- Sodium: 0.8 milligram of sodium
- Saturated Fat: 5 grams saturated fat
- Sugar: 6 grams sugar
- Total Fat: 36 grams fat
- Fiber: 3 grams fiber
- Protein: 17 grams protein
- Total Carbohydrate: 8 grams carbohydrates

228.   Cinnamon Cashew Flapjacks

Serving: Makes 15 | Prep: 15mins | Cook: 40mins | Ready in:

Ingredients

- 140g butter, plus extra for greasing
- 140g light brown soft sugar
- 2 tbsp set honey
- 1 tbsp ground cinnamon
- 140g porridge oats
- 85g desiccated coconut
- 85g sesame seeds
- 50g sunflower seeds
- 1 tbsp plain flour
- 85g cashews or pecans

Direction

- Heat oven to 160C/140C fan/gas 3. Grease and line a 20 x 30cm cake tin with baking parchment. Melt the butter in a large non-stick pan, add the sugar, honey and cinnamon, and stir with a wooden spoon over a low heat for 5-10 mins until the sugar dissolves.
- Remove from the heat and stir in all the remaining ingredients until well coated in the buttery spice mixture. Tip into the tin and press down to an even layer. Bake for 30-35 mins until golden. Cool for 5 mins, then mark into squares – don't remove from the tin yet as they won't hold together until they are cold. Will keep in a sealed container for a couple of days.

Nutrition Information

- Calories: 282 calories
- Sugar: 12 grams sugar
- Fiber: 3 grams fiber
- Protein: 5 grams protein
- Sodium: 0.2 milligram of sodium
- Saturated Fat: 9 grams saturated fat
- Total Fat: 19 grams fat
- Total Carbohydrate: 20 grams carbohydrates

229.   Classic Cheese Scones

Serving: Makes 5-6 | Prep: 15mins | Cook: 20mins | Ready in:

Ingredients

- 225g self-raising flour, plus extra for dusting
- pinch of salt
- pinch of cayenne pepper
- 1 tsp baking powder
- 55g chilled butter, cut into cubes
- 120g mature cheddar, grated
- 90-100ml milk, plus 1 tbsp for glazing

Direction

- Heat the oven to 200C/180C fan/gas 6 with a large baking tray inside. Sift the flour, salt, cayenne pepper and baking powder into a bowl, then sift again to make sure the ingredients are thoroughly combined.
- Add the butter to the bowl and combine with your fingertips to make breadcrumbs. Sprinkle 100g of the cheese into the breadcrumb mixture and rub together until evenly distributed. Try not to mix too much as the heat from your hands may start to melt the butter.
- Make a well in the centre of the mixture and pour in enough milk to give a fairly soft but firm dough. Do not pour in all the milk at once as you may not need it all to get the right consistency.
- Lightly flour a surface and roll out the dough to approximately 2cm thick. Cut out the scones with a medium (about 8cm) cutter, then put on a sheet of baking parchment, glaze with a little milk and sprinkle with the remaining cheese. Slide onto the hot oven tray.
- Bake in the oven for 15-20 mins or until golden brown and cooked through.

Nutrition Information

- Calories: 300 calories
- Sugar: 1 grams sugar
- Total Fat: 16 grams fat
- Sodium: 1.2 milligram of sodium
- Fiber: 2 grams fiber
- Protein: 9 grams protein
- Total Carbohydrate: 30 grams carbohydrates
- Saturated Fat: 10 grams saturated fat

230.   Coconut Chai Traybake

Serving: Cuts into 15 squares | Prep: 25mins | Cook: 30mins | Ready in:

Ingredients

- 100ml vegetable oil, plus a little for greasing
- 300ml coconut milk (not low-fat) - if the cream has separated in the can, give it a good mix before measuring
- 4 large eggs
- 2 tsp vanilla extract
- 280g light brown soft sugar
- 250g self-raising flour
- 75g desiccated coconut
- 1 tsp ground ginger
- 1 tsp ground cinnamon
- ¼ nutmeg, finely grated
- ¼ tsp ground cloves
- 10 cardamom pods, seeds removed and crushed using a pestle and mortar
- 4 tbsp ginger syrup
- For the topping and icing
- 3-4 tbsp coconut milk
- 140g icing sugar
- 2 balls stem ginger, finely chopped
- chopped pistachios and coconut flakes (optional)

Direction

- Grease a 20 x 30cm baking tin with a little oil, and line the base and sides with baking parchment. Heat oven to 180C/160C fan/gas 4. Measure the coconut milk and oil into a jug. Crack in the eggs, add the vanilla and whisk with a fork to combine.
- In a large bowl, mix the sugar, flour, coconut, spices and a pinch of salt. Squeeze any lumps of sugar through your fingers, shaking the bowl a few times so they come to the surface. Pour in the wet ingredients and use a large whisk to mix to a smooth batter. Pour into the tin, scraping every drop of the mixture out of the bowl with a spatula.
- Bake on the middle shelf of the oven for 25 mins or until a skewer inserted into the middle comes out clean. If there is any wet mixture clinging to it, bake for a further 5 mins, then check again. Leave to cool for 15 mins in the tin, then transfer to a wire rack and drizzle over the ginger syrup.
- To make the icing, mix the coconut milk with the icing sugar until smooth. Drizzle the icing over the cake in squiggles, then scatter with the chopped ginger, pistachios and coconut flakes, if using. Eat warm or cold. Will keep for 3 days in an airtight container.

Nutrition Information

- Calories: 340 calories
- Sugar: 31 grams sugar
- Total Fat: 16 grams fat
- Protein: 4 grams protein
- Saturated Fat: 7 grams saturated fat
- Sodium: 0.2 milligram of sodium
- Fiber: 2 grams fiber
- Total Carbohydrate: 44 grams carbohydrates

231.   Coconut Macaroons

Serving: Makes 10-12 | Prep: | Cook: | Ready in:

Ingredients

- 2 eggs, whites only

- 80g caster sugar
- 150g desiccated coconut
- 1 tsp vanilla paste
- 90g dark chocolate

Direction

- Whisk together the egg whites and caster sugar in a large bowl for 2-3 mins until light and frothy, and the sugar has dissolved. Add the coconut, a pinch of salt and the vanilla, then stir until combined. Leave to stand for 10 mins.
- Heat the oven to 170C/150C fan/gas 3½. Line a baking sheet with baking parchment. Scoop teaspoonfuls of the mixture and roll into compact balls, then arrange on the prepared baking sheet. Bake for 10-12 mins until golden.
- Leave on the baking sheet to cool completely. Melt the chocolate in a heatproof bowl over a pan of simmering water, making sure the bowl doesn't touch the water, or in short 20-second bursts in the microwave. Tip the melted chocolate into a small bowl, then dip the bottom of each cooled macaroon into the chocolate and wipe off any excess. Arrange on a sheet of baking parchment, chocolate-side up, then put in the fridge for 20 mins, or until set. You can use any remaining melted chocolate to pipe in zigzags over the top, if you like, then leave to set.

Nutrition Information

- Calories: 154 calories
- Total Fat: 11 grams fat
- Fiber: 3 grams fiber
- Protein: 2 grams protein
- Saturated Fat: 8 grams saturated fat
- Total Carbohydrate: 10 grams carbohydrates
- Sugar: 9 grams sugar
- Sodium: 0.14 milligram of sodium

232.   Coffee Walnut Millionaire's Shortbread

Serving: Serves 18 | Prep: 40mins | Cook: 40mins | Ready in:

Ingredients

- 200g cold unsalted butter, chopped, plus extra for the tin
- 40g walnut halves
- 250g plain flour
- 75g golden caster sugar
- For the caramel
- 4 tbsp espresso powder
- 100g light muscovado sugar
- 2 x 397g cans condensed milk
- For the chocolate topping
- 300g dark chocolate, chopped
- 50g butter
- 30g white chocolate, chopped
- 1 tsp espresso powder
- 30g chocolate-coated coffee beans
- 20 walnut halves (about 50g)

Direction

- Heat the oven to 180C/160C fan/ gas 4. Butter and line the base and sides of a rectangular 20 x 30cm tin with baking parchment.
- To make the base, blitz the walnuts in a food processor until finely chopped. Add the flour, sugar, butter and ½ tsp salt and blitz until the mixture is combined. Tip onto a work surface and bring together into a dough. Press the dough into the base of the tin and bake for 25 mins until lightly golden. Leave to cool.
- To make the caramel, mix the espresso powder in a small bowl with 1 tbsp boiling water to dissolve. Tip the sugar, condensed milk and espresso into a heavy-based saucepan. Bring to a simmer, stirring to dissolve the sugar. Once the sugar has dissolved, boil vigorously for 3 mins, whisking continuously until the colour has darkened slightly and the caramel has thickened. Leave to cool for 20 mins, then pour

the caramel over the biscuit layer and chill in the fridge for 2 hrs.

- To make the topping, heat the dark chocolate and butter in a heatproof bowl in the microwave in 30 second bursts until evenly melted. Pour over the caramel layer. Melt the white chocolate in the same way and mix with the espresso powder. Swirl and drizzle the white chocolate over the dark chocolate layer. Scatter over the coffee beans and walnuts. Chill for a further 2 hrs or overnight to set before slicing into squares.

Nutrition Information

- Calories: 482 calories
- Total Carbohydrate: 52 grams carbohydrates
- Fiber: 3 grams fiber
- Sodium: 0.3 milligram of sodium
- Saturated Fat: 14 grams saturated fat
- Total Fat: 27 grams fat
- Sugar: 39 grams sugar
- Protein: 7 grams protein

233.   Easy Apple Fruit Cake

Serving: Cuts into 12 slices | Prep: 15mins | Cook: 1hours | Ready in:

Ingredients

- 200g butter, softened plus extra for greasing
- 200g dark muscovado sugar
- 3 eggs, beaten
- 1 tbsp black treacle
- 200g self-raising flour
- 2 tsp mixed spice
- 1 tsp baking powder
- 2 eating apples, grated (approx 100g each)
- 300g mixed sultanas and raisins

Direction

- Heat oven to 180C/fan 160C/gas 4. Butter and line the bottom of a deep, round 20cm cake tin with greaseproof paper. Beat the first seven ingredients together in a large bowl (electric hand-beaters are best for this), until pale and thick. Using a large metal spoon, gently fold in the fruit until evenly combined.

- Spoon the batter into the tin and bake for 50 mins-1 hr or until the cake is dark golden, springy to the touch and has shrunk away from the tin slightly. A skewer inserted into the centre will come out clean when it's ready. Cool completely before decorating. Will keep, wrapped in an airtight container or iced, for up to a week, or can be frozen un-iced for up to a month – defrost fully before decorating.

Nutrition Information

- Calories: 350 calories
- Total Fat: 16 grams fat
- Saturated Fat: 9 grams saturated fat
- Sodium: 0.63 milligram of sodium
- Sugar: 18 grams sugar
- Fiber: 1 grams fiber
- Protein: 4 grams protein
- Total Carbohydrate: 51 grams carbohydrates

234.   Easy Caramel Cake

Serving: Serves 12-14 | Prep: 30mins | Cook: 30mins | Ready in:

Ingredients

- 225g softened salted butter, plus extra for the tins
- 125g golden caster sugar
- 100g light brown soft sugar
- 1 tsp vanilla extract
- 4 large eggs
- 225g self raising flour
- 2 tbsp milk
- toffee, chocolate or caramel pieces, to decorate

- For the icing
- 200g softened salted butter
- 400g icing sugar (golden icing sugar if you can find it – it adds a golden colour and caramel flavour)
- 70g caramel sauce, dulce de leche or caramel spread, plus 3 tbsp to serve

Direction

- Heat the oven to 180C/160C fan/gas 4. Butter two 20cm springform tins and line the bases with baking parchment.
- Beat the butter and both sugars in a bowl with an electric whisk for a few mins until lighter in colour and fluffy. Add the vanilla and the eggs, one at a time, adding a spoonful of flour and beating in between each egg. Add the remaining flour and milk. Divide between the cake tins and bake for 25-30 mins until they're golden, spring back when pressed, and a skewer comes out clean when inserted into the middle. Cool in the tins for a few mins, then tip out and leave to cool completely on a wire rack.
- Meanwhile, for the icing, put the butter and icing sugar in a bowl and whisk for a few mins until light and airy. Whisk in the caramel briefly, adding 1 tbsp of boiling water to loosen, if needed. Set aside until the sponges are completely cool before assembling, or the icing will melt.
- Use half the icing to sandwich the cakes together, then spread the remainder over the top, smoothing it out with a knife or the back of a spoon. Leave in a cool place until ready to serve. Drizzle with the 3 tbsp extra sauce (warm briefly in the microwave if it's a little stiff), allowing some to drip down the sides if you like, and scatter over the toffee, chocolate or caramel pieces to serve. Edible glitter, birthday candles or sparklers, optional.

Nutrition Information

- Calories: 517 calories
- Protein: 5 grams protein

- Total Fat: 28 grams fat
- Total Carbohydrate: 62 grams carbohydrates
- Sugar: 49 grams sugar
- Fiber: 1 grams fiber
- Sodium: 0.8 milligram of sodium
- Saturated Fat: 17 grams saturated fat

235. Flaouna Style Hot Cross Buns

Serving: 8 | Prep: 15mins | Cook: 30mins | Ready in:

Ingredients

- 500g strong white bread flour, plus extra for dusting
- 7g sachet fast-action dried yeast
- 50g golden caster sugar
- 1 ½ tsp cinnamon
- 3 tbsp olive oil
- 250g halloumi, chopped into chunks
- 150g raisins
- 2 tbsp chopped mint
- 1 beaten egg
- 2 tbsp sesame seeds
- 50g plain flour

Direction

- Mix the bread flour, yeast, sugar, cinnamon, oil, 2 tsp sea salt and 350ml warm water in a bowl with a spoon first, and then with your hands. Add the halloumi, raisins and mint and continue to knead (or use a mixer fitted with a dough hook) for around 10 mins until it feels less sticky. Shape into a ball, return to the bowl and cover. Leave to rise for about 1 hr or until doubled in size (or leave in the fridge overnight).
- Knock the air out of the dough. On a floured surface, shape into eight buns. Put the buns on a baking tray lined with baking parchment (no more than 2cm apart) and prove somewhere warm for 1 hr or until well risen.

- Heat oven to 220C/200C fan/gas 7. Brush the bun tops with egg. Sprinkle on the sesame seeds. Mix the plain flour with water to make a paste, transfer to a piping bag and pipe crosses on top. Bake for 25-30 mins or until golden and risen. Serve warm.

Nutrition Information

- Calories: 488 calories
- Fiber: 3 grams fiber
- Protein: 18 grams protein
- Saturated Fat: 6 grams saturated fat
- Total Fat: 14 grams fat
- Total Carbohydrate: 71 grams carbohydrates
- Sodium: 2.22 milligram of sodium
- Sugar: 19 grams sugar

---

236. Giant Cookie

Serving: 8 | Prep: 15mins | Cook: 20mins | Ready in:

Ingredients

- 200g butter at room temperature, plus extra for the pan
- 250g light brown sugar
- 2 egg yolks
- ½ tsp vanilla extract
- 275g plain flour
- 1 tsp baking powder
- 150g chocolate chips
- 100g other cookie fillings, such as pretzels, chopped nuts, pieces of fudge or toffee, marshmallows
- vanilla ice cream, to serve (optional)

Direction

- Heat oven to 180C/160C fan/gas 4. Tip the butter and sugar into a large mixing bowl, beat until combined, then stir in the yolks and vanilla. Tip in the flour, baking powder, chocolate chips, a pinch of sea salt and any

other fillings you want to add. Mix until a crumbly dough forms.
- Lightly butter a 25cm ovenproof frying pan. Spoon in and flatten the cookie mixture. For a gooey dessert, bake for 20 mins, leave to rest for 5 mins, then scoop straight from the pan and serve with ice cream, if you like. For a firmer cookie you can cut, bake for 30 mins, then leave to cool completely before cutting into wedges.

Nutrition Information

- Calories: 596 calories
- Saturated Fat: 17 grams saturated fat
- Total Carbohydrate: 76 grams carbohydrates
- Sodium: 1.2 milligram of sodium
- Sugar: 40 grams sugar
- Fiber: 2 grams fiber
- Protein: 7 grams protein
- Total Fat: 29 grams fat

---

237. Ginger & White Chocolate Cake

Serving: Serves 10-12 | Prep: 20mins | Cook: 45mins | Ready in:

Ingredients

- 220g unsalted butter, softened
- 365g self-raising flour
- 200g muscovado sugar
- 50g black treacle
- 150g golden syrup
- 2 large eggs, lightly beaten
- 300ml milk
- 2 balls stem ginger in syrup, finely chopped, plus 50ml of the syrup
- 1 tsp fine sea salt
- 3 tsp ground ginger
- ½ tsp cinnamon
- ½ tsp bicarbonate of soda

- small handful of crystallised ginger pieces, chopped, to decorate
- For the white chocolate icing
- 30ml milk
- 160g icing sugar, sieved
- 150g white chocolate, chopped

Direction

- Heat the oven to 180C/160C fan/gas 4. Melt 1 tbsp butter in a small pan, then stir in ½ tbsp flour to create a wet paste. Brush it over the inside of a 9-inch bundt tin. Put the remaining butter, sugar, treacle and golden syrup in a pan set over a medium heat and stir until everything has melted together. Leave to cool a little.
- Pour the mixture into a large bowl and whisk in the eggs and milk. Fold in the stem ginger, remaining flour, salt, ground ginger, cinnamon and bicarb. Tip into the prepared tin and bake for 40-45 mins, or until firm to the touch. Leave to cool for 10 mins in the tin, then turn out onto a wire rack to cool completely.
- To make the icing, whisk the milk, ginger syrup and icing sugar together. Melt the chocolate in a heatproof bowl in the microwave in 1-min bursts. Leave to cool a little, then whisk into the milk mixture. Spoon the icing over the cake, then decorate with the crystallised ginger pieces.

Nutrition Information

- Calories: 533 calories
- Sodium: 1 milligram of sodium
- Total Fat: 22 grams fat
- Protein: 6 grams protein
- Fiber: 1 grams fiber
- Saturated Fat: 13 grams saturated fat
- Total Carbohydrate: 77 grams carbohydrates
- Sugar: 54 grams sugar

238. Ginger Cookie Sandwiches With Lemon Mascarpone

Serving: Makes 12-15 | Prep: 30mins | Cook: 14mins | Ready in:

Ingredients

- 100g unsalted butter, melted
- 50g golden caster sugar
- 100g light brown soft sugar
- 25g black treacle
- 1 large egg
- ½ tsp vanilla extract
- ¼ tsp bicarbonate of soda
- 175g gluten-free flour blend (I used Doves Farm)
- 1 tbsp ground ginger
- ½ tsp ground black pepper
- ¼ tsp ground nutmeg
- ¼ tsp ground cloves
- ¼ tsp ground cardamom (the seeds from 3 pods, crushed – see tip)
- 75g demerara sugar, to coat
- For the filling
- 175g mascarpone
- 85g lemon curd

Direction

- To make the cookies, put the butter, sugars, treacle, egg and vanilla in a large bowl and mix together with an electric whisk until smooth and combined. In a separate bowl, mix together the remaining ingredients except the demerara. Add the dry ingredients to the egg mixture and mix until a very sticky dough is formed. Cover with cling film and chill for at least 4 hrs.
- Heat oven to 180C/160C fan/gas 4 and line two baking trays with baking parchment. Roll the cookie dough into balls, about a tablespoon in size, then roll in the demerara sugar. Place on the lined trays, leaving about 2.5cm space between cookies.

- Bake for about 14 mins or until just lightly browned around the edges, swapping the trays over halfway through cooking. Allow to cool on the trays for 10 mins before transferring to a wire rack to cool completely.
- To make the filling, beat together the mascarpone and lemon curd in a bowl until smooth and creamy. Transfer to a piping bag fitted with a plain round piping tip. Pipe a layer of the cream onto the base of half the cookies and sandwich together with the other half. Will keep for 3-4 days in a sealed container in the fridge – the texture will turn soft and cakey (this is no bad thing).

Nutrition Information

- Calories: 227 calories
- Saturated Fat: 7 grams saturated fat
- Total Carbohydrate: 28 grams carbohydrates
- Sugar: 18 grams sugar
- Protein: 2 grams protein
- Sodium: 0.1 milligram of sodium
- Total Fat: 12 grams fat

---

239. Gluten Free Scones

Serving: Makes 6-8 | Prep: 20mins | Cook: 15mins | Ready in:

Ingredients

- 250g gluten free self-raising flour
- ½ tsp fine salt
- 1 tsp xanthan gum
- 1 tsp gluten-free baking powder
- 50g caster sugar
- 40g cold butter, cubed
- 75ml whole milk
- 1 large egg and 1 egg yolk
- 50g sultanas (optional)

Direction

- Mix the flour, salt, xanthan gum, baking powder and sugar together in a bowl. Rub in the butter with your fingertips until you have fine breadcrumbs. You can also do this by gradually pulsing the mixture in a food processor until it resembles breadcrumbs.
- Whisk together the milk and whole egg and gradually mix into the flour mixture with your hands until you have a smooth dough. Mix in the sultanas, if using. Knead briefly to come together into a ball.
- Gently roll out the scone dough until 2cm thick. Transfer to a baking tray lined with parchment and chill for 30 mins to firm up the dough – this makes them easier to cut out.
- Remove the dough from the fridge and, using a 5cm cutter, cut out 6-8 scones (press the offcuts together and re-roll when you need to). Put the scones upside down (this will mean you get a neater top when baked) onto another baking tray lined with baking parchment, spread 2cm apart.
- Whisk the egg yolk and evenly brush the tops of the scones, making sure that the egg wash doesn't run down the sides of the scones otherwise they will rise unevenly. Put the scones on a tray and transfer to the freezer for 15 mins. Heat oven to 220C/200C fan/gas 7. Remove the scones from the freezer and brush the tops with the beaten egg again, then bake for 12-15 mins until golden brown. Eat just warm or cold, generously topped with jam and cream, if you like.

Nutrition Information

- Calories: 193 calories
- Fiber: 1 grams fiber
- Protein: 4 grams protein
- Total Fat: 6 grams fat
- Sugar: 7 grams sugar
- Sodium: 0.82 milligram of sodium
- Saturated Fat: 3 grams saturated fat
- Total Carbohydrate: 30 grams carbohydrates

- Once cool, cut into 16 squares. Will keep for 3 days in an airtight container.

Nutrition Information

- Calories: 424 calories
- Total Carbohydrate: 42 grams carbohydrates
- Protein: 6 grams protein
- Total Fat: 24 grams fat
- Sugar: 37 grams sugar
- Sodium: 0.5 milligram of sodium
- Fiber: 2 grams fiber
- Saturated Fat: 11 grams saturated fat

---

240.   Hazelnut Brownies

Serving: Makes 16 | Prep: 15mins | Cook: 45mins | Ready in:

Ingredients

- box of 16 Ferrero Rocher chocolates
- 250g pack salted butter, plus extra for greasing
- 250g golden caster sugar
- 225g light muscovado sugar
- 100g cocoa powder
- 4 large eggs
- 100g self-raising flour
- 85g ready-chopped hazelnuts
- 4 tbsp Frangelico or Fratello hazelnut liqueur (or Disaronno)

Direction

- Unwrap the chocolates, place on a tray and pop in the freezer. Heat oven to 180C/160C fan/gas 4. Lightly grease and line the base and sides of a 21-22cm square tin with baking parchment.
- Put the butter, sugars and cocoa into your largest saucepan and gently melt together, stirring regularly so the mixture doesn't catch. Once the sugar granules have just about disappeared, take off the heat, tip into a bowl and leave to cool for 5 mins.
- Use a whisk or wooden spoon to beat the eggs, one by one, into the mixture. When they're completely incorporated and the mixture is smooth and shiny, stir in the flour, hazelnuts and liqueur. Tip the mixture into the prepared tin and bake for 35 mins.
- Remove the tin from the oven and use a cutlery knife to mark the top of the brownies into 16 squares (don't cut through, it's just as a guide). Use a teaspoon to push a little dent in the centre of each portion and add a frozen Ferrero Rocher chocolate into each dip. Return to the oven for 3 mins, then remove and leave to cool completely.

---

241.   Lamingtons

Serving: Makes 18 | Prep: 1hours | Cook: 30mins | Ready in:

Ingredients

- 125g salted butter, softened, plus extra for the tin
- 250g golden caster sugar
- 3 large eggs
- 250g self-raising flour
- 3 tbsp milk
- ½ tsp salt
- 250ml double cream
- 2 tbsp icing sugar
- 200g raspberry jam
- 350g desiccated coconut
- Icing
- 80g unsalted butter, melted
- 250ml milk
- 50g cocoa powder
- 400g icing sugar

Direction

- Heat the oven to 200C/180C fan/gas 6. Butter and line a 20 x 30cm rectangle tin.
- Beat the butter and sugar in a free-standing mixer until pale and fluffy. Add the eggs one

at a time and beat well. Beat through the flour, milk and salt until fully combined, then spoon into the tin. Bake in the oven for 25 mins or until golden and firm to the touch. Set aside to cool completely.

- Slice the sponge horizontally to create two halves. Trim the edges to make perfect corners. Cut the sponge into 18 squares. Lightly whip the cream with the icing sugar until it reaches soft peaks. Spread a little of the jam on half of the sponge squares then pipe or spread over a little of the cream. Sandwich each one with a second square of sponge then set aside in the fridge to chill.

- To make the icing, whisk together the melted butter and milk in a bowl. Sieve the cocoa powder and icing sugar together in a seperate bowl. Gradually add the cocoa and sugar to the butter and milk mixture, whisking continuously to ensure there are no lumps. If it gets lumpy, whizz with a hand blender until smooth.

- Divide the coconut between three shallow bowls (this keeps it from getting coated in too much chocolate whilst you're dipping).

- Dip each lamington in the icing until completely covered. Roll in the coconut and set on a wire rack. Repeat with the remaining sponges. Chill for a minimum of 1 hr.

Nutrition Information

- Calories: 545 calories
- Sodium: 0.6 milligram of sodium
- Total Carbohydrate: 58 grams carbohydrates
- Saturated Fat: 22 grams saturated fat
- Total Fat: 31 grams fat
- Sugar: 47 grams sugar
- Protein: 6 grams protein
- Fiber: 5 grams fiber

---

242.   Lemon & Buttermilk Pound Cake

Serving: 12 | Prep: 25mins | Cook: 45mins | Ready in:

Ingredients

- 125g butter, plus extra for the tin
- 200g plain flour, plus extra for dusting
- ¼ tsp bicarbonate of soda
- ¼ tsp baking powder
- 200g golden caster sugar
- 4 lemons, finely zested (save a little for the top if you like)
- 2 large eggs, at room temperature, lightly beaten
- 100ml buttermilk, at room temperature
- ½ lemon, juiced
- For the syrup
- 50g granulated sugar
- 2 large lemons, juiced (use the lemons you've zested)
- For the icing
- 150g icing sugar, sifted
- 2-3 tbsp lemon juice

Direction

- Heat oven to 180C/160C fan/gas 4. Butter and flour a loaf tin measuring 22 x 11 x 7cm. Sift the flour with a pinch of salt, bicarbonate of soda and baking powder. Beat the butter and sugar until pale and fluffy, then add the lemon zest. Gradually add the eggs a little at a time, beating well after each addition. Mix the buttermilk with the lemon juice. Fold the flour mixture into the batter, alternating with the buttermilk and lemon mixture.

- Scrape the batter into the loaf tin and bake for 40-45 mins, or until a skewer inserted into the centre of the cake comes out clean. Leave to sit for 10 mins, then turn out onto a wire cooling rack with a tray underneath it. Set the cake the right way up.

- To make the syrup, put the ingredients in a small saucepan and heat until the sugar has dissolved. Pierce the cake all over with a skewer then, while the cake is still warm, pour the syrup over slowly. Leave to cool.

- Gradually add the lemon juice to the icing sugar and mix until just smooth. If runny, put in the fridge for about 10 mins – you don't want it to set, you just want it become a little firmer. Pour or spread the icing over the cake (the bits that drizzle down the side will be caught by the tray under the cooling rack). This icing won't set hard, but do leave it to set a little before serving.

Nutrition Information

- Calories: 291 calories
- Sodium: 0.4 milligram of sodium
- Saturated Fat: 6 grams saturated fat
- Total Carbohydrate: 47 grams carbohydrates
- Protein: 4 grams protein
- Total Fat: 10 grams fat
- Sugar: 34 grams sugar
- Fiber: 1 grams fiber

243. Lemon & Ginger Shortbread

Serving: 12 | Prep: 10mins | Cook: 40mins | Ready in:

Ingredients

- 100g salted butter, softened, plus a little extra for greasing
- 50g golden caster sugar, plus extra for dusting
- zest 1 large lemon
- 8 pieces of crystallised ginger, finely chopped
- 175g plain flour

Direction

- Heat oven to 150C/130C fan/gas 2 and grease a 22cm loose-bottomed fluted tart tin. Put the butter in a bowl and beat with a wooden spoon until soft. Beat in the sugar, then stir in the lemon zest and ginger.

- Stir in the flour and work with your hands to form a soft dough. Tip into the tin and press into an even, flat layer with your fingers. Prick all over with a fork and bake in the oven for 40 mins until pale gold. Cut into wedges then leave to cool completely in the tin. Remove from the tin and dust with caster sugar to serve.

Nutrition Information

- Calories: 142 calories
- Total Carbohydrate: 18 grams carbohydrates
- Sugar: 7 grams sugar
- Sodium: 0.1 milligram of sodium
- Saturated Fat: 4 grams saturated fat
- Fiber: 1 grams fiber
- Protein: 2 grams protein
- Total Fat: 7 grams fat

244. Lemon Curd, Mascarpone & Passion Fruit Tart

Serving: 6 | Prep: 15mins | Cook: 25mins | Ready in:

Ingredients

- 320g sheet of puff pastry
- 1 egg, beaten
- 250g mascarpone
- 150ml double cream
- 6 tbsp lemon curd
- 3 passion fruit, seeds removed
- 30g chopped pistachios

Direction

- Heat the oven to 200C/180C fan/gas 6. Unroll the puff pastry onto a lined baking tray. Score a 2cm border around the edge of the pastry using a sharp knife, then brush the border with the egg.

- Bake for 15-20 mins, or until golden and crisp. Gently push down the middle with the back of a spoon, then leave to cool completely.
- Whisk the mascarpone with the double cream and 3 tbsp lemon curd until soft and spoonable. Fold in another 3 tbsp lemon curd and the seeds of 1 passion fruit.
- Spoon the cream mixture in the centre of the pastry and scatter over the seeds of 2 passion fruit and the chopped pistachios.

Nutrition Information

- Calories: 602 calories
- Sodium: 0.6 milligram of sodium
- Total Carbohydrate: 30 grams carbohydrates
- Fiber: 3 grams fiber
- Total Fat: 50 grams fat
- Sugar: 12 grams sugar
- Saturated Fat: 28 grams saturated fat
- Protein: 8 grams protein

245. Malty Choc Chip Cookies

Serving: Makes 20 | Prep: 15mins | Cook: 10mins | Ready in:

Ingredients

- 140g butter, softened
- 50g golden caster sugar
- 100g soft light brown sugar
- 2 medium eggs
- 200g plain flour
- 175g malted milk drink powder (we used Horlicks)
- ½ tsp baking powder
- 100g bar dark chocolate, chopped

Direction

- Heat oven to 180C/160C fan/gas 4 and line 2 baking sheets with baking parchment. Beat the butter and sugars in a bowl until light and fluffy, then beat in the eggs one at a time.
- Add the flour, malted milk drink powder, baking powder and a good pinch of salt, then stir with a wooden spoon until the mixture forms a dough. Tip out onto the work surface and gently knead in the chocolate. Divide the mixture into 20 pieces, roughly the size of a whole walnut. Roll each piece into a ball and place on the baking trays, leaving plenty of room for the cookies to spread. Flatten each ball slightly with your hand.
- Bake for 10-12 mins until starting to turn golden brown on the edges. Remove from the oven, leave on the baking tray for 5 mins to cool slightly then transfer to a wire rack to cool completely. Will keep in a cake tin or cookie jar for up to 5 days.

Nutrition Information

- Calories: 186 calories
- Sodium: 0.3 milligram of sodium
- Total Fat: 9 grams fat
- Total Carbohydrate: 24 grams carbohydrates
- Fiber: 1 grams fiber
- Protein: 3 grams protein
- Sugar: 14 grams sugar
- Saturated Fat: 5 grams saturated fat

246. Orange & Coriander Drizzle Cake

Serving: Cuts into 10-12 slices | Prep: 5mins | Cook: 1hours45mins | Ready in:

Ingredients

- 1 large orange
- 175g golden caster sugar
- 2 tbsp coriander seeds
- 50g polenta
- 175g butter, softened
- 150g self-raising flour

- 1 tsp baking powder
- 3 eggs
- For the decoration
- 1 orange
- 50g golden caster sugar
- 100g icing sugar

Direction

- To make the cake, put the orange in a saucepan, cover with water, bring to the boil and simmer for 1 hr or until you can pierce the orange easily with a knife.
- Drain, leave to cool, then cut the orange into quarters. Cut each quarter in half so that you have 8 pieces, and remove any pips. Put 75g of the sugar in a small pan and add 100ml water and the orange pieces. Heat gently until the sugar has dissolved, then turn up the heat and simmer for 10 mins. Allow the orange to cool slightly, then either blitz with a stick blender or liquidise to a pulp. Crush the coriander seeds using a pestle and mortar or a spice grinder, then add to the warm orange pulp along with the polenta. Stir to combine, then leave to cool.
- Heat oven to 190C/170C fan/gas 5. Grease and line the base and sides of a 22cm loose-bottomed cake tin. Put the butter, flour, baking powder, eggs and the remaining 100g caster sugar in a large mixing bowl along with the cooled orange pulp. Mix until thoroughly blended using an electric hand mixer. Spoon into the prepared tin and bake for 35-45 mins or until springy to the touch – a skewer inserted into the centre should come out clean. The cake should be pale in colour and just leaving the sides of the tin. Transfer to a wire rack and leave to cool.
- Meanwhile, prepare the decoration. Using a potato peeler, peel half the zest from the orange into large strips, then slice very thinly so that you have lots of orange zest shreds (like you would for marmalade). Put the caster sugar and 100ml water in a small saucepan set over a low heat until the sugar has dissolved, then add the orange shreds. Bring to the boil,

then simmer for 8-10 mins until the shreds are quite soft. Remove using a slotted spoon and set aside on a tray lined with baking parchment.
- When the cake has cooled, sift the icing sugar into a small bowl. Juice the orange and add enough of it to the icing sugar to make a runny icing. Drizzle the icing over the cooled cake and scatter the orange shreds on top.

Nutrition Information

- Calories: 304 calories
- Total Carbohydrate: 41 grams carbohydrates
- Sugar: 28 grams sugar
- Fiber: 1 grams fiber
- Protein: 4 grams protein
- Sodium: 0.5 milligram of sodium
- Total Fat: 14 grams fat
- Saturated Fat: 8 grams saturated fat

247.   PBJ Bakewell Tart

Serving: 15 | Prep: 35mins | Cook: 45mins | Ready in:

Ingredients

- 80g roasted unsalted peanuts, plus 2 tbsp to serve
- 100g peanut butter
- 75g plain flour
- 1 tsp baking powder
- 120g butter, softened
- 150g golden caster sugar
- 1 egg, plus 1 egg white (use the yolk in the pastry)
- 50g raspberry jam, plus 2 tsp to serve
- For the chocolate pastry
- 200g plain flour
- 4 tbsp cocoa powder
- 130g cold butter, chopped into small pieces
- 1 egg yolk
- 2 tbsp icing sugar, plus 5 tbsp for the drizzle

Direction

- First, make the pastry. Tip the flour, cocoa, butter and a pinch of salt into a food processor and blitz until the mixture resembles fine breadcrumbs. Add the egg yolk, icing sugar and 2 tbsp cold water and blitz again until just starting to clump together. Tip onto your work surface (don't worry about washing the bowl), knead briefly into a smooth ball of dough, then flatten into a thick disc shape, wrap in cling film and chill for 30 mins.
- Add the remaining ingredients – except for the jam and the peanuts to serve – to the food processor and blitz until smooth and creamy. Heat oven to 180C/160C fan/gas 4.
- Remove the pastry from the fridge and roll out to the thickness of a £1 coin. Lift the pastry into a 22cm fluted tart tin and press it into the corners, taking care not to rip it. Trim the excess pastry with scissors, leaving an overhang of about 1cm. Line with baking parchment and baking beans, and bake for 15 mins.
- Remove the parchment and beans and return to the oven for 5 mins more, until it looks biscuity. Remove from the oven and use a small serrated knife to trim the pastry to the height of the tin. Discard (or nibble on) the off-cuts.
- Spoon the jam onto the base of the tart and spread to the edges. Top with the peanut mixture, spreading to the edges to cover the jam. Bake for 45 mins until the sponge is cooked and a skewer inserted into the centre comes out clean. Cool in the tin for 15 mins, then transfer to a wire rack to cool completely.
- Mash the remaining icing sugar and jam together to make a smooth icing and drizzle on top. Roughly chop the remaining peanuts and scatter over. Leftovers will keep in an airtight container for 3 days.

Nutrition Information

- Calories: 368 calories
- Fiber: 2 grams fiber
- Sugar: 20 grams sugar
- Protein: 7 grams protein
- Total Carbohydrate: 35 grams carbohydrates
- Sodium: 0.6 milligram of sodium
- Saturated Fat: 11 grams saturated fat
- Total Fat: 22 grams fat

248. Peach Melba Pop Pies

Serving: makes 12 | Prep: 30mins | Cook: 20mins | Ready in:

Ingredients

- 200g raspberries
- 410g can peach slices in fruit juice, drained and chopped
- 1 tbsp cornflour
- 1 tbsp honey
- 2 x 320g shortcrust pastrysheet
- 1 egg, beaten
- 150g icing sugar
- freeze-dried raspberriesor sprinkles, optional

Direction

- Set 6 plump raspberries aside and tip the rest into a bowl. Add the peaches and toss together. In a small bowl mix the cornflour and honey to make a paste, pour over the fruit and combine.
- Unroll the pastry sheets and use a pizza wheel to cut out 6 rectangles from each one. Turn a piece of pastry so the long side is nearest to you, and fold it in half like a book, to create a fold down the middle. Open the pastry out and spoon the fruit filling onto one side, leaving a border of about 1cm around the edge. Brush the beaten egg around the edges and fold the pastry again to encase the filling. Use a fork to seal the edges all the way around, then brush all over with more egg. Poke a few air holes in the top with the fork. Repeat with the remaining pastry and filling.

Arrange the pop pies on a baking sheet lined with baking parchment and chill for at least 30 mins, or for up to 24 hrs. Alternatively freeze for up to 2 months.

- Heat oven to 200C/180C fan/gas 6. Bake the pop pies for 20 mins, or until the pastry is golden and the filling is bubbling through the holes. Remove from the oven and cool for at least 20 mins. If cooking from frozen, bake for an extra 5 mins. Meanwhile crush the remaining raspberries until juicy and mix with the icing sugar to make a thick icing. Spread thinly over the pies and sprinkle with freeze dried raspberries or sprinkles, if you like. Eat warm, or cold, for breakfast or drizzle with cream or custard for dessert.

Nutrition Information

- Calories: 330 calories
- Sugar: 18 grams sugar
- Fiber: 3 grams fiber
- Sodium: 0.3 milligram of sodium
- Total Fat: 17 grams fat
- Saturated Fat: 6 grams saturated fat
- Protein: 4 grams protein
- Total Carbohydrate: 38 grams carbohydrates

---

249. Peanut Butter & Jam Flapjacks

Serving: Makes 9 | Prep: 15mins | Cook: 30mins | Ready in:

Ingredients

- 5 tbsp salted butter, plus extra for the tin
- 250g crunchy peanut butter
- 8 tbsp strawberry or raspberry jam
- 80g light brown soft sugar
- 200g rolled oats

Direction

- Heat the oven to 180C/160C fan/gas 4. Butter and line the base and sides of a 20cm square cake tin with baking parchment.
- Put 3 tbsp each of the peanut butter and jam in separate small bowls and set aside. Tip the remaining peanut butter, the rest of the jam and the butter and sugar into a pan set over a medium heat and stir until everything has melted together. Quickly stir in the oats, then leave to cool for 5 mins.
- Spoon the mixture into the prepared cake tin and gently press down with your hands. Dot over the reserved peanut butter and jam, then bake for 20-25 mins or until golden brown. Leave to cool completely in the tin, then turn out onto a board and cut into squares.

Nutrition Information

- Calories: 399 calories
- Total Carbohydrate: 34 grams carbohydrates
- Sodium: 0.4 milligram of sodium
- Total Fat: 23 grams fat
- Saturated Fat: 7 grams saturated fat
- Sugar: 19 grams sugar
- Protein: 11 grams protein
- Fiber: 4 grams fiber

---

250. Pineapple Passion Bundt

Serving: 16 | Prep: 15mins | Cook: 1hours15mins | Ready in:

Ingredients

- For the sponge
- 1 small, ripe pineapple (300g pineapple after trimmings)
- 250g unsalted butter, softened
- 350g self-raising flour, plus 1 tbsp
- 100ml whole milk
- seeds and juice of 2 passion fruits
- 250g golden caster sugar
- 4 large eggs, at room temperature

- seeds from 1 vanilla pod, or 1 tsp vanilla extract
- For the icing
- 100g icing sugar
- seeds and juice of 1 passion fruit
- 2-3 tsp whole milk

Direction

- Heat oven to 180C/160C fan/gas 4. Top and tail the pineapple, then use a serrated knife to cut away the skin. Cut the flesh into eight wedges and remove the central core from each wedge. Slice the pineapple into small pieces about the thickness of a £1 coin, then roast on a baking tray for 20 mins until drier and golden. Leave to cool.
- Rub 1 tbsp of the butter around the inside of a 25cm bundt tin. Sprinkle in 1 tbsp flour, then turn the pan on its side and roll it, tapping gently, to move the flour around and coat the butter. Tap out any excess.
- Mix the milk with the passion fruit and set aside for a few mins – the acidity of the juice will sour the milk a little. With electric beaters, beat together the rest of the butter and the sugar in a bowl until light and fluffy. Add the flour, milk and passion fruit mixture, eggs, vanilla and ¼ tsp salt. Beat briefly until creamy and smooth, then fold in the pineapple pieces. Spoon the mix into the tin and level the top.
- Bake the bundt for 50-55 mins until risen, golden and a skewer inserted into the deepest part of the cake comes out clean. Sit the tin on a cooling rack until the cake is barely warm.
- Sift the icing sugar into a large bowl, then make a well in the middle and slowly mix in the passion fruit and milk to make a smooth, flowing glaze. Turn the cake onto a plate, brush with the glaze and leave to cool and set.

Nutrition Information

- Calories: 327 calories
- Protein: 5 grams protein
- Sodium: 0.3 milligram of sodium
- Saturated Fat: 9 grams saturated fat
- Total Fat: 15 grams fat
- Total Carbohydrate: 42 grams carbohydrates
- Fiber: 2 grams fiber
- Sugar: 25 grams sugar

---

251. Pink Marble Sandwich Cake

Serving: Serves 10-12 | Prep: 30mins | Cook: 25mins | Ready in:

Ingredients

- 225g butter, at room temperature, plus extra for the tin
- 225g golden caster sugar
- 225g self-raising flour
- 4 large eggs, lightly beaten
- 4 tbsp seedless raspberry jam
- a few drops of pink food colouring (optional)
- 1 tsp vanilla extract
- 1-2 tbsp icing sugar, for dusting
- For the white chocolate layer
- 200g white chocolate, chopped
- 100ml double cream

Direction

- Heat the oven to 180C/160C fan/gas 4. Butter and line the bases of two 18cm sandwich tins. Beat the butter, sugar, flour and eggs together in a large bowl using an electric whisk until it's lump-free.
- Divide the mixture between two bowls. Beat half the jam and the food colouring, if using, into one, and beat the vanilla into the other.
- Spoon alternating dollops of the mixes into the prepared cake tins, then swirl together using a skewer. Do this carefully – if you overdo it, you won't see the pattern. Smooth the tops with the back of a spoon.
- Bake for 20-25 mins until golden and a skewer inserted into the centre comes out clean. Leave to cool in the tins for 10 mins, then turn out.

- Meanwhile, to make the white chocolate layer, put the chocolate and cream in a heatproof bowl set over a pan of just simmering water, ensuring the bowl doesn't touch the water. Stir until the chocolate has melted into the cream and you're left with a smooth, glossy mixture. Leave to cool completely in the fridge, stirring occasionally.
- Sandwich the cakes together with the remaining raspberry jam and the white chocolate mixture, then generously dust the top with icing sugar. Slice and serve.

Nutrition Information

- Calories: 460 calories
- Sugar: 33 grams sugar
- Fiber: 1 grams fiber
- Sodium: 0.6 milligram of sodium
- Saturated Fat: 16 grams saturated fat
- Total Carbohydrate: 47 grams carbohydrates
- Total Fat: 27 grams fat
- Protein: 6 grams protein

252.	Sangria Cake

Serving: 10 | Prep: 45mins | Cook: 1hours20mins | Ready in:

Ingredients

- 100g pears, peeled and chopped
- 100g peaches or nectarines, stoned and chopped
- 100g strawberries, hulled and chopped
- 100g cherries, stoned and chopped
- 280g golden caster sugar
- 225g butter, softened
- 1 orange, zest only
- 150ml red wine
- 225g self-raising flour
- 100g pack ground almonds
- 1 tsp baking powder
- 3 medium eggs
- 50ml orange liqueur (we used Cointreau)
- 1 tbsp granulated sugar
- To decorate
- 1 small orange, cut into wedges
- 1 lemon, cut into wedges
- a handful of strawberries (optional)
- a handful of cherries (optional)

Direction

- Tip the pears, peaches, strawberries and cherries into a bowl and sprinkle over 50g of the sugar. Stir, then set aside for 30 mins to macerate.
- Heat oven to 180C/160C fan/gas 4 and grease and line the base and sides of a 23cm loose-bottomed, round cake tin with baking parchment
- Tip remaining sugar, butter, orange zest and 100ml red wine into a large bowl and beat with an electric whisk until well blended. Add the flour, almonds, baking powder and eggs, then beat again until smooth. Add half the chopped fruit and 1 tbsp of the liquid from the bowl too and mix gently with a spoon to combine. Put the mixture into your prepared tin and smooth the top so the mixture is level.
- Bake in the middle of the oven for 1 hr - 1 hr 15 mins until risen, golden and a skewer inserted into the centre comes out clean. Cover with foil if the cake starts to brown too much on the top. Once baked, leave in the tin for 15 mins before transferring it to a wire rack to cool.
- Once the cake is cool enough to handle, but ideally still a little warm, heat the remaining red wine and orange liqueur together with the granulated sugar in a pan until melted, raise the heat and boil for a few mins until syrupy. Flip the cake over and pile the rest of the fruit on top of the cake with then pour the boozy syrup over.
- Decorate with the orange and lemon wedges along with extra strawberries and cherries if you like. Serve with crème fraiche, or a good quality vanilla ice cream.

Nutrition Information

- Calories: 499 calories
- Total Carbohydrate: 53 grams carbohydrates
- Fiber: 2 grams fiber
- Protein: 7 grams protein
- Total Fat: 26 grams fat
- Sugar: 35 grams sugar
- Sodium: 0.8 milligram of sodium
- Saturated Fat: 13 grams saturated fat

253. Sweet Potato, Avocado & Feta Muffins

Serving: makes 9 | Prep: 20mins | Cook: 20mins | Ready in:

Ingredients

- 1 sweet potato (about 200g), peeled and chopped into small chunks
- drizzle of flavourless oil, such as vegetable or sunflower
- 1 large avocado, peel and stone removed, roughly chopped (about 150g prepared weight)
- 100g ground almonds
- 100g fine polenta
- 80ml maple syrup
- 3 large eggs
- 1 ½ tsp baking powder
- 1 tsp bicarbonate of soda
- 100ml semi-skimmed milk
- 50g feta, crumbled, optional
- 2 tbsp mixed seeds
- ¼ tsp sweet paprika

Direction

- Place the sweet potato in a heatproof bowl, cover with cling film and microwave on High for 8 mins, or until really soft. Leave to cool completely. Grease 9 holes of a muffin tin with a little oil (or line each hole with a square of baking parchment.)

- Chop 1/4 of the sweet potato into even smaller pieces and set aside. Place the sweet potato, avocado, almonds, polenta, maple syrup, eggs, baking powder, bicarb, milk and 1/4 tsp salt in the bowl of a food processor. Blend until completely smooth. Divide the mixture evenly between the muffin tin holes, then top with the reserved chopped sweet potato, feta, seeds and a dusting of paprika. Bake for 22 mins at 180C/160 fan/ gas mark 4, or until risen, browning on top and cooked through – check by inserting a skewer to the centre, it should come out dry. Cool in the tin for 5 mins, then transfer to a wire rack and cool completely. Store in a sealed container for up to 3 days.

Nutrition Information

- Calories: 268 calories
- Fiber: 3 grams fiber
- Saturated Fat: 3 grams saturated fat
- Total Carbohydrate: 22 grams carbohydrates
- Protein: 9 grams protein
- Sodium: 0.9 milligram of sodium
- Sugar: 9 grams sugar
- Total Fat: 15 grams fat

254. Vegan Carrot Cake

Serving: 15 | Prep: 35mins | Cook: 30mins | Ready in:

Ingredients

- For the icing
- 4 sachets (200g) creamed coconut
- 1 tbsp lemon juice
- 2 tbsp cashew nut butter
- 50g icing sugar
- 60ml oat milk
- For the cake
- 250ml jar coconut oil, melted
- 300g light brown sugar
- 1 ½ tsp vanilla essence

- 210ml dairy free milk, we used oat milk
- 420g plain flour
- 1 ½ tsp baking powder
- 1 ½ tsp bicarbonate of soda
- 1 tsp cinnamon, plus extra cinnamon to decorate
- 1 tsp ginger
- 1 tsp ground nutmeg
- 1 orange, zest only
- 4 medium carrots, grated (you want 270g grated weight)
- 75g chopped walnuts, plus extra to decorate
- edible flowers (optional)

Direction

- Start by making the icing first. Mash the coconut cream with 2 tbsp hot water and the lemon juice until smooth. Add the cashew butter then whisk in the icing sugar followed by the oat milk. Continue to whisk until fully combined, set aside in the fridge until needed.
- Heat the oven to 180C/160C fan/gas mark 4. Grease 2 x 20cm cake tins with a little of the melted coconut oil and line the bases with baking parchment. Whisk together the oil and sugar, then add the vanilla and milk. Combine the flour, baking powder, bicarbonate of soda, spices and orange zest in a separate bowl. Add these to the wet mixture and stir well. Finally stir in the carrot and the nuts. Divide the mixture between the prepared tins and bake for 25-30 mins until a skewer inserted into the middle of the cake comes out cleanly. Cool in the tin for 5 mins before transferring to a wire rack to cool completely.
- Sandwich the cakes together with half the icing then cover the top with the remaining icing (add a splash of oat milk if the icing feels too firm). Scatter over the nuts and dust the cake with a little cinnamon and decorate with edible flowers.

Nutrition Information

- Calories: 501 calories
- Total Carbohydrate: 49 grams carbohydrates
- Total Fat: 31 grams fat
- Sugar: 26 grams sugar
- Sodium: 0.45 milligram of sodium
- Fiber: 2 grams fiber
- Protein: 5 grams protein
- Saturated Fat: 23 grams saturated fat

Chapter 8: Awesome Baking Recipes

***

| 255. | Bakewell Tart |

Serving: 8 | Prep: 25mins | Cook: 55mins | Ready in:

Ingredients

- 250g plain flour, plus extra for rolling out
- ¼ tsp fine sea salt
- 2 tbsp icing sugar
- 140g cold butter, cubed
- 2 egg yolks, beaten
- cream or custard, to serve (optional)
- For the filling
- 100g salted butter, softened
- 100g caster sugar
- 50g ground almonds
- 1 tsp almond extract
- 2 medium eggs, beaten
- 3 tbsp raspberry jam
- 50g flaked almonds
- 80g icing sugar

Direction

- Heat the oven to 200C/180C fan/gas 6. To make the pastry, put the flour in a food processor along with the salt and icing sugar. Blitz to combine. Add the butter and pulse in short bursts until it's the texture of fine breadcrumbs. Mix 4 tbsp cold water with the beaten eggs and drizzle into the mixture, then quickly pulse to combine. Tip out the crumbly mixture onto a work surface, then form into a puck, cover and chill for 30 mins.

- Roll the pastry out on a lightly floured surface to around 25cm, and to the thickness of a £1 coin. Line a 20cm fluted tart tin with the pastry, leaving the pastry to overhang. Add a large disc of baking parchment big enough to cover the edges, and some baking beans to weigh it down (use dried rice or lentils if you don't have baking beans). Bake for 15 mins, then remove the parchment and beans and bake for a further 7-10 mins or until the bottom is evenly cooked. Trim off any overhanging pastry with a serrated knife.
- For the filling, beat the butter and sugar until combined. Add the ground almonds, almond extract and eggs and beat for a further minute. Spread the jam over the pastry, then top with the almond filling. Scatter over the flaked almonds and bake for 25-30 mins until golden and firm. Leave to cool in the tin (or eat warm at this stage and leave out step 4).
- Mix together the icing sugar and 1-2 tsp water and drizzle over the tart. Slice and serve with cream or custard, if you like.

Nutrition Information

- Calories: 572 calories
- Saturated Fat: 17 grams saturated fat
- Fiber: 1 grams fiber
- Sodium: 0.77 milligram of sodium
- Total Carbohydrate: 55 grams carbohydrates
- Protein: 9 grams protein
- Total Fat: 35 grams fat
- Sugar: 31 grams sugar

---

256. Best Ever Chocolate Brownies Recipe

Serving: Cuts into 16 squares or 32 triangles | Prep: 25mins | Cook: 35mins | Ready in:

Ingredients

- 185g unsalted butter
- 185g best dark chocolate
- 85g plain flour
- 40g cocoa powder
- 50g white chocolate
- 50g milk chocolate
- 3 large eggs
- 275g golden caster sugar

Direction

- Cut 185g unsalted butter into small cubes and tip into a medium bowl. Break 185g dark chocolate into small pieces and drop into the bowl.
- Fill a small saucepan about a quarter full with hot water, then sit the bowl on top so it rests on the rim of the pan, not touching the water. Put over a low heat until the butter and chocolate have melted, stirring occasionally to mix them.
- Remove the bowl from the pan. Alternatively, cover the bowl loosely with cling film and put in the microwave for 2 minutes on High. Leave the melted mixture to cool to room temperature.
- While you wait for the chocolate to cool, position a shelf in the middle of your oven and turn the oven on to 180C/160C fan/gas 4.
- Using a shallow 20cm square tin, cut out a square of non-stick baking parchment to line the base. Tip 85g plain flour and 40g cocoa powder into a sieve held over a medium bowl. Tap and shake the sieve so they run through together and you get rid of any lumps.
- Chop 50g white chocolate and 50g milk chocolate into chunks on a board.
- Break 3 large eggs into a large bowl and tip in 275g golden caster sugar. With an electric

mixer on maximum speed, whisk the eggs and sugar. They will look thick and creamy, like a milk shake. This can take 3-8 minutes, depending on how powerful your mixer is. You'll know it's ready when the mixture becomes really pale and about double its original volume. Another check is to turn off the mixer, lift out the beaters and wiggle them from side to side. If the mixture that runs off the beaters leaves a trail on the surface of the mixture in the bowl for a second or two, you're there.

- Pour the cooled chocolate mixture over the eggy mousse, then gently fold together with a rubber spatula. Plunge the spatula in at one side, take it underneath and bring it up the opposite side and in again at the middle. Continue going under and over in a figure of eight, moving the bowl round after each folding so you can get at it from all sides, until the two mixtures are one and the colour is a mottled dark brown. The idea is to marry them without knocking out the air, so be as gentle and slow as you like.
- Hold the sieve over the bowl of eggy chocolate mixture and resift the cocoa and flour mixture, shaking the sieve from side to side, to cover the top evenly.
- Gently fold in this powder using the same figure of eight action as before. The mixture will look dry and dusty at first, and a bit unpromising, but if you keep going very gently and patiently, it will end up looking gungy and fudgy. Stop just before you feel you should, as you don't want to overdo this mixing.
- Finally, stir in the white and milk chocolate chunks until they're dotted throughout.
- Pour the mixture into the prepared tin, scraping every bit out of the bowl with the spatula. Gently ease the mixture into the corners of the tin and paddle the spatula from side to side across the top to level it.
- Put in the oven and set your timer for 25 mins. When the buzzer goes, open the oven, pull the shelf out a bit and gently shake the tin. If the brownie wobbles in the middle, it's not quite

done, so slide it back in and bake for another 5 minutes until the top has a shiny, papery crust and the sides are just beginning to come away from the tin. Take out of the oven.

- Leave the whole thing in the tin until completely cold, then, if you're using the brownie tin, lift up the protruding rim slightly and slide the uncut brownie out on its base. If you're using a normal tin, lift out the brownie with the foil. Cut into quarters, then cut each quarter into four squares and finally into triangles.
- They'll keep in an airtight container for a good two weeks and in the freezer for up to a month.

Nutrition Information

- Calories: 150 calories
- Sugar: 12 grams sugar
- Total Fat: 9 grams fat
- Sodium: 0.04 milligram of sodium
- Saturated Fat: 5 grams saturated fat
- Protein: 2 grams protein
- Total Carbohydrate: 15 grams carbohydrates
- Fiber: 1 grams fiber

257. Black Tahini Chocolate Cookies

Serving: makes 20 | Prep: 20mins | Cook: 8mins | Ready in:

Ingredients

- 50g salted butter, softened
- 125g light brown muscovado sugar
- 125g golden caster sugar
- 1 egg, beaten
- 200g self-raising flour
- 2 tbsp cocoa powder
- 200g milk chocolate, broken into chunks
- 100g white chocolate, melted, for drizzling
- For the black tahini

- 100g black sesame seeds (available at Waitrose), plus extra for decorating
- 100g flavourless oil
- 30g maple syrup

Direction

- First, make the black tahini. Toast the sesame seeds in a small pan over a gentle heat until you can smell the sesame aroma. Transfer to a mini processor and blitz. Pour in the oil gradually until a paste forms. Add the maple syrup and blitz again. Tip into a small bowl until ready to use.
- Heat oven to 180C/160C fan/gas 4 and line two baking sheets with parchment. In a large bowl, beat the butter and sugars together until pale and fluffy. Add the egg and 80g of black tahini paste, and beat to combine. Tip in the flour, cocoa and milk chocolate chunks, and beat until fully incorporated.
- Using an ice cream scoop, ball the dough into about 20 pieces and place on the baking sheets. Press each ball lightly so it's a little flatter, leaving plenty of room between them, as they will spread.
- Bake for 6-8 mins until still soft in the middle – they will harden as they cool. Leave to cool on the sheets for a few mins before transferring to wire racks to cool completely.
- Once cooled, drizzle white chocolate zigzags all over the cookies and sprinkle some black sesame seeds on top. Will keep in an airtight container for 3 days.

Nutrition Information

- Calories: 254 calories
- Protein: 3 grams protein
- Total Fat: 13 grams fat
- Saturated Fat: 5 grams saturated fat
- Sugar: 21 grams sugar
- Fiber: 1 grams fiber
- Sodium: 0.2 milligram of sodium
- Total Carbohydrate: 29 grams carbohydrates

258. Bread In Four Easy Steps

Serving: Cuts into 8 thick slices | Prep: 15mins | Cook: 35mins | Ready in:

Ingredients

- 500g granary, strong wholewheat or white bread flour (I used granary)
- 7g sachet fast-action dried yeast
- 1 tsp salt
- 2 tbsp olive oil
- 1 tbsp clear honey

Direction

- Tip the flour, yeast and salt into a large bowl and mix together with your hands. Stir 300ml hand-hot water with the oil and honey, then stir into the dry ingredients to make a soft dough.
- Turn the dough out onto a lightly floured surface and knead for 5 mins, until the dough no longer feels sticky, sprinkling with a little more flour if you need it.
- Oil a 900g loaf tin and put the dough in the tin, pressing it in evenly. Put in a large plastic food bag and leave to rise for 1 hr, until the dough has risen to fill the tin and it no longer springs back when you press it with your finger.
- Heat oven to 200C/fan 180C/gas 6. Make several slashes across the top of the loaf with a sharp knife, then bake for 30-35 mins until the loaf is risen and golden. Tip it out onto a cooling rack and tap the base of the bread to check it is cooked. It should sound hollow. Leave to cool.

Nutrition Information

- Calories: 231 calories
- Sodium: 0.63 milligram of sodium
- Saturated Fat: 1 grams saturated fat
- Protein: 10 grams protein
- Total Carbohydrate: 42 grams carbohydrates

- Fiber: 4 grams fiber
- Total Fat: 4 grams fat
- Sugar: 3 grams sugar

259. Brilliant Banana Loaf

Serving: Cuts into 8-10 slices | Prep: 15mins | Cook: 50mins |Ready in:

Ingredients

- 140g butter, softened, plus extra for the tin
- 140g caster sugar
- 2 large eggs, beaten
- 140g self-raising flour
- 1 tsp baking powder
- 2 very ripe bananas, mashed
- 50g icing sugar
- handful dried banana chips, for decoration

Direction

- Heat oven to 180C/160C fan/gas 4.
- Butter a 2lb loaf tin and line the base and sides with baking parchment.
- Cream 140g softened butter and 140g caster sugar until light and fluffy, then slowly add 2 beaten large eggs with a little of the 140g flour.
- Fold in the remaining flour, 1 tsp baking powder and 2 mashed bananas.
- Pour the mixture into the prepared tin and bake for about 50 mins, or until cooked through. Check the loaf at 5-min intervals by testing it with a skewer (it should be able to be inserted and removed cleanly), as the time may vary depending on the shape of your loaf tin.
- Cool in the tin for 10 mins, then remove to a wire rack.
- Mix 50g icing sugar with 2-3 tsp water to make a runny icing.
- Drizzle the icing across the top of the cake and decorate with a handful of banana chips.

Nutrition Information

- Calories: 268 calories
- Sodium: 0.5 milligram of sodium
- Sugar: 24 grams sugar
- Fiber: 1 grams fiber
- Total Fat: 13 grams fat
- Total Carbohydrate: 34 grams carbohydrates
- Saturated Fat: 8 grams saturated fat
- Protein: 3 grams protein

260. Carrot Cake

Serving: 15 slices | Prep: 1hours15mins | Cook: |Ready in:

Ingredients

- 175g light muscovado sugar
- 175ml sunflower oil
- 3 large eggs, lightly beaten
- 140g grated carrot (about 3 medium)
- 100g raisins
- 1 large orange, zested
- 175g self-raising flour
- 1 tsp bicarbonate of soda
- 1 tsp ground cinnamon
- ½ tsp grated nutmeg (freshly grated will give you the best flavour)
- For the frosting
- 175g icing sugar
- 1½-2 tbsp orange juice

Direction

- Heat the oven to 180C/160C fan/gas 4. Oil and line the base and sides of an 18cm square cake tin with baking parchment.
- Tip the sugar, sunflower oil and eggs into a big mixing bowl. Lightly mix with a wooden spoon. Stir in the carrots, raisins and orange zest.
- Sift the flour, bicarbonate of soda, cinnamon and nutmeg into the bowl. Mix everything

together, the mixture will be soft and almost runny.

- Pour the mixture into the prepared tin and bake for 40-45 mins or until it feels firm and springy when you press it in the centre.
- Cool in the tin for 5 mins, then turn it out, peel off the paper and cool on a wire rack. (You can freeze the cake at this point if you want to serve it at a later date.)
- Beat the icing sugar and orange juice in a small bowl until smooth – you want the icing about as runny as single cream. Put the cake on a serving plate and boldly drizzle the icing back and forth in diagonal lines over the top, letting it drip down the sides.

Nutrition Information

- Calories: 265 calories
- Saturated Fat: 2 grams saturated fat
- Sodium: 0.4 milligram of sodium
- Sugar: 24.8 grams sugar
- Protein: 3 grams protein
- Total Carbohydrate: 39 grams carbohydrates
- Fiber: 1 grams fiber
- Total Fat: 12 grams fat

| 261. | Cheese & Pesto Whirls |

Serving: 12 | Prep: 40mins | Cook: 40mins | Ready in:

Ingredients

- 450g strong white bread flour, plus a little for dusting
- 7g sachet fast-action dried yeast
- 1 tsp golden caster sugar
- 2 tbsp olive oil, plus a drizzle
- 150g tub fresh pesto
- 240g tub semi-dried tomatoes, drained and roughly chopped
- 100g grated mozzarella (ready-grated is best for this, as it is drier than fresh)
- 50g parmesan (or vegetarian alternative), grated
- handful basil leaves

Direction

- Combine the flour, yeast, sugar and 1 ½ tsp fine salt in a large mixing bowl, or the bowl of a tabletop mixer. Measure out 300ml warm water and add roughly 280ml to the flour, along with the olive oil, and start mixing until the ingredients start to clump together as a dough. If the dough seems a little dry, add the remaining water. Once combined, knead for 10 mins by hand on your work surface, or for 5 mins on a medium speed in a mixer. The dough is ready when it feels soft, springy and elastic. Clean the bowl, drizzle in a little oil, then pop the dough back in, turning it over and coating the sides of the bowl in oil. Cover with some oiled cling film and set aside in a warm place to double in size – this will take 1-3 hrs, depending on the temperature.
- Line a baking tray with parchment. Uncover the dough and punch it down a couple of times with your fist, knocking out all the air bubbles. Tip out onto a floured work surface and dust the top with a little flour too, if it is sticky. Roll the dough out to a rectangle, roughly 40 x 30cm. Spread the pesto over the dough, then scatter over the tomatoes, both cheeses and the basil. Roll the dough up from one of the longer sides, into a long sausage.
- Use a sharp knife to cut the dough into 12 even pieces. Place on the baking tray, cut-side up, in a 3-by-4 formation, making sure the open end of each roll is tucked in towards the centre on the arrangement – this will prevent them from uncoiling during cooking. Leave a little space between each roll as they will grow and touch as they prove. Loosely cover with oiled cling film and leave to prove for 30 mins–1 hr until almost doubled in size again. Heat oven to 200C/180C fan/gas 6.
- Uncover the bread when it is puffed up. Bake on the middle shelf in the oven for 35-40 mins until golden brown and the centre looks dry

and not doughy. Remove from the oven and leave to cool for at least 10 mins.

Nutrition Information

- Calories: 293 calories
- Total Fat: 11 grams fat
- Saturated Fat: 3 grams saturated fat
- Protein: 10 grams protein
- Sodium: 1.4 milligram of sodium
- Sugar: 8 grams sugar
- Fiber: 4 grams fiber
- Total Carbohydrate: 36 grams carbohydrates

---

262. Chocolate & Orange Fudge Squares

Serving: Makes 15 | Prep: 10mins | Cook: 30mins | Ready in:

Ingredients

- 200g plain chocolate, broken into cubes (we used Bournville)
- 200g dark muscovado sugar
- 175g butter, plus extra for greasing
- 3 eggs, separated
- 140g plain flour
- 1 tsp vanilla extract
- zest 1 orange
- For the topping
- 200g tub soft cheese (I used Philadelphia Extra Light)
- ½ tsp vanilla extract
- 50g icing sugar

Direction

- Heat oven to 180C/fan 160C/gas 4. Butter and line a traybake tin, 23 x 23cm or thereabouts. Put the chocolate, sugar and butter in a pan, then heat very gently for about 5 mins, stirring every min until the butter and chocolate have melted. Leave to cool for 10 mins. Beat in the

egg yolks, flour, vanilla and half the orange zest.
- Put the egg whites into a large, very clean bowl, then whisk until they stand up in peaks. Stir ¼ of the whites into the chocolate mix to loosen it, then carefully fold in the rest with a metal spoon. Pour the mix into the tin, then bake for 25 mins or until evenly risen and just firm to the touch. Cool in the tin, then cut into squares. Can be frozen for up to 1 month.
- Beat together the cheese, vanilla, sugar and remaining zest until smooth. Spread over each chocolate square and serve. If you're making ahead, spread the topping over just before serving.

Nutrition Information

- Calories: 289 calories
- Fiber: 1 grams fiber
- Protein: 5 grams protein
- Sodium: 0.37 milligram of sodium
- Saturated Fat: 9 grams saturated fat
- Total Carbohydrate: 34 grams carbohydrates
- Total Fat: 16 grams fat
- Sugar: 27 grams sugar

---

263. Chocolate & Raspberry Birthday Layer Cake

Serving: 12 | Prep: 20mins | Cook: 40mins | Ready in:

Ingredients

- 225ml sunflower oil, plus extra for the tins
- 250g caster sugar
- 3 large eggs
- 225ml milk
- 250g self-raising flour
- 4 tbsp cocoa
- 1½ tsp bicarbonate of soda
- For the raspberry layer
- 150g raspberry jam
- 100g frozen raspberries, defrosted

- 300ml double cream
- 2 tbsp icing sugar

Direction

- Heat the oven to 180C/160C fan/gas 4. Oil and line two round 20cm springform cake tins with baking parchment. Whisk the oil, sugar, eggs and milk in a bowl until smooth. Sieve the flour, cocoa and bicarb into another large bowl, then gradually mix in the wet ingredients.
- Divide the mixture between the tins and bake for 35-40 mins until the cakes are risen and spring back when pressed. Leave to cool in the tins for 10 mins, then transfer to a wire rack to cool completely.
- For the raspberry layer, stir the jam and the defrosted raspberries together. Once the cakes are cool, whip the cream with the sugar to soft peaks, then gently fold half the raspberry mixture through the cream to create a ripple effect.
- Spoon most of the reserved raspberry mixture over one of the cakes, then dollop on half of the cream. Smooth over with a palette knife, then place the other sponge on top. Swirl over the remaining cream and swirl the last of the raspberry mixture through it. Will keep in the fridge for two days.

Nutrition Information

- Calories: 549 calories
- Sodium: 0.6 milligram of sodium
- Sugar: 33 grams sugar
- Total Fat: 36 grams fat
- Fiber: 2 grams fiber
- Saturated Fat: 12 grams saturated fat
- Total Carbohydrate: 49 grams carbohydrates
- Protein: 6 grams protein

264.   Chocolate Muffins

Serving: 6 | Prep: 10mins | Cook: 25mins | Ready in:

Ingredients

- 125g plain flour
- 25g cocoa powder
- 1 tsp baking powder
- 1 large egg
- 60g caster sugar
- 2 tbsp vegetable oil
- 100ml whole milk
- 50g chocolate chips (optional)
- 100g icing sugar

Direction

- Heat the oven to 180C/160C fan/gas 4. Line a muffin tin with six muffin cases. Sieve the flour, cocoa and baking powder into a medium bowl. Mix together the egg, sugar, oil and milk together in a jug, then gradually pour into the dry ingredients (add chocolate chips now to make double chocolate muffins, if you like) and mix until combined.
- Spoon the mixture evenly into the cake cases and bake for 20-25 mins until a skewer inserted into the middle comes out clean. Remove from the oven and leave to cool.
- Meanwhile, gradually mix ½-1 tbsp water into the icing sugar until you have a loose consistency that's not too runny. Drizzle the icing over the muffins once cool.

Nutrition Information

- Calories: 257 calories
- Protein: 5 grams protein
- Sugar: 27 grams sugar
- Total Carbohydrate: 44 grams carbohydrates
- Total Fat: 6 grams fat
- Saturated Fat: 2 grams saturated fat
- Sodium: 0.26 milligram of sodium
- Fiber: 2 grams fiber

265. Classic Victoria Sandwich Recipe

Serving: Cuts into 10 slices | Prep: 40mins | Cook: 20mins | Ready in:

Ingredients

- 200g caster sugar
- 200g softened butter
- 4 eggs, beaten
- 200g self-raising flour
- 1 tsp baking powder
- 2 tbsp milk
- For the filling
- 100g butter, softened
- 140g icing sugar, sifted
- drop vanilla extract (optional)
- half a 340g jar good-quality strawberry jam (we used Tiptree Little Scarlet)
- icing sugar, to decorate

Direction

- Heat oven to 190C/fan 170C/gas 5. Butter two 20cm sandwich tins and line with non-stick baking paper.
- In a large bowl, beat 200g caster sugar, 200g softened butter, 4 beaten eggs, 200g self-raising flour, 1 tsp baking powder and 2 tbsp milk together until you have a smooth, soft batter.
- Divide the mixture between the tins, smooth the surface with a spatula or the back of a spoon.
- Bake for about 20 mins until golden and the cake springs back when pressed.
- Turn onto a cooling rack and leave to cool completely.
- To make the filling, beat the 100g softened butter until smooth and creamy, then gradually beat in 140g sifted icing sugar and a drop of vanilla extract (if you're using it).
- Spread the buttercream over the bottom of one of the sponges. Top it with 170g strawberry jam and sandwich the second sponge on top.
- Dust with a little icing sugar before serving. Keep in an airtight container and eat within 2 days.

Nutrition Information

- Calories: 558 calories
- Saturated Fat: 17 grams saturated fat
- Protein: 5 grams protein
- Total Carbohydrate: 76 grams carbohydrates
- Sugar: 57 grams sugar
- Fiber: 0.6 grams fiber
- Total Fat: 28 grams fat
- Sodium: 0.9 milligram of sodium

266. Classic Scones With Jam & Clotted Cream

Serving: 8 | Prep: | Cook: 10mins | Ready in:

Ingredients

- 350g self-raising flour, plus more for dusting
- 1 tsp baking powder
- 85g butter, cut into cubes
- 3 tbsp caster sugar
- 175ml milk
- 1 tsp vanilla extract
- squeeze lemon juice (see tips below)
- beaten egg, to glaze
- jam and clotted cream, to serve

Direction

- Heat the oven to 220C/200C fan/gas 7. Tip the self-raising flour into a large bowl with ¼ tsp salt and the baking powder, then mix.
- Add the butter, then rub in with your fingers until the mix looks like fine crumbs. Stir in the caster sugar.
- Put the milk into a jug and heat in the microwave for about 30 secs until warm, but not hot. Add the vanilla extract and a squeeze of lemon juice, then set aside for a moment.

- Put a baking tray in the oven. Make a well in the dry mix, then add the liquid and combine it quickly with a cutlery knife – it will seem pretty wet at first.
- Scatter some flour onto the work surface and tip the dough out. Dredge the dough and your hands with a little more flour, then fold the dough over 2-3 times until it's a little smoother. Pat into a round about 4cm deep. Take a 5cm cutter (smooth-edged cutters tend to cut more cleanly, giving a better rise) and dip it into some flour. Plunge into the dough, then repeat until you have four scones. You may need to press what's left of the dough back into a round to cut out another four.
- Brush the tops with a beaten egg, then carefully arrange on the hot baking tray. Bake for 10 mins until risen and golden on the top. Eat just warm or cold on the day of baking, generously topped with jam and clotted cream. If freezing, freeze once cool. Defrost, then put in a low oven (about 160C/140C fan/gas 3) for a few minutes to refresh.

Nutrition Information

- Calories: 268 calories
- Saturated Fat: 6 grams saturated fat
- Fiber: 1 grams fiber
- Sugar: 8 grams sugar
- Protein: 6 grams protein
- Sodium: 0.9 milligram of sodium
- Total Fat: 10 grams fat
- Total Carbohydrate: 41 grams carbohydrates

267.　　Doughnut Muffins

Serving: Makes 12 | Prep: 20mins | Cook: 18mins |Ready in:

Ingredients

- 140g golden caster sugar, plus 200g extra for dusting

- 200g plain flour
- 1 tsp bicarbonate of soda
- 100ml natural yogurt
- 2 large eggs, beaten
- 1 tsp vanilla extract
- 140g butter, melted, plus extra for greasing
- 12 tsp seedless raspberry jam

Direction

- Heat oven to 190C/170C fan/gas 5. Lightly grease a 12-hole muffin tin (or use a silicone one). Put 140g sugar, flour and bicarb in a bowl and mix to combine. In a jug, whisk together the yogurt, eggs and vanilla. Tip the jug contents and melted butter into the dry ingredients and quickly fold with a metal spoon to combine.
- Divide two-thirds of the mixture between the muffin holes. Carefully add 1 tsp jam into the centre of each, then cover with the remaining mixture. Bake for 16-18 mins until risen, golden and springy to touch.
- Leave the muffins to cool for 5 mins before lifting out of the tin and rolling in the extra sugar.

Nutrition Information

- Calories: 229 calories
- Saturated Fat: 6 grams saturated fat
- Total Carbohydrate: 29 grams carbohydrates
- Protein: 3 grams protein
- Total Fat: 11 grams fat
- Sugar: 18 grams sugar
- Fiber: 1 grams fiber
- Sodium: 0.4 milligram of sodium

268.　　Easy Sourdough Bread

Serving: Makes 1 loaf (cuts into 10-12 slices) | Prep: 30mins | Cook: 30mins |Ready in:

Ingredients

- For the starter
- 100g strong white bread flour
- 100g organic dark rye flour
- 0.5 x 7g sachet fast-action dried yeast
- For the main dough
- 400g strong white bread flour
- 0.5 x 7g sachet fast-action dried yeast

Direction

- To make your starter, place all the ingredients in a bowl and add 250ml cold water. Mix together thoroughly with a spoon until you have a spongy mixture, then cover with cling film and leave at room temperature at least overnight, but up to 24 hrs if you have time.
- To make the bread dough, tip the ingredients into a clean bowl and add 1 tbsp fine salt, 200ml cold water and your starter. Bring all the ingredients together to a dough, adding a splash more water if too stiff, then tip out onto a lightly floured surface and knead for at least 10 mins until smooth, elastic and springy (this will take 5-7 mins in a mixer with a dough hook). Place the dough in a clean, lightly oiled bowl, cover with cling film and leave until doubled in size – about 1 hr at room temperature, 3 hrs in the fridge (see tips, below).
- Tip the dough onto a floured surface and gently shape into a round – you don't want to knock too much air out of the dough. Dust a piece of baking parchment heavily with flour and sit the dough on top. Cover with a tea towel and leave to prove for 1 hr until doubled in size.
- Heat oven to 220C/200C fan/gas 7. Place a sturdy flat baking tray on the middle shelf of the oven and a smaller tray with sides underneath. Dust the dough with flour and slash with a utility knife. Slide the bread onto the hot tray on top and throw a few ice cubes (or pour some cold water) onto the tray below – this creates a burst of steam, which helps the bread form a nice crust. Bake for 25-30 mins until the loaf sounds hollow when tapped on the bottom. Leave the bread to cool completely.

Nutrition Information

- Calories: 172 calories
- Total Fat: 1 grams fat
- Total Carbohydrate: 33 grams carbohydrates
- Fiber: 3 grams fiber
- Protein: 6 grams protein
- Sodium: 1.3 milligram of sodium

---

269.   Easy Vegan Chocolate Cake

Serving: 16 | Prep: 30mins | Cook: 25mins | Ready in:

Ingredients

- For the cake
- a little dairy-free sunflower spread, for greasing
- 1 large ripe avocado (about 150g)
- 300g light muscovado sugar
- 350g gluten-free plain flour
- 50g good-quality cocoa powder
- 1 tsp bicarbonate of soda
- 2 tsp gluten-free baking powder
- 400ml unsweetened soya milk
- 150ml vegetable oil
- 2 tsp vanilla extract
- For the frosting
- 85g ripe avocado flesh, mashed
- 85g dairy-free sunflower spread
- 200g dairy-free chocolate, 70% cocoa, broken into chunks
- 25g cocoa powder
- 125ml unsweetened soya milk
- 200g icing sugar, sifted
- 1 tsp vanilla extract
- gluten-free and vegan sprinkles, to decorate

Direction

- Heat oven to 160C/140C fan/gas 3. Grease two 20cm sandwich tins with a little dairy-free sunflower spread, then line the bases with baking parchment.
- Put 1 large avocado and 300g light muscovado sugar in a food processor and whizz until smooth.
- Add 350g gluten-free plain flour, 50g cocoa powder, 1 tsp bicarbonate of soda, 2 tsp gluten-free baking powder, 400ml unsweetened soya milk, 150ml vegetable oil and 2 tsp vanilla extract to the bowl with ½ tsp fine salt and process again to a velvety, liquid batter.
- Divide between the tins and bake for 25 mins or until fully risen and a skewer inserted into the middle of the cakes comes out clean.
- Cool in the tins for 5 mins, then turn the cakes onto a rack to cool completely.
- While you wait, start preparing the frosting. Beat together 85g ripe avocado flesh and 85g dairy-free sunflower spread with electric beaters until creamy and smooth. Pass through a sieve and set aside.
- Melt 200g dairy-free chocolate, either over a bowl of water or in the microwave, then let it cool for a few mins.
- Sift 25g cocoa powder into a large bowl. Bring 125ml unsweetened soya milk to a simmer, then gradually beat into the cocoa until smooth. Cool for a few mins.
- Tip in the avocado mix, 200g sifted icing sugar, melted chocolate and 1 tsp vanilla, and keep mixing to make a shiny, thick frosting. Use this to sandwich and top the cake.
- Cover with sprinkles or your own decoration, then leave to set for 10 mins before slicing. Can be made 2 days ahead.

Nutrition Information

- Calories: 452 calories
- Fiber: 3 grams fiber
- Total Fat: 24 grams fat
- Total Carbohydrate: 53 grams carbohydrates
- Sodium: 0.9 milligram of sodium

- Saturated Fat: 6 grams saturated fat
- Protein: 4 grams protein
- Sugar: 34 grams sugar

---

270. Easy Bake Bread

Serving: Makes 1 large loaf | Prep: 30mins | Cook: 35mins |Ready in:

Ingredients

- 500g strong bread flour
- 7g sachet fast-action dried yeast
- 1 tsp salt
- 300ml hand-hot water
- 2 tbsp sunflower oil
- 1 tbsp honey

Direction

- Tip the flour into a bowl and mix in the yeast with the salt. Stir in the water, oil and honey. Now bring together to make a soft dough – I use my hands, but a wooden spoon or knife from the cutlery drawer is fine. Tip onto a lightly floured surface and knead for 10 mins. It is worth putting in the time to do this as it will pay off later with lovely airy bread.
- Don't keep adding flour, a wet dough is better than a dry one, which will bake to a tough texture, so if you don't like the dough sticking to your hands, lightly oil them. If you are adding flavourings, knead them in gently now.
- Turn the dough into an oiled 1kg bread tin and cover with oiled cling film (or better still, a free unused shower cap from your last hotel stay!). Put in a warm place until the bread fills the tin, it should take between 1-2 hrs.
- Uncover and bake your bread at 200C/180C fan/gas 6 for 30-35 mins until golden. Tip out of the tin and tap the base of the loaf. It should sound hollow when fully cooked. If not cooked, put loaf back in the oven out of the tin and test again after 10 mins. Cool.

271.   Gregg's Tangy Lemon Tart

Serving: 8 | Prep: 25mins | Cook: 1hours | Ready in:

Ingredients

- For the pastry (makes double)
- 500g plain flour, plus extra for dusting
- 140g icing sugar
- 250g unsalted butter, cubed
- 4 egg yolks
- For the filling
- 5 eggs
- 140g caster sugar
- 150ml double cream
- juice 2-3 lemon (about 100ml/3.5fl oz) and 2 tbsp lemon zest

Direction

- To make the pastry, mix the flour and icing sugar in a bowl. Rub the butter into the flour with your fingers until crumbly. Mix in the egg yolks. If the pastry is still too dry, add 1-2 tbsp water until it comes together. Roll into a ball and divide in half (freeze one half for another recipe). Flatten out the pastry with your hands, wrap the dough in cling film, then chill for at least 30 mins. While the pastry is chilling, make the filling. Beat all the ingredients, except for the zest, together. Sieve the mixture, then stir in the zest.
- Roll out the pastry on a lightly floured surface to about the thickness of a £1 coin, then lift into a 23cm tart tin. Press down gently on the bottom and sides, then trim off any excess pastry. Stab a few holes in the bottom with a fork and put back in the fridge for 30 mins.
- Heat oven to 160C/140C fan/gas 3. Line the tart with foil and fill with rice or dried beans. Bake for 10 mins, then remove the tart tin from the oven, discard the foil, and bake for another 20 mins until biscuity. When the pastry is

ready, remove it from the oven, pour in the lemon mixture and bake again for 30-35 mins until just set. Leave to cool, then remove the tart from the tin and serve at room temperature or chilled.

Nutrition Information

- Calories: 770 calories
- Total Fat: 44 grams fat
- Sugar: 38 grams sugar
- Total Carbohydrate: 86 grams carbohydrates
- Fiber: 2 grams fiber
- Saturated Fat: 24 grams saturated fat
- Protein: 13 grams protein
- Sodium: 0.18 milligram of sodium

272.   Hazelnut Latte Cake

Serving: 16 | Prep: 1hours30mins | Cook: 25mins | Ready in:

Ingredients

- For the cakes
- 100g unsalted butter, plus extra for greasing
- 100g bag chopped toasted hazelnuts
- 300g light brown soft sugar
- 6 tbsp semi-skimmed milk
- 1 tsp fine instant coffee powder (see tip)
- 6 large eggs, at room temperature
- 2 tbsp cornflour
- 175g plain flour
- For the coffee syrup
- 50g light brown soft sugar
- 1 tsp fine instant coffee powder
- 1 tbsp Frangelico (hazelnut) liqueur, or use Kahlua or Tia Maria
- For the frosting and nuts
- 400g mascarpone
- 300g hazelnut chocolate spread (Nutella has the best texture for this)
- 1 tbsp fine instant coffee powder
- 50g chopped toasted hazelnuts

- For the latte topping
- 150ml pot double cream
- 4 tsp icing sugar
- 3 tbsp semi-skimmed milk
- 1 tbsp fine instant coffee powder, dissolved in 1 tsp boiling water

Direction

- Heat the oven to 180C/160C fan/gas 4. Generously butter two 20cm sandwich tins (ideally about 4.5cm deep or deeper) and line the bases with baking parchment. Put the hazelnuts into a food processor with 2 tbsp of the sugar, then pulse until finely chopped. Don't expect them to go as fine as ground almonds and avoid over-processing, as this can make the nuts greasy.
- Put the butter, milk and coffee powder into a small pan and heat gently until the butter has melted. Set aside.
- Now start the sponge. Crack the eggs into the bowl of a tabletop mixer, add the rest of the sugar and beat for 5-10 mins (or beat with an electric hand mixer in a large deep bowl for 15-20 mins) or until thick and billowy, and the mixture leaves a trail that holds for a couple of seconds. It is really important that the mixture has thickened, almost doubling in size, in order to achieve a light sponge.
- Mix the cornflour, plain flour and 1/2 tsp salt, and sift onto the whisked mixture. Using a large metal spoon, fold in very carefully. Sprinkle in the ground nuts, then fold these in too. Pour the warm milk mix around the edge of the bowl, and fold this in. Don't rush the folding, and continue with a light lifting and cutting motion until ribbons of liquid stop appearing. Divide the batter between the tins, then bake for 25 mins until risen to the middle and a burnished gold.
- Loosen the sides of the cakes with a palette knife, then cool in the tins on a rack for 20 mins (the cakes will level off, and possibly go a bit wrinkly, but that's normal). Carefully remove from the tins and cool, paper-side down.
- Make the syrup and the frosting while you wait. Put the sugar and 4 tbsp water into a small pan. Bring to the boil and leave for 1 min then take off the heat. Stir in the coffee and alcohol. Beat the mascarpone, hazelnut chocolate spread and coffee together with a wooden spoon, until silky and even.
- To assemble, cut the cold cakes horizontally across the middle, using a long serrated knife. With a pastry brush, dampen the cut surfaces all over with the syrup. Use it all. Put one cake layer onto a plate or stand, cut-side up. Spoon on 3 generous dollops of the frosting, then spread to the edges with a palette knife. The frosting should be about 5mm deep. Repeat with the next two layers. When you come to the final layer, place it cut-side down, so that the top of the cake is smooth. Paddle the rest of the frosting over the top and sides of the cake. The layer on the top can be thin. Clean the knife then use it to press a neat ring of nuts into the frosting on the side of the cake. Brush any excess away.
- For the topping, put 3 tbsp of the cream, 1 tsp icing sugar and 1 tbsp milk into a small bowl. Put the rest of the cream, milk and sugar, plus most of the dissolved coffee into a larger bowl. Whip the white cream, then the coffee cream, until they look like soft cappuccino froth, thick but still able to flow from a spoon. Pour most of the coffee cream onto the cake and push it out to cover the top. Whisk a little more coffee into what is left, so that it turns a few shades darker.
- To decorate with a characteristic latte 'tree' shape, load a pointy teaspoon with a little of the white cream. Start at the base of the tree, just right of the centre of the cake. Push the spoon into the coffee cream and let the white cream flow slowly. As it flows, drag the spoon then pull it gently away, to make a leaf-like shape. Repeat with more white cream on the left to make another leaf, then repeat 3-4 times, working up the cake top graduating from large to small leaves. Use the same technique to sweep a couple of arc shapes around the edge of the pattern.

- Use the dark cream to add detail to each leaf – you can paint this on with the tip of a teaspoon or a clean cocktail stick. Use a cocktail stick to drag the points of each leaf up and outwards. Draw a line down from the top of the 'tree' to the bottom to finish. The cake will keep for up to 2 days. Loosely cover any cut edges but avoid covering the cake directly as you could damage the decoration. Serve from the fridge or at cool room temperature.

Nutrition Information

- Calories: 544 calories
- Total Carbohydrate: 45 grams carbohydrates
- Fiber: 2 grams fiber
- Saturated Fat: 18 grams saturated fat
- Protein: 8 grams protein
- Sodium: 0.3 milligram of sodium
- Sugar: 33 grams sugar
- Total Fat: 36 grams fat

---

273. Iced Buns With Cream & Jam

Serving: Makes 10 | Prep: 45mins | Cook: 25mins | Ready in:

Ingredients

- 350ml milk, plus extra for brushing
- 30g butter, cubed
- 500g strong white bread flour
- 10g fast-action dried yeast
- 2 tbsp caster sugar
- 300g icing sugar, plus 1 tbsp
- few drops of yellow, pink and purple food colouring (optional)
- 300ml whipping or double cream
- 200g lemon curd
- 200g raspberry jam
- 200g blackcurrant jam
- glacé cherries, sprinkles or crystallised rose and violet petals, to decorate (optional)

Direction

- Heat the milk until steaming. Add the butter and swirl until melted. Leave to cool slightly. Tip the flour and yeast into a bowl or stand mixer fitted with a dough hook, then add the caster sugar and ½ tsp salt.
- When the milk mix has cooled slightly (it should feel just warm when you stick a finger in) pour into the flour mix. If using a stand mixer, mix for 5-8 mins on a medium speed until springy. Or, knead in the bowl for about 10 mins – when the dough is pulled apart, it should be able to stretch without ripping.
- Put the dough in a clean bowl, cover with a tea towel and leave to rise for 1½ hrs or until doubled in size. Or, transfer to the fridge to slowly rise for up to 24 hrs (this will improve the texture and flavour).
- If the dough is chilled, remove from the fridge 1 hr before shaping. Divide into 10 equal portions (weigh them out if you want to be accurate). To make round buns, roll and shape each piece into a smooth ball, or to make finger buns, roll and shape each piece into a finger shape. Arrange on a lined baking tray, leaving space between each. Cover loosely and leave to rise for 30 mins-1 hr more until doubled.
- Heat the oven to 180C/160C fan/ gas 4. Brush the buns with milk and bake for 25-30 mins until golden. Put on a wire rack and leave to cool.
- Mix the icing sugar with 2-3 tbsp water – it should be thick. Divide between bowls, depending on how many food colourings you're using (we used three). Dye each with a different colouring, adding a splash more water if needed.
- Whisk the cream and 1 tbsp icing sugar until just holding its shape. Don't overwhip, as it will thicken as you pipe (see tip, below). Fit a piping bag with a star nozzle and fill with a third of the cream.
- Split the round buns in half as you would a burger bun, or the finger buns down the middle lengthways. Spoon roughly 60g lemon

curd or jam over the bottom half of each bun (or down the middle), alternating the flavours, then pipe over a swirl of cream. Continue until all the buns are filled, refilling the piping bag with cream as needed. Spoon some icing over each bun, matching the colours to the jam (we used yellow for the curd, pink for the raspberry jam and purple for the blackcurrant). Decorate with the glacé cherries, sprinkles and crystallised petals, if you like, then leave to set for about 20 mins before serving. Best eaten the day they're made, but will keep in the fridge for 24 hrs.

Nutrition Information

- Calories: 647 calories
- Total Fat: 17 grams fat
- Saturated Fat: 10 grams saturated fat
- Sugar: 74 grams sugar
- Fiber: 2 grams fiber
- Protein: 9 grams protein
- Total Carbohydrate: 113 grams carbohydrates
- Sodium: 0.4 milligram of sodium

274.   Lemon Drizzle Cake

Serving: Cuts into 10 slices | Prep: | Cook: 45mins | Ready in:

Ingredients

- 225g unsalted butter, softened
- 225g caster sugar
- 4 eggs
- 225g self-raising flour
- 1 lemon, zested
- For the drizzle topping
- 1½ lemons, juiced
- 85g caster sugar

Direction

- Heat the oven to 180C/160C fan/gas 4.

- Beat together the butter and caster sugar until pale and creamy, then add the eggs, one at a time, slowly mixing through.
- Sift in the self-raising flour, then add the lemon zest and mix until well combined.
- Line a loaf tin (8 x 21cm) with greaseproof paper, then spoon in the mixture and level the top with a spoon.
- Bake for 45-50 mins until a thin skewer inserted into the centre of the cake comes out clean.
- While the cake is cooling in its tin, mix together the lemons juice and caster sugar to make the drizzle.
- Prick the warm cake all over with a skewer or fork, then pour over the drizzle – the juice will sink in and the sugar will form a lovely, crisp topping.
- Leave in the tin until completely cool, then remove and serve. Will keep in an airtight container for 3-4 days, or freeze for up to 1 month.

Nutrition Information

- Calories: 399 calories
- Protein: 5 grams protein
- Fiber: 1 grams fiber
- Total Carbohydrate: 50 grams carbohydrates
- Sugar: 33 grams sugar
- Saturated Fat: 13 grams saturated fat
- Sodium: 0.3 milligram of sodium
- Total Fat: 21 grams fat

275.   Lemon Drizzle Slices

Serving: cuts into 12 slices | Prep: 25mins | Cook: 30mins | Ready in:

Ingredients

- For the cake
- 70g softened unsalted butter
- 120g caster sugar

- 2 medium eggs
- 140g self-raising flour
- 1 tsp baking powder
- finely grated zest 1 lemon
- 1 tbsp lemon curd
- 2 tbsp full-fat milk
- For the drizzle topping
- 30g granulated sugar
- juice 1 lemon
- For the feather icing
- 250g icing sugar
- 3 tbsp water
- splash of yellow food colouring

Direction

- Heat oven to 180C/160C fan/ gas 4. Line a 20 x 20cm square baking tin with baking parchment.
- Using an electric whisk, beat the butter and sugar together until pale, light and fluffy. Add the eggs and mix again. Add the flour, baking powder, lemon zest, lemon curd and milk, and mix with a wooden spoon until all the ingredients are thoroughly combined. Pour the mixture into the prepared tin and bake for 25-30 mins or until a skewer comes out clean.
- Mix the sugar and lemon juice together and pour over the hot cake. Leave to cool in the tin. You can eat the cake as it is, or for a fancy finish, try making this feather icing.
- Mix the icing sugar with just enough water to give a runny, but not watery, icing. Put a small amount of icing in a separate bowl. Add a few drops of the food colouring to the icing until pale yellow. Spoon into a disposable icing bag.
- Remove the cake from the tin and peel off the baking parchment. Sit the cake on a wire rack over a baking tray. Spread the white icing over the top. Pipe thin lines of the coloured icing across the width of the cake. Use a cocktail stick to drag through the lines in opposite directions to create a feathered effect. Leave to set before cutting into slices.

Nutrition Information

- Calories: 236 calories
- Total Fat: 6 grams fat
- Sugar: 34 grams sugar
- Total Carbohydrate: 43 grams carbohydrates
- Saturated Fat: 3 grams saturated fat
- Protein: 2 grams protein
- Fiber: 1 grams fiber
- Sodium: 0.2 milligram of sodium

276.   Lemon Sponge Cake

Serving: Serves 10-12 | Prep: 25mins | Cook: 55mins | Ready in:

Ingredients

- 175g unsalted butter, softened, plus extra for the tin
- 175g golden caster sugar
- 3 large eggs
- 3 large unwaxed lemons, zested, plus 4-4 ½ tbsp juice
- 250g self-raising flour
- ½ tsp baking powder
- 100g Greek yogurt
- 400g icing sugar
- lemon zest or candied peel, to serve (optional)
- For the candied peel
- 2 large lemons
- 200g granulated sugar

Direction

- Heat oven to 170C/150C fan/gas 3. Butter a deep, loose-bottomed, 18cm cake tin and line the base with baking parchment.
- Beat the butter and caster sugar together with an electric whisk until fluffy and pale in colour. Crack the eggs in one at a time, beating well after each addition, then stir in the lemon zest. Fold in the flour, baking powder and ½ tsp salt, then fold in the yogurt.
- Spoon the mixture into the lined tin, smoothing the top with a spatula. Bake in the centre of the oven for 50-55 mins, or until

golden brown on top and firm to the touch. Cool in the tin for 10 mins before turning out onto a wire rack to cool completely. Will keep in an airtight container for up to four days, or in the freezer for up to a month.

- When you're ready to decorate, sieve the icing sugar into a bowl and beat in enough of the lemon juice to create a thick icing. Set the cake on a serving plate or cake stand, then spoon over the icing, allowing it to drip down the sides a little. Top with the lemon zest or candied peel, if using (see below), and cut into generous wedges to serve.

- To make candied lemon peel, peel large, wide strips from the lemons using a vegetable peeler. Remove any pith with a knife, then julienne the peel into very thin matchsticks. Tip the granulated sugar into a saucepan with 200ml water and set over a medium heat until the sugar has dissolved. Add the lemon peel and simmer gently for 15 mins, then scoop the peel out using a slotted spoon and set on a piece of kitchen paper to cool. Use to decorate the top of your cake.

Nutrition Information

- Calories: 409 calories
- Protein: 5 grams protein
- Fiber: 1 grams fiber
- Total Fat: 15 grams fat
- Saturated Fat: 9 grams saturated fat
- Sodium: 0.5 milligram of sodium
- Total Carbohydrate: 64 grams carbohydrates
- Sugar: 48 grams sugar

---

277. Lighter Gingerbread

Serving: Cuts into 21 pieces | Prep: 35mins | Cook: 40mins | Ready in:

Ingredients

- 140g dried pitted whole dates preferably Medjool, chopped into small pieces
- 75ml rapeseed oil, plus a few drops for greasing
- 75g black treacle
- 50g maple syrup
- 1 tsp finely grated fresh ginger
- 1 large egg
- 175ml buttermilk
- 250g plain flour
- 1 tsp bicarbonate of soda
- 1 tbsp ground ginger
- ½ tsp ground cinnamon
- 50g dark muscovado sugar

Direction

- Put the dates in a small bowl and pour over 125ml of boiling water. Leave to cool for 30 mins. Lightly oil a 28 x 19 x 3cm traybake tin, then line the base with baking parchment.

- Meanwhile, put the oil, black treacle, maple syrup and freshly grated ginger in a bowl and beat together with a fork to mix well. Set aside. Beat the egg in a small bowl and stir in the buttermilk. In a large bowl, mix the flour with the bicarbonate of soda, ground ginger, cinnamon and sugar – rub the mixture between your fingers to break down any lumpy bits of sugar. Heat oven to 160C/140C fan/gas 3.

- Blend the dates and their liquid to a thick purée in a small food processor. Pour the egg, the dates and the treacle mixture into the bowl with the flour. Stir together briefly with a wooden spoon just until well mixed – the mixture will be soft like a thick batter. Pour it into the lined tin, gently level the mixture and bake for 40-45 mins. To test if it's done, insert a skewer in the centre – if the skewer comes out clean with no uncooked mixture on it, and the cake feels firm but springy to the touch, it should be done.

- Leave in the tin for a few mins before removing to a wire rack, peeling off the parchment and leaving to cool completely. If you can wait, wrap it well in parchment, then foil. Leave for a day before cutting, as it will become stickier – it will keep moist for 3-4 days.

Nutrition Information

- Calories: 116 calories
- Saturated Fat: 0.4 grams saturated fat
- Total Carbohydrate: 17.5 grams carbohydrates
- Protein: 2 grams protein
- Sugar: 8.6 grams sugar
- Sodium: 0.2 milligram of sodium
- Fiber: 0.7 grams fiber
- Total Fat: 4.1 grams fat

---

278. Luscious Lemon Baked Cheesecake

Serving: Cuts into 10 slices | Prep: 10mins | Cook: 40mins | Ready in:

Ingredients

- 225g digestive biscuits
- 100g butter, melted
- 250g tub mascarpone
- 600g soft cheese
- 2 eggs, plus 2 yolks
- zest 3 lemons, juice of 1
- 4 tbsp plain flour
- 175g caster sugar
- For the topping
- ½ a 284ml pot soured cream
- 3 tbsp lemon curd
- handful raspberries, to serve (optional)

Direction

- Heat oven to 180C/fan 160C/gas 4. Line the bottom of a 23cm springform tin with greaseproof paper. Tip the biscuits and melted butter into a food processor, then blitz to make fine crumbs. Press into the tin and chill.

- Whisk all the other ingredients in a large bowl until completely combined, pour into the tin, then bake for 35-40 mins until the cheesecake has a uniform wobble.
- Turn off the oven and leave the cake inside until cool. When it is completely cooled, remove from the tin and top with soured cream. Swirl lemon curd over the top and decorate with raspberries, if you like.

Nutrition Information

- Calories: 705 calories
- Saturated Fat: 34 grams saturated fat
- Total Carbohydrate: 43 grams carbohydrates
- Sugar: 25 grams sugar
- Protein: 7 grams protein
- Sodium: 1.08 milligram of sodium
- Total Fat: 57 grams fat

---

279. Mary Berry's Orange Layer Cake

Serving: Cuts into 8 slices | Prep: 15mins | Cook: 20mins | Ready in:

Ingredients

- For the cake
- 225g baking spread
- 225g self-raising flour
- 1 level tsp baking powder
- 100g golden caster sugar
- 100g brown sugar
- 4 large eggs
- finely grated zest of 2 oranges
- For the butter icing
- 150g butter, softened
- 300g icing sugar, sifted
- finely grated zest of 2 oranges
- For the glaze
- 25g caster sugar
- juice of 2 oranges

Direction

- Heat oven to 180C/160C fan/gas 4. You will need 2 x 20cm loose-bottomed sandwich tins, greased and bases lined with baking parchment. Measure all the cake ingredients into a large bowl (reserve a little orange zest for decoration) and beat with a wooden spoon or electric hand mixer until combined and smooth.
- Divide evenly between the 2 tins. Bake for 20-25 mins or until well risen, lightly golden and shrinking away from the sides of the tins. After 5 mins, remove from the tins and leave to cool on a wire rack.
- To make the icing, put the butter and icing sugar into a bowl and mix with an electric hand mixer until light and fluffy. Stir in the orange zest.
- Remove the paper from the cakes. Sit 1 cake upside down on a plate. Make the glaze by putting the caster sugar and orange juice into a saucepan, stirring over a low heat until the sugar has dissolved. Boil until reduced by half, then brush half on the upside-down cake, using a pastry brush. Spread half the butter icing over the glazed cake. Sit the other cake on top, brush with the remaining glaze, then spread with the remaining butter icing. Scatter with the reserved orange zest. The cake is best eaten on the day, but will keep for up to 3 days in a cool place. It freezes well un-iced or filled.

Nutrition Information

- Calories: 745 calories
- Sugar: 67 grams sugar
- Total Fat: 42 grams fat
- Total Carbohydrate: 86 grams carbohydrates
- Fiber: 1 grams fiber
- Protein: 6 grams protein
- Sodium: 1.3 milligram of sodium
- Saturated Fat: 15 grams saturated fat

---

280.   Millionaire's Chocolate Tart

Serving: 10 | Prep: 30mins | Cook: 55mins | Ready in:

Ingredients

- 375g pack dessert shortcrust pastry
- 1 tsp vanilla paste or extract
- flour, for dusting
- 250g/9oz caramel (we used Carnation caramel from a can)
- 100g 70% plain chocolate, broken into pieces
- 100g white chocolate, broken into pieces
- 6 tbsp melted butter
- 2 eggs, plus 3 egg yolks
- 4 tbsp golden caster sugar
- icing sugar and single cream, to serve (optional)

Direction

- Break the pastry into chunks and drop into a food processor. Drizzle over the vanilla paste and pulse until the vanilla is speckled through the pastry (the extract should be completely absorbed). Tip out onto a floured surface, bring together into a ball, then roll out to line a 23cm tart tin (leave any overhanging pastry as you will trim this away when the tart is baked). Chill for 30 mins.
- Heat oven to 200C/180C fan/gas 6. Line the pastry with greaseproof paper. Fill with baking beans, bake blind for 15-20 mins, then remove the paper and beans and bake for 5-10 mins more until pale golden. Carefully spread caramel over the base and set aside while you make the filling. Lower oven to 180C/160C fan/gas 4.
- Melt the chocolates in a bowl over a pan of barely simmering water, then stir in the melted butter. Whisk the eggs, yolks and sugar together with an electric whisk in a large mixing bowl for 10 mins, until pale and thick enough to leave a trail when the beaters are lifted up. Fold in the melted chocolate with a large metal spoon, then scrape into the tin.

- Bake for 20-25 mins – the surface should be set and puffed but still with a slight wobble. Cool, then chill for at least 3 hrs or overnight, before dusting with icing sugar and serving.

Nutrition Information

- Calories: 618 calories
- Total Carbohydrate: 62 grams carbohydrates
- Saturated Fat: 18 grams saturated fat
- Fiber: 2 grams fiber
- Sodium: 0.59 milligram of sodium
- Total Fat: 39 grams fat
- Protein: 9 grams protein
- Sugar: 41 grams sugar

281.   Monkey Bread

Serving: 12 | Prep: 1hours15mins | Cook: 35mins | Ready in:

Ingredients

- For the dough
- 200ml semi-skimmed milk
- 85g unsalted butter
- 2 large eggs
- 550g strong white bread flour, plus extra for kneading if doing it by hand
- 2½ tsp fast-action dried yeast
- 50g golden caster sugar
- oil, for greasing
- To assemble
- 125g unsalted butter, plus extra for greasing
- 1 tbsp ground cinnamon
- 1 tsp ground ginger
- 1 tsp ground nutmeg
- 225g light muscovado sugar
- 140g pecans, toasted then roughly chopped
- For the glaze
- 100g icing sugar, sifted
- ½ tsp vanilla extract
- 1 tbsp semi-skimmed milk
- pinch of ground cinnamon

- 2 tbsp unsalted butter, melted

Direction

- Start with the dough. Put the milk and butter into a medium pan and heat gently until the butter melts and the milk is at a simmer. Cool for a few mins, then beat in the eggs with a fork. Mix the dry ingredients in a large bowl with 1 1/2 tsp fine salt, then add the liquid and stir to a sticky dough. Leave for 5 mins, then tip onto a floured worktop and knead for 5-10 mins until smooth and springy. Use a little oil to grease a large bowl, add the dough, turn it in the oil to coat, then cover the bowl with clingfilm. Leave in a warm place for 1 hr or until doubled in size. Knead in a tabletop mixer with a dough hook if you prefer.
- To assemble, grease a 25cm bundt pan with butter. Melt the rest of the butter in a pan. In a medium bowl mix the spices and sugar plus a pinch of salt. Spoon 2 tbsp melted butter, 3 tbsp spiced sugar and 4 tbsp pecans into the bottom of the tin.
- Pull the dough into about 65 small pieces and roll into balls. Taking 4 or 5 at a time, dunk the dough balls into the melted butter, let the excess drain off, then tip them into the spiced sugar. Roll to coat, then put haphazardly into the tin. Repeat until there's a full layer of dough in the tin. Scatter with the rest of the chopped nuts, then carry on filling the tin with the coated dough balls. Tip any leftover sugar and butter over the dough. Can be frozen now for up to 1 month. Defrost in the fridge then let prove.
- Cover the pan with oiled clingfilm then leave to rise in a warm place for 1 hr, or until risen and the dough no longer springs back when you poke it.
- Heat the oven to 180C/160C fan/gas 4. Bake the monkey bread for 35 mins, or until well risen and golden. Let the pan cool for 5 mins, then give it a sharp rap on the counter. Leave in the tin until just warm.
- Whisk all of the ingredients together to make the glaze. It will thicken as the melted butter

cools. Turn the monkey bread onto a serving plate, then drizzle with the glaze. Let it set, if you can bear the wait.

Nutrition Information

- Calories: 546 calories
- Total Carbohydrate: 65 grams carbohydrates
- Fiber: 2 grams fiber
- Sugar: 32 grams sugar
- Protein: 9 grams protein
- Sodium: 0.7 milligram of sodium
- Total Fat: 27 grams fat
- Saturated Fat: 12 grams saturated fat

282.   Raspberry Bakewell Cake

Serving: 8 | Prep: 10mins | Cook: 50mins | Ready in:

Ingredients

- 140g ground almond
- 140g butter, softened
- 140g golden caster sugar
- 140g self-raising flour
- 2 eggs
- 1 tsp vanilla extract
- 250g raspberry
- 2 tbsp flaked almond
- icing sugar, to serve

Direction

- Heat oven to 180C/160C fan/gas 4 and base-line and grease a deep 20cm loose-bottomed cake tin. Blitz the ground almonds, butter, sugar, flour, eggs and vanilla extract in a food processor until well combined.
- Spread half the mix over the cake tin and smooth over the top. Scatter the raspberries over, then dollop the remaining cake mixture on top and roughly spread – you might find this easier to do with your fingers. Scatter with flaked almonds and bake for 50 mins until

golden. Cool, remove from the tin and dust with icing sugar to serve.

Nutrition Information

- Calories: 411 calories
- Total Fat: 28 grams fat
- Sugar: 21 grams sugar
- Total Carbohydrate: 35 grams carbohydrates
- Saturated Fat: 10 grams saturated fat
- Protein: 8 grams protein
- Sodium: 0.5 milligram of sodium
- Fiber: 3 grams fiber

283.   Raspberry Honey Flapjacks

Serving: Makes 9-12 | Prep: 10mins | Cook: 25mins | Ready in:

Ingredients

- 150g butter
- 150g light brown soft sugar
- 4 tbsp honey (we used heather honey)
- 300g porridge oats
- 100g frozen raspberries

Direction

- Heat oven to 200C/180C fan/gas 6 and line a 20 x 20cm baking tin with parchment. Melt the butter, sugar, honey and a pinch of salt in a pan. Once the mixture is bubbling and combined, stir in the oats.
- Tip the oat mixture into the lined baking tin and press down with the back of a spoon. Scatter over the raspberries, then lightly press them into the oat mixture. Bake for 25-30 mins until golden brown. Leave to cool, then cut into 9 or 12 flapjacks.

Nutrition Information

- Calories: 265 calories
- Fiber: 2 grams fiber
- Total Fat: 12 grams fat
- Total Carbohydrate: 34 grams carbohydrates
- Sugar: 17 grams sugar
- Sodium: 0.3 milligram of sodium
- Saturated Fat: 7 grams saturated fat
- Protein: 3 grams protein

284. Red Velvet Cupcakes

Serving: Serves 12 | Prep: 25mins | Cook: 15mins | Ready in:

Ingredients

- 150g plain flour
- 1 tbsp cocoa powder
- 1 tsp bicarbonate of soda
- 50g butter, softened
- 150g caster sugar
- 1 large egg, beaten
- 1 tsp vanilla paste
- 100ml buttermilk or kefir
- 50ml vegetable oil
- 1 tsp white wine vinegar
- 1 tbsp red gel food colouring
- For the cream cheese icing
- 100g slightly salted butter, softened
- 225g icing sugar
- 100g full fat cream cheese, stirred to loosen

Direction

- Line a cupcake tin with 12 cupcake cases and set aside. Heat oven to 180C/160C fan/gas 4. Sieve the flour, cocoa, bicarb and a pinch of fine salt into a medium bowl and mix to combine.
- Using a stand mixer or an electric hand whisk, beat together the butter and sugar until light and fluffy, then beat in the egg, vanilla, buttermilk, oil and vinegar until combined. Gradually mix the wet ingredients into the dried. Once combined, mix in the red food

colouring until you have a deep red mix – the colour may vary depending on what brand you use.
- Divide the batter between the cupcake cases and bake for 15 mins, or until a skewer inserted into the centre of a cake comes out clean.
- While the cakes are cooling, make the icing. Beat together the butter and icing sugar using an electric whisk or by hand until pale and fluffy, about 3 mins, then beat in the cream cheese for a further 1-2 mins until well combined.
- Once the cakes are cool, use a piping bag fitted with a star nozzle to cover the cakes with the cream cheese icing, or dollop the icing on top using a spoon.

Nutrition Information

- Calories: 339 calories
- Total Carbohydrate: 42 grams carbohydrates
- Fiber: 1 grams fiber
- Sodium: 0.59 milligram of sodium
- Total Fat: 17 grams fat
- Protein: 3 grams protein
- Sugar: 32 grams sugar
- Saturated Fat: 8 grams saturated fat

285. Rhubarb & Custard Sandwich Biscuits

Serving: MAKES 16 | Prep: 30mins | Cook: 35mins | Ready in:

Ingredients

- 175g unsalted butter, cubed
- 50g caster sugar
- 50g icing sugar
- ¼ tsp fine sea salt
- 250g plain flour, plus extra for dusting
- 50g custard powder
- 2 egg yolks

- 1 tbsp vanilla bean paste
- For the rhubarb jam filling
- 200g rhubarb, trimmed and chopped
- 200g caster sugar
- ¼ lemon, juiced

Direction

- To make the jam, put the rhubarb, sugar and lemon juice in a pan over a medium heat. Bring to a simmer and cook for 15 mins, or until the rhubarb has broken down and released its liquid. Blitz using a hand blender until smooth, then simmer for another 5-10 mins until thick and jammy. To test it's ready, run a wooden spoon over the base of the pan – it should leave a trail rather than filling in straightaway. Leave to cool (it will set more as it does), then chill until ready to use. Will keep in a sealed container or jar in the fridge for up to one week.
- To make the biscuit dough, put the butter, both sugars and salt in a food processor and pulse a few times to a coarse paste. Scrape down the sides, then add the flour and custard powder and pulse again to a damp, sandy consistency. Add the egg yolks and vanilla and pulse again until the dough comes together into a ball. Add ½-1 tbsp water to bring it together, if needed. Tip the dough out, then wrap and put in the fridge to chill for at least 30 mins.
- Roll the dough out on a floured surface to a 5mm thickness. Stamp out as many biscuits as you can using a 6mm round cutter – you should get about 32 in total.
- Cut circles or hearts out of the centres of half the biscuits using the wide end of a plain piping nozzle (about 1.5cm), or a small heart cutter. Transfer all the biscuits to lined baking sheets, then transfer to the fridge and chill for 15 mins. You can also cook the cut-out shapes to make mini biscuits – if doing so, put these on their own baking sheet.
- Heat the oven to 200C/180C fan/ gas 6, then bake the biscuits for 8-10 mins until golden (5-6 mins for the mini biscuits). Put on a wire rack and leave to cool completely.
- Transfer the jam to a piping bag, snip off the end, and pipe a small layer of jam onto the plain biscuits (those without the centres cut out). Or, use a teaspoon. Spread the jam out – it may squidge out of the sides when sandwiching the biscuits, so don't go too far to the edge.
- Sandwich the remaining biscuits over the jam (don't press down too firmly), then transfer to an airtight container in a single layer and leave to set overnight. This ensures the jam won't leak when you bite into them, but they can be eaten straightaway if you can't resist. Will keep in an airtight container for up to three days, but the biscuits will start to soften over time.

Nutrition Information

- Calories: 237 calories
- Fiber: 1 grams fiber
- Total Carbohydrate: 34 grams carbohydrates
- Saturated Fat: 6 grams saturated fat
- Protein: 2 grams protein
- Total Fat: 10 grams fat
- Sugar: 19 grams sugar
- Sodium: 0.1 milligram of sodium

286.   Rhubarb & Pear Crumble

Serving: 6 | Prep: | Cook: | Ready in:

Ingredients

- 3 ripe pears
- 600g rhubarb
- 100g golden caster sugar
- finely grated zest and juice of 1 orange
- For the topping
- 200g wholemeal flour
- 200g cold butter, diced
- 140g soft, light brown sugar

- 50g muesli or porridge oats
- 25g Grape-Nuts or Clusters breakfast cereal

Direction

- Heat oven to 200C/fan 180C/gas 6. For the topping, tip all the ingredients together and rub with your fingers until you have a rough pastry, then set aside in the fridge.
- Peel the pears and chop into large chunks, then chop the rhubarb into finger-length batons. Tip into a large ovenproof dish and toss with the sugar and orange zest and juice. Crumble over the topping and bake for 40 mins until golden and bubbling at the sides. Leave to cool for 5 mins before spooning into bowls and serving with custard or ice cream.

Nutrition Information

- Calories: 591 calories
- Protein: 7 grams protein
- Sodium: 0.69 milligram of sodium
- Saturated Fat: 18 grams saturated fat
- Sugar: 54 grams sugar
- Fiber: 7 grams fiber
- Total Carbohydrate: 81 grams carbohydrates
- Total Fat: 29 grams fat

287.   Shortbread Recipe

Serving: Makes 24 slices | Prep: 15mins | Cook: 25mins | Ready in:

Ingredients

- 300g butter, softened
- 140g golden caster sugar, plus 4 tbsp
- 300g plain flour
- 140g rice flour

Direction

- Place the butter and 140g sugar in a food processor and whizz until smooth.

- Tip in both the flours and a pinch of salt, then whizz until mixture comes together.
- Using your hands, roughly spread the mixture out in a 20 x 30 x 4cm baking tray. Cover with cling film and smooth over until there are no wrinkles. Place in the fridge, uncooked, for at least 30 mins and up to 2 days.
- Heat oven to 180C/160C fan/gas 4. Remove cling film, then lightly mark the shortbread all over with a fork.
- Sprinkle with the remaining sugar, then bake for 20-25 mins.
- Leave to cool in the tin, then cut into 24 thin slices. Shortbread will keep in an airtight container for up to 1 week.

Nutrition Information

- Calories: 188 calories
- Sodium: 0.2 milligram of sodium
- Total Fat: 11 grams fat
- Saturated Fat: 7 grams saturated fat
- Total Carbohydrate: 23 grams carbohydrates
- Sugar: 9 grams sugar
- Protein: 2 grams protein

288.   Spiced Honey Drizzle Cake

Serving: 8 | Prep: 15mins | Cook: 45mins | Ready in:

Ingredients

- 100g salted butter, plus extra for the tin
- 100g light brown soft sugar
- 100g runny honey
- 1 large egg
- 100ml milk
- 1 tsp mixed spice
- ½ tsp ground ginger
- 150g self-raising flour
- For the glaze
- 25g salted butter
- 25g runny honey

Direction

- Heat oven to 180C/160C fan/gas 4. Butter and line a 900g loaf tin with baking parchment. Beat the butter and sugar with an electric whisk until creamy. Whisk in the honey, egg, milk, spices and a pinch of salt (don't worry if it curdles slightly, it will become a loose batter), then fold in the flour.
- Tip into the prepared loaf tin and bake for 45 mins until a skewer inserted in the middle comes out clean. Leave the cake to cool for 10 mins, then transfer to a wire rack to cool completely.
- For the glaze, melt the butter and honey in a small pan until smooth. Leave to cool until thickened, then drizzle over the top of the cooled cake. Leave to set before serving.

Nutrition Information

- Calories: 298 calories
- Fiber: 1 grams fiber
- Total Carbohydrate: 38 grams carbohydrates
- Total Fat: 14 grams fat
- Sodium: 0.5 milligram of sodium
- Sugar: 24 grams sugar
- Protein: 3 grams protein
- Saturated Fat: 9 grams saturated fat

289. Sticky Stem Ginger Cake With Lemon Icing

Serving: 12 | Prep: | Cook: 1hours | Ready in:

Ingredients

- 225g self-raising flour
- 1 tsp bicarbonate of soda
- 1 tbsp ground ginger
- 1 tsp ground cinnamon
- 1 tsp ground mixed spice
- 115g butter, cut into cubes, plus extra for greasing
- 115g dark muscovado sugar
- 115g black treacle
- 115g golden syrup
- 250ml whole milk
- 85g drained stem ginger, finely grated
- 1 egg
- For the icing
- 50g icing sugar, sifted
- 1 tsp finely grated lemon zest
- 1 tbsp lemon juice

Direction

- Preheat the oven to fan 160C/conventional 180C/gas 4. Butter and line an 18cm round, 7cm deep cake tin with greaseproof or parchment paper.
- Put the flour, bicarbonate of soda and all the spices into a large mixing bowl. Add the butter and rub it into the flour with your fingertips until the mixture resembles fine breadcrumbs.
- Put the sugar, treacle, syrup and milk in a medium saucepan and heat, gently stirring until the sugar has dissolved. Turn up the heat and bring the mixture to just below boiling point.
- Add the stem ginger to the flour mixture, then pour in the treacle mixture, stirring as you go with a wooden spoon. Break in the egg and beat until all the mixture is combined and it resembles a thick pancake batter. Pour this into prepared tin and bake for 50 minutes-1 hour, until a skewer pushed into the centre of the cake comes out fairly clean. Leave to cool completely in tin before turning cake out. (To freeze: wrap in greaseproof paper, then in cling film. Freeze for up to 1 month.)
- To make the icing, mix together icing sugar and lemon zest, then gradually add lemon juice until you have a smooth, slightly runny icing, adding more juice, if needed. Drizzle icing in a zig-zag pattern over surface of cake, turn cake around and drizzle again to create the cross-hatched finish (see below). Cake keeps for up to 2 weeks stored in an airtight container.

Nutrition Information

- Calories: 285 calories
- Total Carbohydrate: 50 grams carbohydrates
- Fiber: 1 grams fiber
- Sodium: 0.81 milligram of sodium
- Saturated Fat: 6 grams saturated fat
- Protein: 3 grams protein
- Total Fat: 10 grams fat
- Sugar: 31 grams sugar

290. Sticky Toffee Banana Bread

Serving: 10 | Prep: 25mins | Cook: 1hours15mins | Ready in:

Ingredients

- 125g soft butter, plus extra for the tin
- 75g caster sugar
- 50g dark brown soft sugar
- 3 medium eggs
- 2 large ripe bananas, mashed
- 50g natural yogurt
- 200g plain flour
- 2 tsp baking powder
- 50g pitted dates, chopped (about 10)
- 50g pecans or walnuts, chopped (or mixed chopped nuts)
- For the toffee sauce
- 100g light brown soft sugar
- 25g butter, cut into cubes
- 100ml double cream
- For the banana & nut brittle
- 150g caster sugar
- 50g pecan or walnuts (or mixed nuts)
- 50g banana chips
- ½ tsp sea salt flakes

Direction

- Heat the oven to 160C/140C fan/gas 3. Butter and line a 900g loaf tin with a strip of baking parchment.
- Beat the butter and both sugars in a bowl for 5 mins with an electric whisk until really fluffy. Whisk the eggs, banana and yogurt in a separate bowl until mostly smooth, then whisk this into the butter and sugar mixture. Fold in the flour and baking powder until just combined, then fold in the dates and nuts. Spoon into the tin, smooth over the top and bake for 1 hr-1 hr 15 mins until a skewer inserted into the middle comes out clean. Leave to cool in the tin for 10 mins, then lift out using the strip of parchment. You can serve it warm now, or leave to cool completely on a wire rack. Will keep for four days in an airtight container.
- Meanwhile, make the toffee sauce. Put the sugar in a heavy-based frying pan and melt over a medium-low heat until light golden brown and liquid – don't stir, just tilt the pan to melt the sugar. Carefully whisk in the butter until smooth, then pour in the cream slowly and bring to a bubble. Mix until the sauce is smooth and shiny. Pour into a heatproof bowl, cover and leave to cool to room temperature.
- For the brittle, put the sugar in a frying pan with 2 tbsp water over a medium heat, stir briefly, then simmer for 10 mins until the caramel turns amber. Don't stir after the initial mix, just tilt the pan to get an even deep golden colour.
- Meanwhile, line a baking tray with baking parchment. Carefully stir the nuts, banana chips and salt into the caramel, until well coated, then pour onto the tray. Tip the tray (or use a spoon) to make sure the nuts are in a single layer – or they will be harder to separate later. Leave to cool completely before breaking the brittle into shards.
- Stir the toffee sauce to loosen if it's become stiff, or warm for a few seconds in the microwave (add a splash more cream if you need to), then drizzle over the cake so it drips down the sides. Top with the shards of brittle. Will keep for two days in an airtight container.

Nutrition Information

- Calories: 464 calories
- Total Carbohydrate: 57 grams carbohydrates
- Sugar: 44 grams sugar
- Protein: 5 grams protein
- Sodium: 0.6 milligram of sodium
- Total Fat: 24 grams fat
- Fiber: 1 grams fiber
- Saturated Fat: 14 grams saturated fat

291. Triple Chocolate & Peanut Butter Layer Cake

Serving: 14 | Prep: 45mins | Cook: 1hours | Ready in:

Ingredients

- 225ml rapeseed oil, plus more for the tins
- 250g self-raising flour
- 4 tbsp cocoa
- 1 ½ tsp bicarbonate of soda
- 225g caster sugar
- 3 tbsp golden syrup
- 3 large eggs, beaten
- 225ml milk
- For the pretzel bark
- 200g dark chocolate, chopped
- 2 tbsp chocolate chips
- small handful pretzel pieces
- 2 tbsp honeycomb pieces
- For the icing
- 65g dark chocolate
- 250g soft salted butter
- 500g icing sugar
- 45g smooth peanut butter
- 1-2 tbsp cocoa
- For the ganache drip
- 200ml double cream
- 100g dark chocolate, finely chopped
- For the decoration
- chocolate eggs, some hollow, some filled, gold lustre, toffee popcorn and pretzels

Direction

- Heat oven to 180C/160C fan/gas 4. Oil and line the base of three 19cm sandwich tins. Mix the flour, cocoa, bicarb and sugar in a bowl. Make a well in the centre and beat in the syrup, eggs, oil and milk with an electric whisk until smooth.
- Divide the mix between the tins, and bake for 25-30 mins until the cakes are risen and firm to the touch. Cool in the tins for 10 mins before turning out onto a cooling rack and cooling completely. At this stage, they can be frozen, well wrapped, for up to eight weeks.
- Make the bark while the cake is cooling. Melt the chocolate in short bursts in the microwave, stirring every 20 secs, until smooth. Spoon onto a parchment-lined baking tray and smooth over with a spatula to make a thinnish layer, around 35 x 20cm. Sprinkle over the chocolate chips along with the pieces of pretzel and honeycomb, then chill until solid. Remove the bark from the fridge and leave for a minute to come to room temperature before using a sharp knife to cut it into shards (if it's fridge cold, the chocolate will snap rather than cut). Chill again until you're ready to decorate the cake.
- To make the icing, melt the chocolate in the microwave, stirring between short blasts, then leave to cool a little. Meanwhile, beat the butter, icing sugar and 1 tbsp boiling water with an electric whisk or stand mixer, slowly at first, then turn up the speed and beat until you get a pale, fluffy icing. Spoon out a third of the mix into a separate bowl and stir in the peanut butter. Whisk the melted chocolate into the remainder of the icing, then beat in the cocoa if you want a darker, more chocolatey-coloured icing.
- Sandwich the three cakes together with the peanut butter icing. Use half the chocolate icing to coat the sides and top of the cake and fill in the edges between the layers, scraping off any excess. Chill for 20 mins. This is called a crumb coating, allowing you to get a really smooth finish when it comes to the final icing.
- Spread the remaining chocolate icing over the lightly chilled cake, smoothing over the sides

and top so you get a neat finish. Chill again for 20 mins.

- To make the ganache, heat the cream in a small pan until steaming. Tip the dark chocolate into a bowl, then pour over the cream. Mix well until smooth and shiny. Transfer to a piping bag and leave to cool for a few mins at room temperature.
- Pipe the ganache on top of the cake, nudging it over the edge and allowing it to drip down neatly. Do this all the way round the cake, then fill in the centre with more ganache. Smooth the top with a knife. Chill for 1 hr for the ganache to set.
- Press the bark shards into the cake, sticking up. Add lots of chocolate eggs, popcorn and pretzels in and around the shards. Cut into slices to serve. Will keep for up to three days kept in a cool place in an airtight container.

Nutrition Information

- Calories: 870 calories
- Protein: 8 grams protein
- Sugar: 68 grams sugar
- Sodium: 1 milligram of sodium
- Saturated Fat: 23 grams saturated fat
- Total Carbohydrate: 85 grams carbohydrates
- Total Fat: 54 grams fat
- Fiber: 4 grams fiber

---

292. Tropical Upside Down Cake

Serving: 9 | Prep: 15mins | Cook: 45mins | Ready in:

Ingredients

- 80g unsalted butter, softened, plus extra for the tin
- 50g light brown soft sugar
- 8 canned pineapple rings in syrup (syrup reserved)
- 7 maraschino cherries
- 2-3 tbsp coconut rum (optional)
- 2-3 tbsp coconut flakes, toasted
- whipped cream or coconut yogurt, to serve
- For the sponge
- 150g unsalted butter, softened
- 150g golden caster sugar
- 150g self-raising flour
- 50g desiccated coconut
- 4 limes, zested, 1 juiced
- 2 large eggs

Direction

- Heat the oven to 180C/160C fan/gas 4. Butter a 20cm square or 22cm round cake tin. Beat 50g of the butter with the brown sugar, then spread into the base and halfway up the sides of the prepared tin. Cut one of the pineapple rings into quarters, then arrange the whole rings in the tin, putting a cherry in the centre of each. Put a pineapple ring quarter into each corner.
- To make the sponge, tip the butter, sugar, flour, desiccated coconut, ½ tsp fine sea salt, most of the lime zest and the eggs into a large bowl. Beat together using an electric whisk until smooth and creamy. Spoon the batter over the pineapple and level with the back of a spoon. Bake for 35-40 mins. Leave to cool in the tin for 5 mins, then turn out onto a cake board or serving plate.
- Bring the reserved pineapple syrup to the boil in a medium pan, then stir in the coconut rum (if using), remaining butter and the lime juice. Leave to cool slightly. Drizzle over the cake, then scatter over the coconut flakes and remaining lime zest. Serve with whipped cream or coconut yogurt, if you like. Will keep in an airtight container for up to five days.

Nutrition Information

- Calories: 488 calories
- Fiber: 3 grams fiber
- Protein: 5 grams protein
- Sodium: 0.5 milligram of sodium
- Total Fat: 29 grams fat

- Total Carbohydrate: 51 grams carbohydrates
- Sugar: 38 grams sugar
- Saturated Fat: 19 grams saturated fat

293. Ultimate Chocolate Cake

Serving: 14 slices | Prep: 40mins | Cook: 1hours30mins | Ready in:

Ingredients

- For the chocolate cake
- 200g dark chocolate (about 60% cocoa solids), chopped
- 200g butter, cubed
- 1 tbsp instant coffee granules
- 85g self-raising flour
- 85g plain flour
- ¼ tsp bicarbonate of soda
- 200g light muscovado sugar
- 200g golden caster sugar
- 25g cocoa powder
- 3 medium eggs
- 75ml buttermilk
- 50g grated chocolate or 100g curls, to decorate
- For the ganache
- 200g dark chocolate (about 60% cocoa solids), chopped
- 300ml double cream
- 2 tbsp golden caster sugar

Direction

- Heat the oven to 160C/fan140C/gas 3. Butter and line a 20cm round cake tin (7.5cm deep).
- Put 200g chopped dark chocolate in a medium pan with 200g butter.
- Mix 1 tbsp instant coffee granules into 125ml cold water and pour into the pan.
- Warm through over a low heat just until everything is melted – don't overheat. Or melt in the microwave for about 5 minutes, stirring halfway through.
- Mix 85g self-raising flour, 85g plain flour, ¼ tsp bicarbonate of soda, 200g light muscovado sugar, 200g golden caster sugar and 25g cocoa powder, and squash out any lumps.
- Beat 3 medium eggs with 75ml buttermilk.
- Pour the melted chocolate mixture and the egg mixture into the flour mixture and stir everything to a smooth, quite runny consistency.
- Pour this into the tin and bake for 1hr 25 – 1hr 30 mins. If you push a skewer into the centre it should come out clean and the top should feel firm (don't worry if it cracks a bit).
- Leave to cool in the tin (don't worry if it dips slightly), then turn out onto a wire rack to cool completely. Cut the cold cake horizontally into three.
- To make the ganache, put 200g chopped dark chocolate in a bowl. Pour 300ml double cream into a pan, add 2 tbsp golden caster sugar and heat until it is about to boil.
- Take off the heat and pour it over the chocolate. Stir until the chocolate has melted and the mixture is smooth. Cool until it is a little thicker but still pourable.
- Sandwich the layers together with just a little of the ganache. Pour the rest over the cake letting it fall down the sides and smooth over any gaps with a palette knife.
- Decorate with 50g grated chocolate or 100g chocolate curls. The cake keeps moist and gooey for 3-4 days.

Nutrition Information

- Calories: 541 calories
- Sodium: 0.51 milligram of sodium
- Protein: 6 grams protein
- Total Fat: 35 grams fat
- Total Carbohydrate: 55 grams carbohydrates
- Sugar: 40 grams sugar
- Fiber: 2 grams fiber
- Saturated Fat: 20 grams saturated fat

294. Vintage Chocolate Chip Cookies

Serving: Makes 30 | Prep: 15mins | Cook: 10mins | Ready in:

Ingredients

- 150g salted butter, softened
- 80g light brown muscovado sugar
- 80g granulated sugar
- 2 tsp vanilla extract
- 1 large egg
- 225g plain flour
- ½ tsp bicarbonate of soda
- ¼ tsp salt
- 200g plain chocolate chips or chunks

Direction

- Heat the oven to 190C/fan170C/gas 5 and line two baking sheets with non-stick baking paper.
- Put 150g softened salted butter, 80g light brown muscovado sugar and 80g granulated sugar into a bowl and beat until creamy.
- Beat in 2 tsp vanilla extract and 1 large egg.
- Sift 225g plain flour, ½ tsp bicarbonate of soda and ¼ tsp salt into the bowl and mix it in with a wooden spoon.
- Add 200g plain chocolate chips or chunks and stir well.
- Use a teaspoon to make small scoops of the mixture, spacing them well apart on the baking trays. This mixture should make about 30 cookies.
- Bake for 8–10 mins until they are light brown on the edges and still slightly soft in the centre if you press them.
- Leave on the tray for a couple of mins to set and then lift onto a cooling rack.

Nutrition Information

- Calories: 121 calories
- Sodium: 0.2 milligram of sodium
- Total Fat: 6.3 grams fat
- Protein: 1.3 grams protein
- Saturated Fat: 3.8 grams saturated fat
- Sugar: 9.5 grams sugar
- Fiber: 0.5 grams fiber
- Total Carbohydrate: 14.7 grams carbohydrates

295. Yummy Golden Syrup Flapjacks

Serving: Makes 12 | Prep: 15mins | Cook: 15mins | Ready in:

Ingredients

- 250g jumbo porridge oats
- 125g butter, plus extra for the tin
- 125g light brown sugar
- 2-3 tbsp golden syrup (depending on how gooey you want it)

Direction

- Heat the oven to 200C/180C fan/gas 6. Put the oats, butter, sugar and golden syrup in a food processor and pulse until mixed – be careful not to overmix or the oats may lose their texture.
- Lightly butter a 20 x 20cm baking tin and add the mixture. Press into the corners with the back of a spoon so the mixture is flat and score into 12 squares. Bake for around 15 mins until golden brown.

Nutrition Information

- Calories: 212 calories
- Protein: 2 grams protein
- Sodium: 0.3 milligram of sodium
- Fiber: 2 grams fiber
- Total Fat: 10 grams fat
- Total Carbohydrate: 27 grams carbohydrates
- Saturated Fat: 6 grams saturated fat
- Sugar: 13 grams sugar

Index

Conclusion

Thank you again for downloading this book!

I hope you enjoyed reading about my book!

If you enjoyed this book, please take the time to share your thoughts and post a review on Amazon. It'd be greatly appreciated!

Write me an honest review about the book – I truly value your opinion and thoughts and I will incorporate them into my next book, which is already underway.

Thank you!

If you have any questions, **feel free to contact at:** _author@thymerecipes.com_

Sandra Neal

thymerecipes.com

Printed in Great Britain
by Amazon